MARTHA OYLER
ANDERSON, IND.

D1769974

PORTUGUESE FOOD

PORTUGUESE FOOD

CAROL WRIGHT

LONDON
J. M. DENT & SONS LTD

© Text, Carol Wright, 1969
© Illustrations, J. M. Dent & Sons Ltd
All rights reserved. No part of this publication may be reproduced, stored in a retrieval system, or transmitted, in any form or by any means, electronic, mechanical, photocopying, recording or otherwise, without the prior permission of
J. M. Dent & Sons Ltd

Made in Great Britain
at the
Aldine Press · Letchworth · Herts
for
J. M. DENT & SONS LTD
Aldine House · Bedford St · London
First published 1969

SBN: 460 03835 4

CONTENTS

ACKNOWLEDGMENTS vii
CONVERSION TABLE viii
American, Metric and British Measures
INTRODUCTION ix
1 Portugal on a Platter 1
2 The Minho 13
3 Oporto, the Douro, Trás-os-Montes 33
4 The Beiras 59
5 Lisbon 80
6 North-west of Lisbon 99
7 The Arrábida 120
8 The Alentejo 133
9 The Algarve 147
10 Madeira 171
11 Translating for the Table 182
12 Capturing the Flavour: Basic Portuguese Recipes 189
13 Table Talk: A Menu Dictionary 199
14 Menu Planner: Index to Recipes 204

MAPS
General Map of Portugal 2
The Minho 12

P O R T U G U E S E   F O O D

Oporto, the Douro, Trás-os-Montes 46–7
The Beiras 58
Central Lisbon 79
North-west of Lisbon 100
The Arrábida 121
The Alentejo 134
The Algarve 148
Madeira 172

ACKNOWLEDGMENTS

The author would like to thank the following people for their kindness and help in the preparation of this book:

IN LONDON: Mr Jorge Dias, Director, Casa de Portugal, and his wife Betty; Mr Antonio Luis Castelo Branco; Mr José Agnelo, Mr José Osorio, Mrs Virginia Heredia, Miss Catarina McMillan and Miss Ellen Barnes of the Casa de Portugal; Mr Harry Dickens; Mr G. Battley and Chef Anthony Bell of Cross Caterers; Mrs Sue Pereira; and Mr Tim Sandeman of George Sandeman and Sons.

IN PORTUGAL: Maria Villar, Ministry of Tourism, Lisbon; Dona Maria Amaral, of the Oporto Tourist Office; José Macedo Correia of the Barcelos Tourist Office; Daniel Constant, gastronomical writer, Oporto; Maria Modesto, television food writer, Lisbon; Peter Johnston, manager, Hotel Eva, Faro; Mr and Mrs J. Hill of Seis Marias, Algarve; Ian Sinclair, director, Sandeman's, Oporto; José Pinto de Gouvea and his family, Régua; Robin Reid, director, Croft and Company, Oporto; Mr and Mrs Brito e Cunha, Oporto; Mrs Philippa Couto of the John Bull, Cascais; and all the chefs, hotel managers and restaurateurs who gave up their busy time to demonstrate and tell me about the recipes they make.

CURRENCY NOTE

At the time of going to press the rate of exchange is 69 escudos to the £ sterling, 29 to the dollar.

American visitors may flinch at printed prices in Portugal, since the escudos symbol is the same as that for the dollar, but it follows the escudo monetary unit instead of preceding it; centavos, however, are preceded by the symbol; thus: 50$20.

CONVERSION TABLE

American and British Measures

1 US pint = 16 fl. oz.

1 British pint = 20 fl. oz.

1 US cup = 8 fl. oz.

1 US cup flour = $4\frac{1}{2}$ oz.   1 US tablespoon flour = $\frac{1}{2}$ oz.

1 US cup sugar = 7 oz.   1 US tablespoon sugar = $\frac{3}{4}$ oz.

1 US cup butter = 7 oz.   1 US tablespoon butter = $\frac{3}{4}$ oz.

Metric and British Measures

1 pint = approx. $\frac{1}{2}$ litre   1 oz. = approx. 30 grams

1 gallon = approx. $4\frac{1}{2}$ litres   1 lb. = approx. 450 grams

INTRODUCTION

This is both guide-book and cook book, although you won't be told the history of castles or churches you should see, or how to make up witty little dinner parties. What it will do, I hope, is teach stay-at-homes some basic recipes of the ever creative Portuguese way of eating, and help the tourist to travel with delight in Portugal. Napoleon discovered that armies marched on their stomachs; so too the tourist sightsees as much with his palate as with his camera.

Portugal has been sadly overlooked in publicity for its food, which is amongst the most creative and pleasing I know. It is always difficult to translate a recipe from its natural surroundings – in this case, sun, sea and high mountains – and expect the total recall of the same palate pleasures when on our own dining-table in everyday surroundings. It is easy to write down a chef's recipe and take it home; but the flavour, like many wines, may not always travel. The recipes must sometimes be adapted to different kitchen conditions: I trust my purist Portuguese gourmet friends will forgive me for any liberties taken with some of their recipes. But I hope this book will be used as a preliminary essay to suggest what to expect and enjoy on holiday; to guide you to some of the best cooking while in Portugal, and to enable you on your return home to produce an aroma of holiday souvenirs. Some substitutions and shopping guides are given at the end of the book to

PORTUGUESE FOOD

help home culinary prologues and epilogues to a Portuguese holiday.

The recipe routes and places have been selected more in accordance with areas most frequently visited by tourists than with an eye for food alone. The Alentejo, one of the most individual and prolific culinary areas of Portugal, is virtually untouched by tourism. I record those of its recipes that can be tasted in other parts of the country. Madeira is included but not the Azores, simply because the English-speaking tourist has wintered in Madeira for decades and knows it well; the Azores have yet to be 'discovered'.

I make no mention of Portugal's excellent wines in this book except where they are related to a recipe. This subject is admirably covered in the companion volume to this book, *Portuguese Wines* by Raymond Postgate.

1

PORTUGAL ON A PLATTER

Lack of communication can hardly be blamed for the singular lack of knowledge of Portuguese cooking which exists in the English-speaking world. Portugal is Britain's oldest proclaimed ally; the centuries-old friendship was sealed historically with exchanges of princesses, commercially with a passion for port wine that sent many English merchant families to Portugal to make their fortunes; and now, touristically, with growing numbers of English tourists to the Algarve, Cascais, Ofir, Esposende and Madeira. In the latter spot the word 'foreign' until the 1950s meant simply 'English'. Lisbon is particularly loved by Americans.

Both London and New York ignore Portuguese cuisine. While other national foods are represented by restaurants in abundance, only one small, off-centre Portuguese restaurant waves the flag in London; in New York there is none.

In Portugal, on the other hand, there is a touch of England in several restaurants, and in pubs in Albufeira and Cascais, though in English-run restaurants chefs produce superb Portuguese dishes as well. Tearooms – *casa de chá* – exist everywhere, the Portuguese still maintaining the habit of tea time and cakes fast declining in Britain and America.

No one can allege that the Portuguese cuisine is either dull or over-exotic. In any case, Spanish restaurants find favour by the

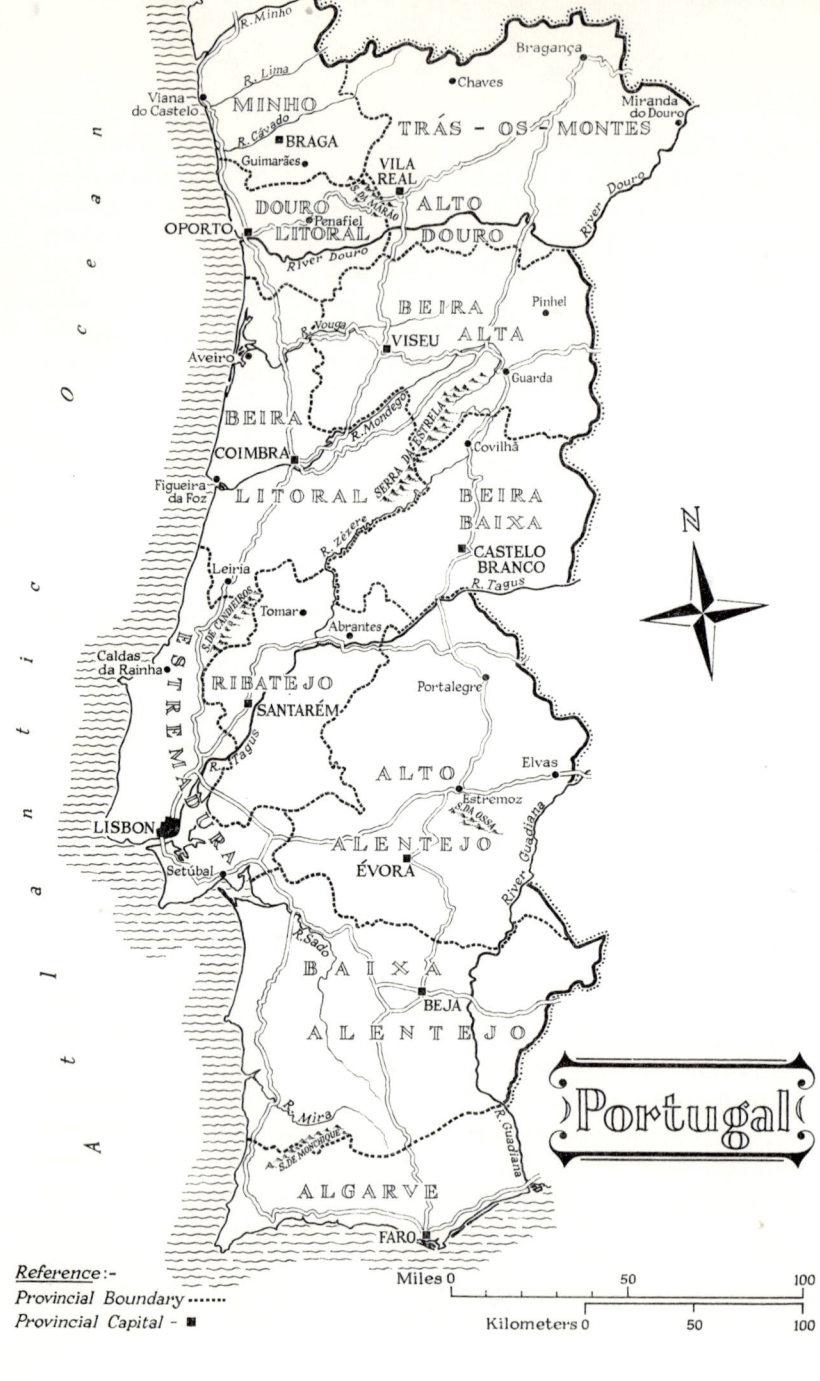

dozen. The Portuguese cuisine is rich and varied and was given an early spur in its history by the Portuguese discoveries of the New World, from which they brought back rice and spices to enrich their food. In the south, the Algarve and Alentejo have Moorish touches and Madeira has been influenced by African ideas to the extent of producing a local *couscous*. Spain too has left her imprint in her neighbour's kitchen, and experts attribute the ubiquitous crème caramel to Spanish chefs. In the north, pilgrimage routes into Spain have left a trail of Spanish-run restaurants on the Portuguese side of the border.

But Portuguese cuisine, like the country, should never be intermingled with Spain in English thinking. The two are far apart; Portugal is not a Latin Mediterranean country but an Atlantic area; its basic staple food is dried cod or fish, usually served northern style with boiled potatoes cooked in the Irish manner, the skins removed only after cooking. Roast pork in a wide variety of guises is the national favourite meat, followed by chicken and veal dishes. Lamb is little eaten, sheep being reared more for their wool. Beef steaks are often topped with an egg. An egg can be poached in tomato soup. Another popular dish is a stew made with beans and sausages. All these dishes are solid and produce warmth to combat the harshness of the sea or the hardness of the interior mountains. It is food for toilers, not for lazier Latin temperaments.

Merged with this sterner side of a gallant country, determined to make the best of what it has, is the influence of a hot climate and sun. The *refogado*, or roux, is made from cooking finely chopped onion to a pulp in olive oil, usually with garlic liberally added. This is the starting point of a good many of the country's recipes. Portugal has given its name to the classic culinary sauce to serve with meat or fish made from tomato *purée* with the above ingredients. Olive oil, which in Portugal has a slight salty tang, is used in everything, even a little added to *caldo verde* (potato and cabbage soup) of the north. Nowadays, domestically, more margarine is being substituted for olive oil and in many country districts pig lard is the favourite cooking fat.

Maria Modesto, the leading Portuguese television chef, divides the country from a culinary point of view vertically into seaboard and mountain areas. In this book I have divided it into the provincial regions from a tourist point of view; though each has its kitchen characteristics. Maria Modesto explained to me how poverty in the past influenced dishes which are now adopted by all classes in the country. In the mountain areas bread plays an important part in cookery, with the bread soups of the Alentejo and the *rabanadas* of the Douro. The rich, heavy pork dishes, smoked sausages and thick soups based on inexpensive ingredients are found in the eastern half of the country. To the seaboard there are the many fish soups, originally made by fishermen from the small fish caught in their nets; the sardines, the lobster and other sea food arouse intense pride and salivation when talking to a Portuguese gourmet. In the large cities a modest ingredient is again adopted as a popular dish; in Lisbon the liver; in Oporto the tripe; and in Braga boiled offal.

Portuguese eating habits combine practicality with overtones of intense delight in food; a national dedication to the creation of recipes found elsewhere perhaps only among the French. I found when travelling through Portugal researching this book that an explanation of my mission was enough to make everyone stop what they were doing to discuss regional recipes, suggest restaurants. The mention of a recipe would bring expressions of rapt desire; lips pursed in anticipation, they would explain 'my dear, it's delicious' with an extra tongue lick around the second syllable.

In general, Portugal's cookery is a strong, virile peasant food, refined over the years with the advance of civilization and sophistication. The most common example is *bacalhau*, the dried cod found everywhere. Originally produced to preserve the cod catches through winter by drying and salting, and found serviceable on the voyages of discovery to the New World, the *bacalhau* was the food of the poor. Now, in a country where the superb fresh fish stimulates the palate of the tourist nourished on frozen fish fingers to new tastes, the dried cod is still national dish number one. It is served in hundreds of ways; whole books are devoted to it. It is enriched with sauces and eggs and vegetables. Although there are regional variations, which I have indicated where I found them, the major ways are described in Chapter 12 (see page 189). Until the cook has mastered the art of *bacalhau* preparation and also the *refogado* (see page 196) she cannot begin to work in the Portuguese manner.

Another striking characteristic is the Portuguese *pudim*: a stage in the meal when the masculine character of main dishes turns to feminine frippery. Though the word recalls our heavy pudding, the Portuguese *pudim* is basically an egg custard with sauce. This *pudim flan* turns up everywhere; it is cheap and easy to make, so much so that it is alternatively called the '365' after the number of days on which most restaurants serve it.

As with *bacalhau*, the *pudim flan* demonstrates the Portuguese genius for endless variations on a recipe theme. My personal favourites are the creamy wedding pudding given me in the Douro Mountains and Dona Tihina's ham pudding served in Monção (see pages 53, 32). Surely Mrs Beeton must have had some Portuguese blood in her veins; her classic phrase, 'take 12 eggs', is the basis of the dozens of sweets created in Portugal from eggs, almonds and sugar. The tourist may find these a little bad for his waistline and wearying to his palate. But these sweets are often served in mid afternoon with a cup of tea instead of after a meal. In many places, particularly in the north, I have given the name of the local sweet to ask for in the pastry shops and *casa de chá*. Some of the names suggest that the Portuguese, for all their stern appearance, have a *risqué* sense of humour; e.g. 'Angel's Breasts', or 'Nuns' Tummies'.

As well as superb vegetables of all kinds, Portugal produces excellent fruit: lemons, grapefruit and oranges are found in most parts of the country, even among the harsh Douro Mountains. Pineapples are imported from the Azores. When they have something edibly perfect the Portuguese show a remarkable restraint in not messing it about for the plate. Port wine is rarely used in cooking – it is for drinking. So the orange is little used in creating great dishes, it is used to make preserve for flavouring sauces. A wedge served with pork is excellent. A slice of lemon often accompanies meat. However, the most common dessert in Portugal, at all times of the year, is a plain peeled orange. To me it is one of the great joys of the country. I head for a favourite tearoom in the Rua Garrett shopping area of Lisbon (usually after a spree in a local shoe shop or boutique) secure in the knowledge that whatever time of day it is I can get the meal I feel like: sticky cake and tea at lunch time or wine and cooked meal at 10 a.m. or 4 p.m.; toasted cheese sandwiches and a beer, coffee and fruit; the customer must be pleased. The final touch in both these tearooms and restaurants of all levels all over the country is the peeled orange. A young waiter in clean white apron (the Portuguese are very clean people where food is concerned: even sugar for coffee must, by law, be served in sealed paper packets; bread rolls are always wrapped in thin greaseproof paper) slices off the peel with a sharp knife and neatly dissects the fruit into a water-lily or a daisy and presents it ready to eat. The most charming presentation was that of the waiter at the Hotel Nazaré in Nazaré. My orange was cut into thin segments and arranged with precise care to form a large petalled daisy, and the centre was filled with a mound of sugar.

In some restaurants one feels the waiter creates the orange arrangement as one would offer a posy to a pretty woman. Time is no object in the dining-room. The waiter is as dedicated as his client; no rush to get rid of guests, lunch goes on all afternoon, dinner into the night. Service and pleasing the customers' palate is another part of Portuguese eating that endears it to the tourist. You can ask for anything. A restaurateur may think the tourist odd in his requests, but provided he has the ingredients he will do his best.

The traveller will notice a lack of cheese-based dishes, and although cheese is always available in restaurants the selection is small. The country lacks rich dairy herds and the cheeses are in the main made from the milk of sheep or goats. *Serra* is a creamy, smooth cheese, and like most of the other native cheeses has its season in winter and so is rarely discovered by the summer traveller. The *serra* is made in the wooded hill area of Serra da Estrela in the north, and is probably the most acclaimed cheese in Portugal. It is at its best when runny inside (usually in the period December to July). *Castelo branco* is similar to *serra*. The Alentejo cheese (also known as *serpa*) is more salty and piquant in flavour and is long keeping.

The tiny village of Azeitão south of Lisbon (see page 121) produces small $1\frac{1}{2}$-lb. cheeses of a creamy golden nature when they are fresh, with a slightly sharp taste. More ubiquitous is the

Portuguese reproduction of Dutch gouda-style cheese called *flamengo*. *Rabacal*, made near Pombal, is smooth without being creamy. *Tomar* and *alcobaca* have a slightly smoky flavour. *Tomar* is smaller, about an inch in diameter. The other 'native' cheeses known as *queija das ilhas* ('cheese of the islands') come from the Azores, principally from São Miguel and São Jorge, though these are used mostly in cooking.

Ask for *queijinhos frescos*, small white cream cheeses made of sheep's milk, which are very fluffy and must be eaten on the day they are made. They are similar to *petit suisses* and can be eaten with sugar or with fruit. Some people eat them with *hors d'œuvre*, salted and, as a texture contrast, with thin, crispy toast. The peasants cradle these delicate creams in straw baskets or wrap them in leaves. Yoghurts should also be asked for since these are rarely offered to visitors.

I found virtually no cheese recipes on my travels, unless a little grated parmesan is added as a finish or in a sauce. Hardly by tradition Portuguese, since it was invented by an English girl living in Cascais, is a recipe for using the small round shells of Azeitão cheese. It is so delicious that I had to include it in the book (see page 128) if only to inspire other Portuguese chefs.

As in England, cheese is served after the meal. It is often accompanied by a slice of *marmelada*. This is not our marmalade at all, but a quince preserve, *marmelos* being the Portuguese for quince. In a restaurant the slice is often presented in a greaseproof packet. The consistency is quite thick, jelly-like and fairly sweet. On a visit to the Gouvea family, who look after the Sandeman port interests in the Douro area, I was told how to make the quince jelly served along with a slice of cheese and, of course, a glass of port. Maria Gouvea told me it should not be eaten until two to three days after making; but covered in greaseproof paper it will keep for one to two years. As cheese will come so rarely into my traveller's tales of Portuguese food, the recipe for its accompaniment must stand here alone.

MARMELADA (QUINCE PRESERVE)

Put quinces in a pan and cover completely with water. Simmer the fruit till cooked, avoiding breaking the skin. Remove from heat, drain, skin and core when fruit is cool. Return the skin and core to the cooking liquid and boil till reduced by one-third. Strain. Weigh and slice fruit and put into a preserving pan with an equal amount by weight of sugar and the strained fruit juice. Boil gently until setting point is reached. Leave to set – the Portuguese use a thick pudding basin for setting – then turn the *marmelada* out on to a plate.

POOR MAN'S CHAMPAGNE

Although the tap water in Portugal is generally safe to drink, a chilled mineral water on a hot day is refreshing with a meal, as well as being helpful to a digestion perhaps confused by change of diet – some of the most common ones to ask for are:

SPARKLING (*gaseous*)	NON-SPARKLING
Carvalhelhos	Luso
Vimeiro	Agua da Bela Vista (Setúbal area)
Vidago	
Melgaco	Monchique (Algarve)
Pedras Salgadas	

The phrase 'poor man's champagne' generally refers in Portugal to a glass of white wine to which sparkling mineral water is added. COFFEE, shipped in from Portuguese overseas colonies, is excellent. Served *demi-tasse*, hot and strong, it is a fine antidote for the heavy-on-the-liver food and is much consumed by the Portuguese, very often from stand-up bars, where prices are minimal.

Earlier in this chapter I referred to the femininity of sweet-making compared with the general virility of the national recipes. The thing I found unusual and charming was the number of women chefs in Portugal. They mostly work in the small establishments, and many are wives whose husbands have started a restaurant. In comparison with the many internationally trained chefs, whose native recipes have overtones of classic cuisine, I found their dishes perhaps more reflective of purely traditional cookery. I enjoyed their enthusiasm; the laughter of Dona Tihina in her dark

PORTUGAL ON A PLATTER

kitchen full of women and cats; the treasured exercise book of recipes brought out in the most beautiful commercial kitchen I know: in the Pousada de São Brás in the Algarve. Here huge local pottery plates decorate the high, old-fashioned range chimney; the copper pots gleam in the sun pouring in from windows that give views of almond-tree orchards down to the coast. The enthusiasm of Mrs Souza Martins at Esposende was for the conversion of her English guests to local cooking and pride in requests for recipes; and, above all, I admired the splendour of Clotilde's professionalism. Clotilde has worked in many restaurants round Lisbon and is well known enough not to need to use her surname. She has cooked at the regal Queluz Palace near Lisbon, during which time she discovered and adopted several recipes created by the former queens of Portugal. She also has recipes culled from the nuns of several convents who are important as early creators of superb dishes mostly on the sweet side.

PUT ON A PLATTER

Presentation of food is another important factor in eating out in Portugal. The Portuguese gourmet insists his dishes taste better in the traditional earthenware pottery (see page 22) and indeed the brown and yellow decorated dishes laid on clean white tablecloths look appetizing.

A slightly fan-shaped bowl is customarily used for serving rice with meats, and most of the big serving pots have a white napkin tied around them for serving. Alternatively some are set in native wickerwork baskets. In the north the plaited straw baskets are used for presenting fruit and bread; thick linen napkins, often embroidered white on blue or mushroom beige on white with fanciful hearts in the corners, with matching tablecloths, grace many restaurants; toothpick-holders are usually made from local pottery, predominantly blue and orange on white.

The tourist will find it much easier than in most countries to drop into an unprepossessing place and get a good meal, though obviously the more purely native the clientèle the less likely the oil and garlic content will be toned down by contact with the international jet set. The tourist hotels in Portugal serve international food, and it is now possible to get excellent Portuguese steaks from herds of British origin in the Minho area.

However, the Portuguese are justly proud of their native cooking, and include it in most hotels for the visitor. This characteristic has done much to maintain a feeling of regional ambience lost in other tourist-conscious countries; hotels use local materials, and architectural styles are thoughtfully planned by the Ministry of Tourism not to spoil an area of country. While this attitude has probably slowed down the development of Portugal's tourist industry it has left her with a character which gives the visitor a definite feeling of identification with the country.

IN PRAISE OF POUSADAS

A prime example of the value-for-character hotels which the country possesses is the small chain of state-sponsored inns called *Pousadas*. These were originally started before the war when the government decided to set up inns so that motorists could visit areas of the country not already served by suitable hotels. The inns have individual management and prices are low and subsidized; a well-furnished room with modern bathroom and three meals a day costs around 35*s* ($4.20). The *Pousadas* are either modern in design but use local architectural ideas, such as the one at Valença on the border with Spain, or are skilfully converted from old castles as at Óbidos, manor houses as at Serém, or old fortresses as on the island of Berlenga. While their architecture is regional so is their cuisine. Although stays are limited to five nights and must be booked well in advance in high season, the *Pousadas* make a pleasant meal stop-over point. An *estalagem* is also an inn, and is found more frequently and usually in settings full of character. All hotels, *estalagems* and *Pousadas* are listed by the tourist board with rates and addresses for easy reference. Pensions are usually clean and comfortable; a lack of modern plumbing can be compensated for by good regional cooking. Prices can be under £1 ($2.40) a day, inclusive terms or 9*s* ($1.08) a night, bed only; so touring Portugal can be managed even on a strict budget.

The motorist comes into his own in Portugal. Communications by train are slow and difficult; local coaches can help, but self-drive hire cars are plentiful and include many English makes. The roads are good and well-surfaced and in the north enhanced by the carefully tended clipped hedges and flowers in deep country areas maintained by the local road tender. Traffic is light off the main through roads, and the traveller can actually enjoy the drive and scenery without strain. In this book I have assumed the tourist will be approaching the restaurants principally by car.

COST OF CUISINE TOURING

It is still possible to eat well in Portugal without spending a lot. A great number of restaurants charge about 10*s* ($1.20) or less for a three-course meal; in large restaurants in smarter city quarters the average cost with a bottle of wine is around £1 ($2.40); de luxe tourist spots may cost more.

The local tourist boards in Portugal are listed throughout the guide sections of this book. For further information on Portugal, and for details of where to get Portuguese products at home, contact the Casa de Portugal, 20 Lower Regent Street, London, S.W.1. or, in the United States, Casa de Portugal, 570 Fifth Avenue, New York, N.Y. 10036.

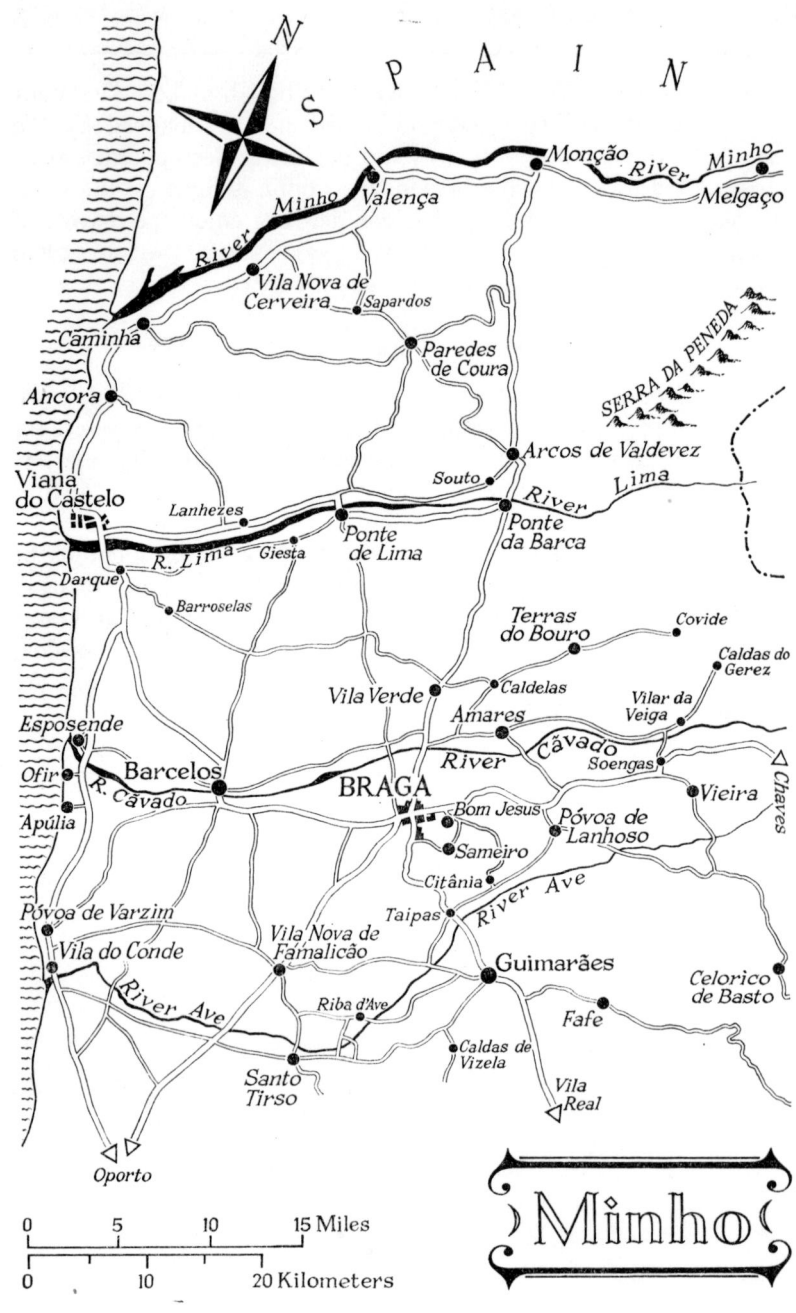

2

THE MINHO

The Minho River forms Portugal's northern border line with Spain, cutting its way inland over soft sandbanks or more ruthlessly further inland, creating a gorge through the mountains. The Minho province, however, covers the coastal plains and foothills of the mountains from the border almost to Oporto.

The Minho is an area which arouses great affection in visitors; its greenness and lushness among the four rivers that meander east–west across the coastal plains is deceptive. It is a frugal, hard-working region. Although the oldest part of Portugal, it never prospered till the voyages of discovery brought back an Indian corn (maize) which survived the cool wet winters and the harsh summer sun. Grape vines trained on trellises produce a grape which is slightly acid, but which becomes the *pétillant vinho verde*. Careful irrigation from wells and terrace cultivation of maize necessitated the help of oxen, lumbering Disney-eyed beasts with a noble span of horn behind which still rumble the solid-wheeled carts.

The oxen's contribution to fertilizing the land is eked out by seaweed, high in iodine content, raked in from the beaches. The poverty of the land drove the fisherfolk of Viana to build boats and sail to Newfoundland for cod; *Margarida da Praça*, a cod dish, is still the city's speciality, found in restaurants along the Lima banks.

PORTUGUESE FOOD

As well as richness in vegetables and soft fruit, modern methods of breeding are creating good cattle herds on the coastal plains to provide the tables of Portugal with good-quality beef steaks. But do not let the hospitality and addiction to rich eating – a veritable dictionary of sweet recipes can be made up for the north – delude the visitor into thinking it is too soft an area. Industry is in the character of the people, noticeable in the road tenders who on those straight, cobbled, pine-shaded roads have added a welcome in the form of colourful flower beds and tenderly arranged clipped hedges. These are for the passer-by's delight, but could win the workman a prize in national competitions. Individual smallholdings – and they are small, split up among the large families – are painstakingly separated out with a neat hedge or grape-vine trellis. In some cases gardens are marked out with a row of tall cabbages, the *couve* from which the soup of the area, *caldo verde*, is made.

Along these straight roads of the coast the visitor sees in the distance a woman advancing, her head piled high with hay, like a caricature of an eighteenth-century bewigged lady of fashion. Her carriage is superb; it comes from toil. The women do everything in this area from working in the field, running their houses and producing superb recipes to engaging in the handicrafts for which the area has become nationally famous. Somehow they find the time to carve candlesticks and the wide, arched oxen yokes, one of which I yearn to possess as a bedhead. (They cost around £10 for one suitable for a single bed.) Filigree jewellery is fashioned. The flax of the area is woven into the blue-and-white tablecloths, napkins and characteristic rounded aprons with pouchy pockets embroidered with heart motifs originating from Viana do Castelo. Some turn their hands to pottery, and the area has produced several natural sculptors: peasant women with a gift for simplicity and charm of form, making primitive figures of animals, fairy-tale people, or religious figures. The light plaster cock figure, symbol of Barcelos, is now the national 'trade mark'. The thick Aran-style sweaters of the Minho are knitted in Esposende for fishermen.

THE FOUR RIVERS

A woman's work is never done and, as well as all this activity which finds its way into the souvenir shops of the area, the Minho mesdames have contributed handsomely to their country's cookery history; and still do, as the reader will learn. The principal relaxation of the area seems to be a pilgrimage or a religious festival, judging by the hundreds of churches and chapels in the area. Festivals give an opportunity to sample the sweets and puddings. Daily food makes use of the maize, vegetables and fish from the sea, particularly the lamprey in season in late spring, or, inland, the salmon and shad from the Cãvado and Ave rivers.

To simplify the tourist routes in the area the Minho divides into a neat rectangle crossed by four rivers in an east–west line. The sides of the rectangle are formed by the good coastal road and a main road going south from Monção through Ponte da Barca and Braga to Guimarães. The whole area is criss-crossed with secondary roads, and although these, as throughout Portugal, are passable, the tourist without too much time to stand and stare would be advised to choose the main roads, at least for speed and comfort.

The guide notes throughout this book are intended to paint a word picture of the scenery of the area and act as a palate stimulator for what to eat where. Specialities with recipes reproduced in full are given in cross-reference. Where tourist boards exist they are mentioned; here the visitor may pick up information on sightseeing. I have also indicated some major fair days when some tempting local shopping may be done in traditional surroundings.

THE COAST NORTH FROM OPORTO TO VIANA DO CASTELO

The road is a rolling easy road taking at the most an hour to Viana, from Oporto.

About $6\frac{1}{4}$ miles from Oporto there is an unpretentious restaurant/pension, the Estalagem Lidador, situated alongside a Sacor petrol station on the main road at Guardeiras Maia. This has a high reputation with the inhabitants of Oporto, who will often drive out for a meal. Regional cooking is served in a modest little dining-room with plain white cloths, brown wood chairs and old calendars on the walls. In summer, meals can be served outside underneath a trellised side roof. Tea is also served here. Specialities include *pescada à Maiata*, hake baked with a mayonnaise cream with potatoes (see page 28), and *penna de porco assada*, a Lidador roast leg of pork. The leg is marinated before roasting, carved into slices and these are then rearranged round the bone and recooked with a sauce and served with rice. Cost of each dish is around 8s (96 cents). A meal is around 12s ($1.44) and bed and breakfast per night costs £1 ($2.40).

Beyond Oporto – about 15½ miles – the first resorts are Vila do Conde and Póvoa de Varzim, both strictly speaking in the Douro area. Vila do Conde is a fishing village with good sandy beach and tearooms where the local *bom doce*, 'good sweet', may be sampled. The Palácio Hotel has a pleasant beach restaurant. Póvoa de Varzim has a small casino and bullring for visitors' delight (the bulls are not killed in Portugal). Apart from sardine canning it is known for being a centre of regional dancing and folklore. Its culinary specialities include local *caldeirada* – fish stew – made with fish, egg yolks, potatoes, garlic and lemon; and hake cooked with chilli powder, vegetables and eggs.

Tourist offices at Vila do Conde and Póvoa de Varzim

Beyond Apulia, a village of windmills where the seaweed gatherers wear baggy costumes based on Phoenician origins, the small resorts of Ofir and Esposende watch each other across the mouth of the Cávado River. These make a convenient stopping point for a meal half way between Oporto and Viana. Both are well served with good hotels, and, for quiet and comfortable holidays, are popular with English visitors (particularly with children) who like a large beach, and they make a good centre for exploring the Minho area.

Ofir: the Hotel Do Pinhal (open only in summer) and Hotel Ofir are on a straight road leading down to the beach from the village itself. The Do Pinhal was opened about three years ago and is a charmingly decorated hotel set in pine trees with its own swimming-pool and view over the Cávado estuary to Esposende. Its cuisine is fairly international, and it served the best steaks I have ever had in Portugal. On the same side of the road as the Do Pinhal, set well back among the trees, is a delightful swimming-pool area with restaurant and snack bar for modest meals.

At the end of the road is the old block of the Ofir Hotel and, right on the beach, a new block with well-furnished modern rooms, wide sun-terrace and a restaurant attached. This restaurant was described by a Portuguese gourmet as 'the balcony of Portugal', and certainly the views from the huge picture windows are exhilarating. The immense sand beach sweeps down the coast with grandeur; the waves breaking over the 'Cavalos de Fão' (horses of Fão) rock reefs near the shore gave rise to the legend of the 'white horses'. Specialities to choose from the local chef are the *peixe assado à Ofir* (roast fish Ofir style); hake or other fish roasted with potato balls, onion and dry white wine. The house style of cooking steak is to top it with a sauce (see page 29) and serve on fried bread with sliced mushrooms and potatoes – *bife à estalagem*. Lobster are good and are boiled alive; *lagosta à bar de Ofir* is described on page 30.

Returning to the main road, the motorist turns north again and crosses the arched bridge of the Cãvado River to Esposende. The river estuary softens the grandeur of the sea at Esposende, screened behind huge sand spits, while the village curls out protectively round the sea wall. There is a strange impression of minimal flat land dominated by the intense clear light of a vast heaven at Esposende which is exhilarating. The fishermen, including tourists, gather on the flat Foz de Cãvado to try their luck, but more peaceful is to watch the locals paddling in the estuary sand searching for clams or lamprey, the local delicacy.

The forty-one roomed Hotel Suave Mar at the edge of the village deserves the high reputation it holds with travel writers and its mainly professional class English clientèle. It has an air of dignified home comfort, not fussily protective but a gentle pampering without ornate luxury. The country style bedrooms with their carved wood bed frames, whiter-than-white coverlets, posies of flowers and wooden shutters, look out across the bay or over the sheltered courtyard swimming-pool. Prices from just under £2 ($4.80) for a double room and £3 ($7.20) for pension.

The hotel is run by the motherly Mrs Souza Martins (who speaks good English) and her husband. They create delicious dishes for the two dining-rooms. The smaller one on the first floor, with its window views over the Cãvado estuary, is my favourite. Here a meal will cost around 15*s* ($1.80) for four courses. Choice is limited, but the regional food is excellent and plenty of helpings –

if you can cope – are offered. Specialities include *açorda de camarão* – a shrimp bread soup, Cãvado style roast *robalo* (sea bass), tripe done in the local manner, chicken cooked in a blood sauce (typical of the Minho area) and the *pièce de résistance* in season, lamprey cooked in the red *vinho verde* of the region.

As a dessert or with morning coffee or tea on the sun terraces round the pool or overlooking the beach, *clarinhas* beat the strongest diet resolutions. These are sweetmeats made from a pumpkin preserve mixture called *chila*, which tastes a little like pineapples. Covered with a thin choux pastry, pumpkins are often used as an inexpensive sweetmeat ingredient in the Minho; the doughnut-sized pastries are deep fried and dusted with fine sugar. This delicacy comes from Fão, a tiny village just outside Ofir. Although I am not fond of the sweet egg and sugar concoctions and prefer fresh fruit when in Portugal, these are irresistible. After a *clarinha* I can, with as much honesty as politeness, put my fingers to clasp my ear lobe to signify, in the Portuguese way, that the food was good.   *Tourist office at Esposende*

Viana do Castelo lies across the estuary of yet another river, the Lima, and is about forty-five miles north of Oporto. It faces south, nestling around the river banks under the shadow of the high hill that dominates the town. On top of the hill is the renowned Hotel Santa Luzia, a palatial design built with an insolence belonging to an earlier age that is most impressive. Now sponsored by the state, its prices for the luxurious rooms with their sweeping balconies above the terraced gardens are modest. The view calls for 'royal purple' prose. Dismissing the tiny town below, and the river estuary, it soars along the sandy beaches of the coast which stretch flat and luminous till they blend with the horizon. Round the hotel are thick gardens containing swimming-pool and sports facilities.

The hotel is worth visiting, preferably at tea time, to sample some of the local cakes for which the town is famous. Ask for *torta de Viana, meia lua, fidalguinhas* or the local biscuits *vianas, Santa Luzia* or *delicias*.

Viana do Castelo is important for drying cod as well as for building the boats that go to Newfoundland to collect it. There are famous *bacalhau* dishes from the area, the best known being *bacalhau à Margarida da Praça* at the restaurant of that name. Like Zefa Carquela, this is a small well-known inn near the Lima banks. After lunch the visitor will find the arched Council House with its sixteenth-century fountain a cool, timeless spot in which to soothe away a huge meal. Viana's biggest annual festival is the week-end nearest to 20th August. *Tourist office at Viano do Castelo*

THE MINHO RIVER

North of Viana the road starts to curve inland along the Minho estuary. Before that there is the charming tiny seaside resort of Ancora with good bathing from a sandy beach at high tide.
Tourist office at Praia de Ancora

The scenery round here is soft and gentle; the impression is of apple orchards, duckponds and small whitewashed farms – almost a touch of old rural England. The village of Caminha at the mouth of the Minho is a straggling palette of different-colourwashed houses; a mixture of fishing and farming. Although the impression is of unspoilt charm the tourist is not unknown. Frequent signs along the way indicate antiques for sale, usually at modest looking farmhouses. The bargain is driven fairly hard, however, though there are some small, delightfully primitive granite saint statues to be bought if you can transport them.

Along the Minho there are two places of importance on the recipe route: Valença and Monção. Valença forms a border point with Spain, the road being carried north over the river bridge. The town maintains its sturdily defensive attitude of tiny Portugal versus gigantic Spain. Massive Vaubanesque ramparts in a wonderful state of preservation surround the small town. Entering at dusk is like going back a couple of hundred years. The old shuttered houses cuddle up along the narrow cobbled streets, shrinking together within the walls against the perils of the night. The pocket handkerchief squares and streets are lit by flickering gaslight; the car just squeezes through between buildings. The well-signposted, one-way streets guide the visitor through the town to the Pousada de São Teotonio, a superbly designed modern building; like the town all forbidding granite and grey outside; inside warmth and helpfulness.

The *Pousada*, although very modern, blends in its solidity with its surroundings. It is set in the ramparts with a marvellous view down over the river and across to Spain. Its twelve rooms are fitted with dark, hand-carved wooden bedposts, white drawn-thread covers, polished tiled floors with soft rugs, lamps and ornaments made from local antiques and a modern bathroom. I felt unwell on my first visit here, and the tender care with which the maids served my meal in my room, arranging the table so that I had the best view while eating, is typical of local hospitality and helpfulness.

If you are inspired by the *décor* of your *Pousada* room to search for a coverlet as a souvenir (around £5 – $12 – for a double bedspread), Valença is a charming shopping centre. There is no need to fuss about finding the right shop; ask for virtually anything at either of the two main general stores and they will send a boy to the other shop if they haven't got it in stock. Among the heaps of fascinating items in these shops I found such treasures as large wooden forks, perfect for serving spaghetti; locally woven napkins and aprons, and, for around 12s ($1.50), a *fogareiro*, a small cast-iron barbecue on which the Portuguese grill their sardines, but which is excellent for terrace or garden barbecues at home.

About 10½ miles from Valença is Monção. This small and rather featureless town has acquired a fair gastronomic interest in Portugal out of all proportion to its importance and beauty. The cooking of lampreys and trout earns rave notices from gourmets, and there are several puddings born of the area.

Cooking on the home-from-home scale, that tourists in the know make an excursion to sample, is offered at the Pensão Vaticano in Monção. Past its exterior, shaded in spring with a purple-flowering creeper, the dining-room is small and unpretentious, nothing chi-chi here. The kitchen, over which Dona Tihina presides fussily, anxious that her foreign guests should be pleased, is dim and full of women scurrying to and fro. Food is piled in mounds as ample as Dona Tihina's bosom; lampreys squirm on huge platters, their primeval sucker faces nuzzling each other; the crisp huge *couve* leaves for the *caldo verde* wait to be shredded; yellow puddings gleam like candlelight in the dark recessed pantry and saffron rice is piled high into earthen pots. Everywhere there is bustle and confusion, but the results are superb and low priced. Specialities are – in spring – the lamprey cooked in red wine, or in a rich pie; back of pork cooked with chestnuts and served with saffron rice; grilled trout; Monção egg custard or Monção egg pudding made with a flavouring of ham in it (see pages 31–2). It is wise to fast a while before eating here; Dona Tihina judges appreciation in terms of the amount eaten. If you feel too weak to move after a substantial meal, a bed at the eighteen-roomed pension costs about 10*s* ($1.20) a night. Full pension is about 22*s* 6*d* ($2.70).

SOUTH TO BRAGA

From Monção the main road leads south via Ponte da Barca to Braga, and then to Oporto. At Ponte da Barca another main road links this little riverside town to Ponte de Lima and Viano do Castelo. Ponte de Lima has a lazy rural charm, with its wide, low, arched river bridge alongside which women scrub their clothes near the municipal wash-house. Outside the chocolate and white churches men sell sweet, thirst-quenching oranges. In the castle keep, which is still used as a prison, prisoners will let down a basket on a rope for cigarettes or food.

Braga, south on the main road, is the capital city of the Minho district. A lively, bustling town, mazed with mellow streets and stuck with towers, it is much given to *festas* and pilgrimages. Just outside the town are two popular pilgrimage places, Sameiro and Bom Jesus, the latter having pleasant tearooms where some of the local sweetmeats can be eaten. None of the restaurants are particularly outstanding from a tourist point of view, but produce reliable local food, the specialities of the area being *bacalhau Narcisa*, *pescada* (hake) in the Braga manner, sardines grilled on charcoal and served with maize and (a dish liked by the men, which takes an age to cook) *papas de carrabulho*, assorted offal, ham and meat boiled together in a casserole with pig's blood, bread and vegetables. Lamb, little favoured in Portugal, is found roast here, and a local custom is to serve roast pork with orange or lemon segments. The chopped *rojoes*, a pork dish, is also popular here.

Recommended restaurants in Braga: Narcisa, near the cemetery, Inacio Filho, Inacia das Hortas, Restaurant Pimento, Benamar and Ragu. *Tourist office in Braga*

BRAGA BACK TO OPORTO

Midway between Braga and Esposende is Barcelos, which deserves a visit from the kitchen-conscious if only to buy some of the local earthenware in russet brown, flecked with yellow decorations of flowers and fish designs. Every Thursday here there is a big market fair devoted mainly to the sale of crockery. On other days, including Sundays, local arts and crafts, including pottery, can be bought from the well-arranged displays inside the tourist office housed in the old castle fortress – the Torre do Porta Nova. Plates and bowls cost only a few shillings each; a typically shaped bowl for serving rice is only about 2s (24 cents), a fish-decorated serving dish 4s 9d (57 cents). Also on sale are local woven and embroidered goods, carved candles, peasant sculptures, carved oxen yokes from £8 ($22.40), pottery cocks, woven feather carpets and baskets.

Barcelos is an ancient town piled over the steep banks of the Cãvado River. Fine views of the river, which has a bathing beach, can be enjoyed from the little formal municipal gardens laid out outside the city walls, near the market site and the elegant round church, Senhor da Cruz.

Restaurants: Do Turismo, Porta Nova, Noite e Dia, Pérola da Avenida.

Confectioners selling local sweetmeats are Galo Negro, Colonial and Salvação.

The town has two small inexpensive pensions. The Bagoeira, run by another substantial matronly figure, is near the market-place and near the round church. Here you can eat in the rather scruffy surroundings of a huge room with kitchen at one side divided off by a serving counter. A meal here will cost only around 10s ($1.20), (bed 13$s$, $1.56), recommended for those on a budget and with stomachs amenable to rougher Portuguese cooking. Typical dishes are pork and vegetables boiled together, the *papas de carrabulho*, roast *bacalhau* and the national dish *cozido*, a great boiling together of meats and vegetables.

From Braga the road leads south-west to Oporto, an easy hour's drive unless a pause is made at Santo Tirso just off the main road to sample their renowned sweet, the *jesuitas*, large triangular pastries with various sweet fillings. A diversion can be made to visit the town of Guimarães, famous as being the cradle of Portuguese nationality in the twelfth century. The small town peers up at the imposing tenth-century castle, which is much restored but impressive in its simple exterior lines of strength.

To nourish the visitors who come to see this national monument, almost a shrine, a popular eating place, large like a students' refectory, is the Jordoa, which serves modestly priced but good food.

RECIPES OF THE MINHO AREA
CALDO VERDE

This cabbage and potato soup has spread its fame farther than the Minho region, but remains essentially of the north. It is made from huge cabbage leaves (*couve*), but any good, dark green cabbage or kale could be used. Remove stalks and any tough membrane. The Portuguese shred the leaves to grass fineness and even have gadgets to do this. It does take time and patience, but makes it more flavoursome and easier to eat. The easiest way I've found to cut the leaves is to roll them tight and cut as fine as possible with a super-sharp knife.

FOR FOUR

1 lb. potatoes	slice of continental sausage
1 lb. cabbage	(see page 185 – optional)
1 large onion	1 tablespoon olive oil
seasoning	(optional)

Boil potatoes in water (chicken stock increases flavour). When cooked, blend to a *purée* and reheat. When boiling add finely shredded cabbage and seasoning. The cabbage should be added only 10–15 minutes before serving for best flavour. A Portuguese touch is to add a slice of sausage and chopped onion or 1 tablespoon olive oil per four people to the boiling potatoes.

In the north of Portugal the *caldo verde* is usually served with a thick piece of maize bread, *broa*, pleasantly nutty in flavour and crumbly in texture.

OVOS À MINHOTA (MINHO EGGS)

FOR TWO

1 onion   2 eggs
1 tomato   olive oil and butter as required

Place the sliced onion in a saucepan together with the skinned and de-pipped and roughly chopped tomato with sufficient oil to cover, and cook gently till tender. Meanwhile butter two small tins or cocotte dishes and break an egg into each. Cook in the oven till whites are set; remove from dishes. Serve on top of the onion and tomato mixture.

COSTELETAS DE CARNEIRO À BARCELENSE
(BARCELOS LAMB CHOPS)

lamb chops (1–2 per person)   1 egg for every 2 chops
olive oil   salt, pepper, crushed garlic to
breadcrumbs   taste

Trim the chops. Beat the eggs together with salt, pepper and crushed garlic. Dip the chops in this mixture and then roll in breadcrumbs. Heat the oil in a frying-pan and fry the chops until golden brown.

ARROZ DE FRANGO DE CABIDELA
(JUGGED CHICKEN WITH RICE)

FOR FOUR

1 chicken, jointed   ½ garlic sausage (*chouriço*)
10 oz. rice   cut into slices (see page 185)
5 soupspoons olive oil   2 soupspoons vinegar
2 large onions chopped   salt to taste
1 sprig parsley   2 pints stock

Put the oil, chicken, onions, parsley, sliced garlic sausage, salt and stock in a saucepan. Bring to the boil and then add the rice (drained) and simmer. Add any chicken blood, mixed with the vinegar to prevent its congealing, stirring well. Cook gently on a low heat till tender. The rice is served separately after drying.

LOMBO DE PORCO DE MONÇÃO
(MONÇÃO PORK)
FOR FOUR

2 lb. loin of pork
scant ½ cup white wine (about 6 tablespoons)
4 cloves
1 bay leaf
salt and pepper

Place the meat in an oven dish with the wine, cloves, pepper, salt and bay leaf. Cook in moderate oven for about 1½ hours, basting occasionally. Strain liquid and use as a gravy accompaniment. This dish is superb served with roasted, skinned chestnuts.

ENTRECOSTO DE VIANA
(VIANA CUTLETS)
FOR FOUR

8 lamb cutlets
2–3 large onions
2 tomatoes
2 carrots
1 sprig parsley
1–2 cloves garlic
salt, pepper, butter

Rub the cutlets with salt and garlic to taste. Grill them, then fry peeled tomatoes from which seeds have been removed, chopped onions, parsley and pepper. When cooked, blend to a *purée* with cooked carrots. Serve cutlets topped with this sauce.

COSTELETAS À MODA DE BRAGA
(BRAGA CUTLETS)
FOR FOUR

8–12 pork cutlets
1¾ lb. potatoes
3½ oz. butter
1–2 large onions
3 soupspoons white wine
3½ oz. cooking fat
5 oz. ham
salt and pepper

Trim the cutlets and season with salt and pepper. Sprinkle with the wine. Fry in butter and fat. In another pan, lightly fry potatoes cut in thin slices. Add chopped ham and onion to the fat in which the cutlets were fried and cook till golden brown. Add the cutlets, the rest of the wine and the potatoes to the pan and simmer gently together for ½ hour.

ARROZ MONÇÃO (MONÇÃO RICE)

A rich rice base for chicken. The Portuguese use the chicken blood to enrich the rice, but chicken stock can be substituted.

FOR FOUR

1 chicken, jointed
1 sprig parsley
5 oz. ham
1 onion
6 tablespoons olive oil
pepper and salt

RICE BASE

8 oz. rice
2 cups chicken stock
2 tablespoons wine vinegar
1 onion
2 oz. butter

Put a sliced onion in a pan with butter and fry till golden brown. Add the joints of chicken, chopped ham and seasoning. Fry till golden. Reduce heat, cover with lid and continue cooking until tender. In a separate pan melt 1 oz. butter, add the chopped onion and cook gently without colouring for 2–3 minutes. Add the rice and cook gently for 2–3 minutes. Add a little chicken stock and the wine vinegar and continue cooking, adding stock each time it is absorbed by the rice, until the rice is cooked. Carefully mix in the remaining butter. Have ready a large heated dish, pile in the rice and place on top the fried chicken, ham and onion. Serve sprinkled with parsley.

COELHO À MINHOTA (MINHO RABBIT)

Make a marinade of wine, vinegar, garlic, pepper and salt and soak the rabbit meat in this for 24 hours. Then remove rabbit and simmer it in water seasoned with salt, to which has been added a piece of raw ham or garlic sausage (*chouriço*, see page 185), and chopped onion. When the rabbit is nearly cooked remove from the water (this can be used for soup-making), cut into chunks and fry in butter till golden.

Make a tomato sauce (see page 195), and place the pieces of rabbit, covered with tomato sauce, in the centre of a dish and surround with fried bread triangles.

COZIDO À PORTUGUESA (MEAT STEW)

SCALED-DOWN VERSION TO SERVE SIX

2 lb. shin of beef 1 lb. turnips
½ lb. fat or streaky bacon 1 large cabbage
2 lb. potatoes 12 oz. rice
1 lb. carrots 1 smoked sausage

Put the meat in a very large pan of boiling water. Add the bacon and simmer slowly. After it has been cooking for about 2 hours add the peeled potatoes, carrots, turnips and the cabbage cut into quarters. When these are half cooked add slices of smoked sausage. Remove some of the liquid and cook the rice separately in this and, when all is cooked, serve in a large dish with the meat in the centre, the vegetables around. The rice will be served in a separate dish. The liquid in which everything has cooked makes an excellent soup just as it is. The local habit is to serve the meats and vegetables set out on the huge platter in separate little mounds.

BACALHAU À MODA DE VIANA
(DRIED VIANA COD)

FOR FOUR

1 lb. dried cod   garlic (optional)
large cabbage leaf   bay leaf
1 lb. onions

Prepare dried cod for each person (see page 189). Drain and, while still moist, wrap in the cabbage leaf which has been freshly washed in cold water. Tie with thin string. Place in an ovenproof dish and cook in a moderate oven till the leaf is browned and the cod risen.

Meanwhile make a side dish of the thinly cut onion fried in olive oil with a little crushed garlic (optional) and bay leaf. Discard the browned cabbage leaf and finish cooking the cod with the onion sauce on top. Serve with boiled potatoes peeled, Portuguese style, after boiling.

ROJOES À MODA DO MINHO
(CHOPPED MINHO PORK)

as described to me by Oporto gourmet Daniel Constant

FOR TWO TO THREE

1 lb. pork (from the leg)	1 clove garlic
6 small halved onions	1 bay leaf
bunch parsley	a little paprika
½ pint dry white wine	

Chop pork in small 2-inch-long pieces. Marinate in dry white wine for 6 hours, allowing ½ pint wine to 1 lb. of meat. Add to the marinade the onions, parsley, garlic, bay leaf and paprika. Drain meat and fry lightly in fat till brown. Add the marinade little by little: enough to fry the meat. When meat is well fried remove to heated dish. Sauté small or diced potatoes (parboiled) in the same pan. Serve meat surrounded by ring of potatoes with a slice of lemon or bitter orange.

PESCADA À MAIATA (MAIA HAKE)

from the Estalagem Lidador

FOR FOUR

1 lb. hake fillets	1 lb. potatoes
(about ½ in. thick)	1 cup mayonnaise
lemon juice	chopped onion (optional)
salt	

Prepare fillets of hake and place in an ovenproof dish sprinkled with lemon juice and salt. Boil potatoes, dice and fry lightly in a little olive oil. Add to fish. Place mayonnaise on top, working it in to the mixed fish and potatoes. Spread a layer over the top with the back of a spoon. Bake, and when it rises like a soufflé on top it is ready – usually ½ hour in a medium oven. Chopped onion can be added on top of the potatoes and olive oil added during baking if necessary.

PEIXE ASSADO À OFIR
(ROAST OFIR FISH)

from Chef Abilio Rodrigues, Hotel Ofir

1 lb. any flaked fish   1 lb. potatoes
(hake is ideal)   tomato (optional)

SAUCE
1–2 onions   ⅓ pint dry white wine

Scoop balls from potatoes, boil and then fry lightly in oil or fat. Meanwhile gently fry the onions in a little olive oil till soft and almost mushy; add the wine. Put this in the bottom of an ovenproof dish; add potatoes and fish. Sliced tomato can also be added. Bake in a hot oven for 12–15 minutes till fish is cooked.

BIFE À ESTALAGEM
(STEAK À LA MAISON)

from Chef Abilio Rodrigues, Hotel Ofir

FOR EACH PERSON
1 fillet steak about an inch thick   butter for frying
slice of fried bread

SAUCE
chicken stock   cream to taste
a little dry white wine

Fry the steak and then the bread in butter. Remove from pan and keep hot while making the sauce. This should be made in the same pan in which the steak was fried. Mix together wine, stock and cream. Cook gently, pour over steak placed on top of the fried bread and garnish with sliced mushrooms and potatoes. Thin ham slices and fried egg served on steak is common in Portugal. The same sauce can be used with veal escalope or chicken.

LAGOSTA À BAR DE OFIR
(LOBSTER FROM THE BAR DE OFIR)
Chef Abilio Rodrigues

As in many Portuguese lobster recipes, a live lobster is recommended, but in Britain or America it will mostly be only possible to start with a prepared lobster in its shell, though live lobsters are available in a few areas.

Remove the lobster meat and chop the white and coral finely. Mix together with a *béchamel* sauce (see below). Line the bottom of the lobster shell with some of the sauce and pile the lobster back into the shell. Scatter a little grated cheese and butter on top and grill or bake in a very hot oven till cheese bubbles.

BÉCHAMEL SAUCE. Put blade of mace, bay leaf, slice of shallot and 4–5 peppercorns in $\frac{1}{2}$ pint milk in covered pan on low heat for 7–8 minutes. Melt $\frac{3}{4}$ oz. butter in a thick saucepan, remove from the heat, add flour, cook for a minute and add the strained, flavoured milk. Stir continuously till smooth and boiling. Simmer 2–3 minutes, adding seasoning and a little cream as required.

FIDALGUINHOS
(the word Fidalguinhos means 'small noblemen')

1 lb. sieved flour   6 tablespoons milk
8 oz. sugar   1 teaspoon baking powder
8 oz. butter

Blend the flour with baking powder. Rub in butter and sugar. Mix with milk and knead into a dough. Cut the dough in pieces and shape into thin plaits. Place the plaits on a greased baking sheet and cook in a moderately hot oven till golden.

SONHOS (DREAMS)

a nationally found dish, but typical of the especially sweet tooth of the north

FOR FOUR

4 oz. butter   oil or cooking fat
2 oz. sugar   pinch of salt
5 oz. plain flour   ½ pint water
4 eggs

SYRUP

1 lb. sugar   stick cinnamon or lemon
½ pint water   peel

In a saucepan put ½ pint water, butter, sugar and salt. Bring to the boil. Add flour, mixing quickly. Remove from the heat, beat till cold. Add the eggs, one by one, and beat till well mixed and smooth. Leave for 15 minutes. Boil cooking fat or oil in a deep fryer and drop in spoonfuls of the dough mixture. Fry slowly to make them puffy. When pale brown, remove and drain on kitchen paper. Eat hot or cold, sprinkled with sugar and cinnamon or with light sugar syrup flavoured with cinnamon or lemon. The syrup is made by boiling sugar in water. Simmer for 5 minutes. Add cinnamon stick or slivers of lemon peel before it boils. Pour over 'dreams' while still warm. N.B. The dough can be shaped with the help of 2 spoons.

PUDIM FLAN DE MONÇÃO
(MONÇÃO EGG CUSTARD)

a creation of Dona Tihina's at the Pensão Vaticano

FOR FOUR TO SIX

1 lb. sugar   6 eggs
grated lemon rind   1 pint water

Mix sugar with water and boil slowly till a thick syrup is formed. Make sure sugar is dissolved before the water boils to avoid crystallization. Cool, add lemon peel and well-beaten eggs. Cook gently on low heat or in double cooker; stir till it becomes thick cream or custard. Serve cold with wafer biscuits or sponge fingers.

PUDIM DE PRESUNTO DE MONÇÃO
(MONÇÃO HAM PUDDING)

another Dona Tihina creation

This is very much of the Mrs Beeton 'take a dozen eggs' school of cookery, to which Portugal wholeheartedly subscribes. The amounts will serve about 10 people at a dinner party and can be scaled down as required.

1 lb. 3 oz. sugar	14 egg yolks
1¼ gills water	2 egg whites
4½ oz. uncooked ham (in one piece)	1 cinnamon stick
	1 small glass port

Boil sugar and water to thin syrup, making sure sugar dissolves before boiling – add more water if necessary. Let it get cold. Add ham, still in one piece, cinnamon and port. Bring to boil, and boil at 215° F. – 217° F. till syrup drops from spoon in narrow ribbons. Remove ham and cinnamon and let the mixture cool. Add egg yolks and whites beaten together. Mix well and pour into a large mould or several small ones lined with caramel (see page 197). Place in *bain-marie* or double boiler and boil gently until firm or when an inserted knife comes cleanly away. Alternatively half fill a large meat tin with water. Place moulds in it and cook slowly in a moderate oven.

3

OPORTO, THE DOURO, TRÁS-OS-MONTES

Oporto and Bragança spread the width of the country and are separated by 160 miles of hilly road. The two places represent two extremes of Portuguese life: the bustling, prosperous city of Oporto, rich in its international port wine trade, and the tiny, scruffy, village town of Bragança, kept alive by history and some recipes. The two towns of the north are dear to the Portuguese; they say Oporto gave its name to the country and Bragança gave her a king. The hard, harsh mountainous country which rises almost immediately outside Oporto and climbs relentlessly towards the Spanish border is poor, and the active, quick and loud-tongued peasants are workworn souls who nourish themselves on hearty food, making much use of kid, as well as pig, the nation's favourite meat, made into sausages and hams or the unique smoked pigs' tongues. The sausage centre is Chaves. The pigs of these areas run semi-wild and produce leaner and richer meat.

It is difficult to believe such a hard area could produce the rich and gloriously hued port wine. The Douro Mountains were described to me as a 'gigantic rockery' by the director of a port firm. Man has worked hard on this rockery, terracing it at every possible spot for vineyards, planting maize, potatoes and cabbages in between the houses. The cabbages often act as a rough hedge, and surprisingly in this harsh place oranges, lemons and grapefruit abound among the farms, as well as olive trees. The Portuguese love of dried cod does not abate in this inland area, and fresh fish is carried up into the Douro area towns like Régua. But the fish restaurants really come into their own around the seaside parts of Oporto's Douro estuary. The north-west of the area is walled in behind high mountains, hard and taciturn, full of strange legends and primitive folklore and, once upon a time, the wild boar, off which most of the inhabitants still live, was worshipped. Many traces of ancient cults still remain, giving the area a chill fascination.

OPORTO

Oporto has a little of the gloom that surrounds many northern industrial cities. Its buildings are towering, worthy and solid; its grey cobbled streets full of hurrying, sombrely dressed people – the town seems always to be full of bank clerks – and one sees few bright secretary birds strolling in the streets. Everyone is in a hurry. It is one of the worst, or most challenging, cities I know for driving; the jostling of the traffic in the cobbled streets, which switchback over the hills on which the city rests, combined with one-way systems and a jumbled centre, makes it difficult to drive, impossible to park and hazardous to cross a road where traffic seems to pour from every orifice between buildings. The yellow trams and their treacherous skidding lines add to the confusion as they do in Lisbon. Oporto is vast and has absorbed the seaside areas of Leça, Matosinhos and the Leixões port of the Douro into its embrace; transport is needed, but, as in Lisbon, resort to the cheap taxis is the best solution for the tourist.

Originally the name 'Portugal' is supposed to have come from 'Portus Cale', once the name of a small town near Vila Nova de Gaia. Oporto and Vila Nova de Gaia, separated by the Douro gorge, are now linked by most impressive bridges. My favourite is the high iron Don Luiz bridge, from whose soaring arches the visitor gets a bird's-eye view of the cities; a lower bridge also links the two.

VILA NOVA DE GAIA is the area in which all the port firms have their 'lodges', and the tourist is very welcome to see round them and sample the wares. Appointments can be made through shippers in Britain and America or by application to the Port Wine Institute, Rua de Ferreira Borges. While in Vila Nova de Gaia, cheap and pungently regional catering can be had at the Castelo Branco restaurant.

From the windows of such lodges as that of Sandeman there are superb views across the Douro to the piled-up buildings of Oporto. The view always reminds me of a film set for London-before-the-Great-Fire; old wooden buildings heaped high up around the arched supports of the iron bridge; stone-cobbled, narrow streets and an impression of colour, vibrant humanity and refuse. The vegetable and fish markets in this north bank area are worth visiting for their colour and the darting, coarse humour of the fishwives who, in this part of Portugal, have a reputation for their quick tongues and ability to make amusement out of anything that strikes their eye as unusual.

In spite of being such an industrious city, there is some night life in Oporto to entertain the visitor. The clubs tend to be on the outskirts of Oporto, mostly in the old narrow streets of Foz do Douro on the river's edge. I am not a discothèque admirer, but the most pleasant one I have ever visited was in Oporto. The Dona Urraca at Foz do Douro is spacious, with music pervading enough but not so loud that one has to shout above it. The *décor* is pseudo-baronial-hall but well thought out, and there was the most superb log fire conversation area away from the dance floor. Other clubs in the area are the Coutada at Leça; the restaurant Arco Iris at Rua Roberto Ivens, 108; at Matosinhos, where there is dancing; the Xeque Mate and Ricardo 3rd, both at Foz do Douro.

Oporto shows its practicality as a hard-working city in its food. The most typical dish is tripe done in the Oporto manner. The dried tripes are seen like shrivelled yellow oilskins hanging bunched at every grocer's door. The legend of the origin of the taste for tripe dates back to the days when Henry the Navigator was setting off to make his discoveries. Oporto loyally built and victualled the ships for the prince. Their herds were slaughtered, salted and stowed in the ships, and when the fleet had sailed the citizens were left with little to eat except the tripe from the cattle.

Tripe is usually cooked here with haricot beans and smoked sausage. Other specialities of the town include *febras de porco*, leg of pork cooked in red *vinho verde*, *aguardente* (a rough native brandy) and spices. Roast chicken – *frango no forno* – is very popular, and round the area one sees plenty of small restaurants or snack bars with their roast chicken signs up. In some areas you can even have the slightly unnerving experience of eating a casseroled hen complete with unlaid egg. More formally, chicken is roast with port wine and very old local brandy. *Bacalhau* turns up local style with rice, onions and tomatoes.

The restaurants in Oporto are modest in *décor*, sturdy in value. The top favourite is Escondidinho, whose chef, José Goncalves, has been forty years in the same restaurant. Some of his specialities are described on pages 55 and 92. The restaurant reproduces the atmosphere of an old inn with plentiful tiling on floor and walls and dark oak furniture. Specialities include *pescada frite* (fried hake), *linguado à Escondidinho* (sole à la maison), *crepes* (*pancakes*), *filetes* (fish fillets) with madeira wine and *bife de frigideira*. The latter appears in many restaurants all over Portugal, but does not mean frozen beef. *Frigideira* means 'frying-pan' and usually refers to the type of earthenware dish in which it is cooked.

Other notable restaurants within the city proper include Tres Irmãos (the three brothers) and the Montenegro, where roast chicken, roast kid and roast *bacalhau* are popular, though the chef is likely to decide what you will have. At Restaurante Freitos an *açorda* bread soup made with shrimp (*camarão*) is served. Such meals can also be obtained at the Hotel Infante Sagres and Bona Chiva, Praça Dom João.

In general Oporto restaurants are, to make a decided understatement, generous with their portions. It is one of the few places where courses are so large that the half portion is costed alongside the full on the menus. It is not an expensive place to eat, and a lunch in many of the ordinary restaurants, with wine, will cost around 7*s* (84 cents).

The popular part of Oporto to visit for dining out, particularly in summer, is the mouth of the river round Leça, where the restaurants have a strong seafood bias. One of the favourites is the Boa Nova, built into the rocks, with plate-glass windows looking out over the sea at Leça. Also at Leça is the Garrafão, where shellfish is the speciality, and the Bem Arramjadinha. Down by the river in Oporto one or two of the rough local restaurants, where gipsies dine with locals, regional food is served and the menu is chalked on a blackboard, are being redecorated with tourists in mind, and should be reopened by the time this book appears.

In summer the visitor may well prefer to stay in one of the several small village resorts clustering round Oporto. Matosinhos is practically part of the city, with good train connections, and it has an excellent camping site set in heady pine woods by the sea at Amgeiras, where there is a restaurant worthy of a visit. To the south of Porto, using the new fast motorway, Miramar, Aguda, Granja and Espinho (all with their own tourist offices) can be reached quickly.

At Miramar there is the Areal restaurant in an historical old building serving *pescada com chouriço* (hake and sausage), *porco em boa companhina* and *torta royale*. Fish canning is an important industry in this area and all the resorts have good sandy beaches.

Oporto Tourist office: Praça dom João I, 25. Matosinhos also has a tourist office.

THE DOURO

The vast Douro River has gashed a gorge right across Portugal from its source in Spain. By the time it reaches Oporto much of its frenzy of rapids and rock-strewn foam has calmed. The Douro is not a city river, broad and stately, but a wild mountain river which at once hides itself from the passer-by yet by its power commands him to see it. Exploration of the Douro district is not quick and easy for the visitor. The only way is by car – the puffing billy train takes far too long – twisting and turning up across the valleys in a south-easterly direction from Oporto. To reach the town of Régua, the centre of the port-wine-producing country, takes a good $2\frac{1}{2}$ to 3 hours' drive from Oporto, especially as you may get trapped behind a road tanker unromantically carrying wine.

It was a Scotsman, Baron Forrester, who in the mid nineteenth century discovered the possibilities of navigating the Douro, adapting for the job flat-bottomed boats with square sails called *rebelos*. The danger of rapids, and Forrester's own drowning in one, ensured the move to mechanized land transport when that came into being. Today there are only a few *rebelo* boats left. To journey on one would be to see the Douro at its best and most beautiful: this opal grey water seething in its haste to escape the hot, arid mountain valley for the cooler Atlantic. Croft, the port company, have plans for converting a *rebelo* into a restaurant and pleasure craft for their visitors and this idea would be welcomed by tourists. A plan for damming the Douro is under way, mainly so that the steel barges from the mines in the Douro can sail down to the coast and thence to the steelworks at Lisbon. When this plan is complete it may well be that port wine will again travel down the river.

The Douro divides into the lower Douro, rising from Oporto to the Serra do Marão, which forms the dividing line with the Trás-os-Montes region of which the upper Douro has been described as a ditch making the southern border. As far as the tourist is concerned, I have treated the upper Douro with the Trás-os-Montes area.

OPORTO TO THE SERRA DO MARÃO

The main road from Oporto leads right across the country through Vila Real and up to Bragança. After Valongo, the salt-producing town, the road curves gently up over wooded hills. On the roadside around Paredes near Penafiel children and women thrust square or round-shaped parcels towards the car. This is not another case of someone trying to make a sucker out of a tourist, they are offering a fine white bread called *regueifa*, freshly made by the local women and sold to passers-by. Like the sweetmeats, Portuguese local breads attain a reputation which draws people away from home to buy them at the spot where they are made. One of the richest, yet light and most delicious, 'breads' of the north is the *pão do ló*, more like a light sponge cake (see page 76).

The Portuguese of this area are accustomed to travelling around with and for their food. In such a tough, hard-working area the festivals achieve a special significance. The *romaries*, or pilgrimages, round the countryside are eagerly anticipated and people take their food with them or join feasts in the area. Fairs of every kind abound; cattle fairs, vegetable fairs, seed and pottery fairs, ironmongery fairs and even in certain areas the old-fashioned marriage fair. At Penafiel, next on the road from Paredes, there is a wide central road lined one side by shops; on the other a terrace drops down to a wide fairground where horse and cattle fairs are well worth visiting.

Amarante, the next town of size along the main road, has old houses with wooden balconies and wrought-iron work, a three-arched Roman bridge over the Tâmega River (good for bathing and for camping by) and views of the glowering pile of the Serra do Marão. The town's curious festivals and customs have earnt it an odd reputation. On Corpus Christi day a cardboard serpent is 'killed' in the streets and everyone enjoys huge banquets. In June and September festivals are held in honour of São Gonçalo, whose saintly work is to find suitable matches for bachelors and spinsters. Amarante, as its name suggests, has a strong interest in love that is more earthly than heavenly, and some of the local fertility customs include the giving of cakes shaped like phallic symbols.

Amarante (branch tourist office) has also gained a reputation for gastronomy. Sweetmeats are made here from almonds which manage to grow in the softer, sheltered valleys. Names such as *foguetes*, rocket-shaped cylinders of almond paste coated with syrup, and *papos de anjo* – angel's breasts, once charmingly translated for me as 'tit-bits' – reflect local humour.

The traveller can come under the care of the match-making saint, São Gonçalo, when he stays at the Pousada de São Gonçalo in the Serra do Marão. This little *Pousada* crouches low into the bare hillside to escape its wintry blasts. The isolated building is built sturdily from local granite and the best, if not liked, word to describe it is 'cosy'. The rooms are small, well-heated, with wooden, country style carved furniture, liberally decorated with flowers; the managers are welcoming, as is the hot nourishing food.

VILA REAL, RÉGUA, LAMEGO AND ALIJÓ

The *Pousada* is within easy reach by car of Vila Real (district head tourist office) the great table-wine town, and Régua the centre for the port wine industry. The latter can make the goal, with nearby Lamego, of a day's drive from Oporto to see the Douro proper. These towns are not great sightseeing towns, but they well represent the character of this hardy land which produces such a rich and famous wine.

The best way to approach the Douro is to drive past Penafiel on the main road, turning off right to Marco de Canaveses, Baião, Carneiro, through Mesão Frio, where there is a stupendous cliff-top view of the Douro gorge, and so into Régua.

The road twists and turns and soars up and over valleys to reach the Douro. On the summit of some of these heath-covered, wind-swept passes, on a crisp, clear morning or evening, the view is limitless and strangely oriental, with swathes of mist hanging over the deeper valleys through which the terraced vineyards rise, looking more like a relief model than real mountains. Most frequent sight on the road is not cars but the Douro oxen, horned like those of the Minho but more stocky, with huge leather padded yokes on their foreheads, straining on their creaking wooden carts.

Régua itself is not a remarkable town for the tourist; it clings to the side of a sloping hill rising from the Douro and achieves its wealth as the centre for the port wine trade, a railhead for shipping goods down to Oporto and the legal centre for the Casa do Douro which governs the making of port wine. Its rather gloomy offices can be seen with vast stained-glass windows showing the making of the wine. There is little point in stopping long in Régua; on the outskirts the new market place is lively (markets on Wednesday) for displays of local agricultural produce – huge oranges, lemons and grapefruit – and the fish market, where even so far from the coast fresh fish can be bought. Alongside the market is a new coffee lounge where hot, strong, black coffee is sold with local sweetmeats.

The Régua surroundings are beautiful, glancing down to the Douro or up to the high vineyard terracing; so far the town has lacked suitable visitor accommodation apart from the private establishments maintained by the port companies. It is hoped, however, that a small *Pousada* may soon be built, supported by the port industry.

From Régua it is about 9 miles south to Lamego, famous for its smoked ham specialities. Like Régua, it is a small market town, but has the dignity of former episcopal palaces, with a wealth of baroque buildings set on a sloping hillside. Just outside the town, at the pilgrimage church of Nossa Senhora dos Remédios, a great fair is held in the first two weeks of September. The town has the first-class modern Estalagem de Lamego, of seven rooms.

Eight miles north of Lamego, on the way to Régua, the road branches east and then follows the Douro bank to Pinhão, where the best port vineyards are, and then on to Alijó, where there is a charming small *Pousada* of twelve rooms in a converted old house named after the Barão de Forrester, who first opened the Douro to navigation. Here local hams are served with river trout or roast kid.

TRÁS-OS-MONTES

(Beyond the Mountains)

Strictly speaking the Régua–Lamego–Alijó area is in Trás-os-Montes, since this starts on the eastern side of the Serra do Marão. The southern extent of Trás-os-Montes is marked by the chasm of the Douro and this is the richest part; the people from the harder, mountain-fringed borderlands come down to help with the port vintage and gradually work their way back towards home as the terraces of grapes get higher and are later harvested as they go eastward.

Trás-os-Montes is as hard and bleak as the granite on which it is formed. But like this granite, great boulders of which are littered over the bare mountainsides, it has a brighter gleam of quartz caught winking by the sun. It is an area rarely explored by the tourist except for the occasional motorist. It is cut off by its square of mountains, gloomier than the rest of Portugal. Its people are sombre in approach but vigorous and extremely hard-working, relaxing only for feasts and festivals. On the harsh hills pigs wander almost wild; they are the staple of the regional cooking, which is particularly expressed in the smoked hams of Chaves and the sausages (*alheiras*) from Bragança. Goats' milk and chestnuts are important local ingredients, and in some of the sheltered dips in the mountains, such as Mirandela, oranges and almonds grow – at Moncorvo the latter end as sugared almonds. Potatoes and black bread are much eaten; sheep and the game of the heath – partridge and hare – are made into tasty recipes.

Vila Real forms a jumping-off point for the two spearheads of main road; the tourist routes flow across the region. Vila Real itself is famous for the table wine which bears its name. Near by is the renowned villa of Mateus. Vila Real's festivals are held in the third week of June. There is a camping ground near by, and trout fishing for the visitor to enjoy. Shopping souvenirs include the Bisalhaes pottery, and food specialities are *morcelas* (sausages), dried cod done in the local way and sweetmeats, *viuvinhas* ('little widows') and marzipan.

Bearing north from Vila Real the road passes through the little spa towns of Pedras Salgadas and Vidago. These names are seen all over Portugal on the mineral water bottles served in hotels and restaurants. Both are slightly gassy and excellent chilled on a hot day.

Another way of cooling off on a hot day is a visit to the swimming-bath at the spa of Vidago, which is pleasantly set in pine woods near a golf-course and tennis facilities. There are several hotels, including the first-class Vidago Palace Hotel.

Chaves is an old spa town with hot springs, Roman bridge and fortified keep and city walls of the kind characterizing the border towns along this tough frontier, epitomized in Bragança as the determination to be a nation separate from Spain. Pottery is made here; and there are religious festivities in July and September. The Chaves ham is famous, and at Easter meat pies are made locally in the shape of loaves.

A circular drive may be made back to Braga and Oporto from Chaves, turning west towards the lake district beyond the Serra do Barroso. Returning to Vila Real and turning east the road sweeps across the barren Trás-os-Montes to Bragança. There is little of interest on the way apart from the tiny market town of Murça, famous for its worship of the pig in ancient times. All the visitor now sees is a tubby porcine stone statue in the main square; a pleasantly Thurberesque change from the usual statues of unknown men on prancing horses. Having made obeisance to the pig, the traveller can slip through Mirandela's more lush area to Bragança, dominated by its hundred-foot-high medieval tower. The view of this and the little town is best seen from the terraces and windows of the modern Pousada de São Bartolomeu; a haven of comfort in this stark area.

Here the specialities are the local *alheiras* (sausages), *caldo verde* (vegetable soup), the roast meats of the region, and trout from nearby rivers which can be caught by tourists. In the rooms local pottery can be admired.

Bragança itself, in spite of its proud name which seems to evoke a flourish of trumpets and of setting forth to war in the crisp, chilly air of the mountains, is not an attractive town to me. Its narrow, broken streets are scruffy and rutted. When you get out of the car to see the charming Domus Municipalis, a uniquely well-preserved building from the twelfth century, grubby children pester for money. (This, incidentally, is not allowed by law in Portugal; the children will usually run away on approach of a policeman who can fine the parents of the child caught begging.)

As a border town Bragança, unlike the welcoming charm of Valença, has an impenetrable defensiveness which, examining its fine old buildings and churches, made me happily turn south for the drive into the Beira areas of central Portugal, which act as a gentler transition from the highlands to the softer plains around Lisbon.

To the south-east, Miranda do Douro is 52 miles away. In spite of its lovely, appealing name, it is a neglected sixteenth-century styled town out on a road link near the Spanish border, isolated enough to be the only Portuguese area to have retained a dialect of its own. Pottery, woollen blankets and wrought-iron items are made here; its festivals occur on the last Sundays in April and August. The Pousada de Santa Catarina offers the usual standard of welcome and tourist comfort, where the local products of smoked ham and garlic sausages can be tasted.

RECIPES FROM OPORTO, DOURO AND TRÁS-OS-MONTES

PORT RECIPES

The Portuguese do not use port much in their cooking. These ideas have, in fact, been produced by the Port Wine Institute to increase interest in and consumption of port abroad; but these few fairly simple suggestions for adding a touch of local flavour to international dishes I thought of sufficient interest to act as a kind of culinary tribute to the wine which moulds the lives and character of this region.

MELÃO COM VINHO DO PORTO
(MELON WITH PORT)

Remove pips from centre of melon. Fill cavity with port. Cover with cap of melon. Chill.

MEXILHÕES À FRANCILLON
(FRANCILLON MUSSELS)

Put cooked, drained, shelled mussels into a serving dish with some potato salad. Add 1 glassful of the juice in which the mussels were cooked, blended with port. Sprinkle with freshly chopped herbs.

MOLHO À PORTUGUESA
(PORTUGUESE SAUCE)

Reduce some port to half its amount. Add the same quantity of meat juice, a little lemon juice and some lemon and shredded bitter orange. Boil and thicken the sauce with cornflour mixed with a little water. Reduce slightly. Add some dried raisins, blanched sweet almonds, a little chopped red pepper, green orange peel and more lemon juice to taste.

MOLHO DE AVES (POULTRY SAUCE)

Use the juice from roast poultry, heat together with a little port and stock and thicken with cornflour (stirring well).

CAMARÕES COM CREME E VINHO DO PORTO
(SHRIMPS WITH CREAM AND PORT)

An idea for an *hors d'œuvre* dish. Chop shelled shrimps into small pieces. Add onions, fried in butter. Pour a little port over the mixture in a pan and simmer for a few minutes. Add about a tablespoon of fresh cream and one egg yolk (per person), salt and pepper. Spoon into small ovenproof or cocotte dishes and reheat in the oven till set.

PEIXE ASSADO (ROAST FISH)

Prepare fish, arrange in baking dish covered with sieved tomatoes and finely chopped onions. Salt to taste. Sprinkle with port and bake in a moderate oven.

VITELA ASSADA (ROAST VEAL)

Trim any fat off veal slices, cover each piece of veal with a piece of ham. Place in a roasting tin, cover with chopped tomatoes and onions. Season to taste, sprinkle with port. Cook in a moderate oven.

MORANGOS COM VINHO DO PORTO (STRAWBERRIES WITH PORT)

A delicious way of eking out a few strawberries for a dinner dessert. Pour dry port over strawberries and leave to soak for a while. Add a few peeled slices of orange and some sugar.

PUDIM RAPIDO DE BANANAS (QUICK BANANA SOUFFLÉ)

Put three finely sliced bananas into a baking dish with one tablespoon sugar and a glass of port. Top with 4 beaten egg whites to which sugar and vanilla have been added to taste. Bake in a moderate oven for 20 minutes.

SOPA DE LEGUMES (CREAMED VEGETABLE SOUP)

from Maria Henrietta Pinto de Gouvea of Régua

In some water to cover cook 3 potatoes, 5 carrots, 1 large onion, 2 small turnips, some cabbage leaves, all chopped or shredded finely, parsley, salt and olive oil (to taste for non-Portuguese stomachs). When well cooked, sieve or put through a blender. 6 good servings.

Oporto, Douro, Trás-os-Montes

PERDIZ AÇORDA
(PARTRIDGE AÇORDA)

Although the *açorda* bread soup really comes from the Alentejo area (see page 137), this one was made for me by Maria Henrietta Pinto de Gouvea, using the partridge common in the area. It would be

suitable for an invalid who could only cope with soft foods or for a cold day when the cupboard is low on stocks. Any cooked or chopped meat could be used instead of partridge. For 4 people, allow 1 partridge or about ½ lb. meat.

Cook finely chopped onions to a pulp in a little oil. Season with salt and pepper. Cook the meat in this. Use the equivalent of one dinner roll per person, crumbling smoothly and finely. Add bread to the meat and onion mixture, making sure the mixture is fairly liquid (about ½ pint liquid for 4 people); add water if necessary. Mix together and heat gently before serving.

SOPA TRANSMONTANA
(SOUP FROM 'BEYOND THE MOUNTAINS')

FOR FOUR

1 white cabbage	2 oz. butter
2 medium potatoes	1 onion
1 turnip	salt
6 carrots	toasted bread
1 lb. pork	water to cover

Put the water, roughly chopped vegetables, salt and the pork cut in 4 portions in a large saucepan. Simmer for about 2 hours. Dice toasted bread, and, when serving the soup, add this and the butter to it.

BACALHAU À DOURO
(DOURO COD)

In the inland mountain districts the dried cod dishes are even more prized and varied. In the Douro town of Régua I was served a delightful lunch by the young daughter-in-law of the Sandeman commissario. Maria Henrietta and her mother-in-law were both enthusiastic and excellent cooks.

This is a frequent dish served in their dining-room overlooking the vineyards sloping down to the Douro.

FOR FOUR

1 lb. dried cod	green cabbage
1 large onion	fat or olive oil
2 lb. potatoes	

CREAM SAUCE

1 oz. butter	½ pint milk
1 tablespoon flour	pepper, salt

OPORTO, THE DOURO, TRÁS-OS-MONTES

Cook the onion in the fat or oil, add the prepared cod (see page 189) and cook together. Place in an ovenproof dish. Put layers of sliced, parboiled potatoes and sliced cabbage in the oven dish. Make the sauce by melting the butter, stir in the flour and add the milk gradually. Season. Bring to boil, stirring all the time. Cover vegetables and fish with the sauce. Cook for ½ hour in a medium oven: sliced hard-boiled eggs can also be added if wished.

Maria's mother also gave me her recipe for *Bacalhau Pudding*. In the Vila Real district *bacalhau* is cooked over charcoal; Oporto adds a little wine to the fish.

BACALHAU ASSADO À VILA REAL
(ROAST VILA REAL COD)

A change for a summer barbecue dish. Put a fillet of cod in to soak for 24 hours, changing the water twice. Wash well, dry and roast on charcoal. When cooked, sprinkle with plenty of olive oil and finely chopped garlic. Serve with baked potatoes in their jackets.

PUDIM DE BACALHAU (COD PUDDING)

Other fish could also be used. Cook a sizable piece of prepared cod (see page 189) and mince well. Chop a large onion finely and cook in 5 tablespoons olive oil until golden. Add 2 soupspoons breadcrumbs to 1 pint of milk and boil. Fry the minced cod in the olive oil with the onion, adding salt, white pepper and finely chopped parsley. Mix well with the milk containing the bread and 4 beaten eggs and bake in a well-buttered tin or dish for about 1½ hours in a slow to moderate oven.

BACALHAU À MODA DO PORTO
(PORTO COD)

FOR FOUR

1 lb. dried codfish beaten eggs and dry white
seasoning crumbs for coating
¼ lemon (juice) oil for frying

SAUCE

3 carrots	2½ tablespoons gravy from roast meat
2 onions	
3 oz. bacon	2 soupspoons port wine
1 tablespoon oil	5 tablespoons white wine
1 tablespoon wine vinegar	½ lemon (juice)
3 egg yolks	sprig parsley, pepper

Prepare the fish as on page 189. Trim and dice it, sprinkle with pepper and some of the lemon juice and leave for 30 minutes. Dip fish pieces in flour and some of the beaten egg and coat with breadcrumbs. Fry in fat. For the sauce, fry grated carrots, finely chopped onions, diced bacon in oil. When cooked add white wine, gravy, port, rest of the lemon juice, chopped parsley and beaten egg and blend into a smooth sauce. Do not let it boil.

EMPADA DE SARDINHAS À MODA DA BRAGANÇA
(BRAGANÇA SARDINE PIE)

Even so far removed from the sea, Bragança has produced fish recipes. Conger eel is sliced into steaks fried on bread and covered with an egg yolk sauce. Ingredients more available at home are sardines, which are used with bread dough to make an economical and satisfying pie.

FOR FOUR

1 lb. bread dough with yeast already added	6 sardines (large tinned or fresh: double amount of small English tinned ones, see page 183)
6 eggs	
7 tablespoons oil	
salt, flour	2–3 onions

Add beaten eggs, salt and warmed oil to the dough. Mix well till an even and soft dough is produced. Gradually add enough flour to blend with the dough till it is dry. Divide dough in two. Roll out one piece lightly into a rectangle to fit a greased baking sheet. Brown sliced onions in oil or fat in frying-pan. Remove from pan, add trimmed sardines and fry lightly on both sides. Place with onions on the dough, pouring on any oil used for frying. Cover with the second piece of dough. Make sure the sides are firmly joined.

Make decorative grooves in the top. Leave the pie for an hour or two to swell slightly. Cook in a hot oven till golden brown.

A similar Douro recipe was given me by Mrs Gouvea, senior, using a meat filling.

BOLA DE CARNE (GOLDEN MEAT BALL)

FOR FOUR TO SIX (to be eaten cold)

1 cooked chicken – about $3\frac{1}{2}$ lb.
4–6 oz. cooked smoked ham
$10\frac{1}{2}$ oz. flour
5 or 6 eggs (less 1 white) beaten with 5 spoons warm olive oil
salt to taste in $\frac{1}{2}$ cup warm water
1 oz. baker's yeast softened in a little warm water to liquefy. The dough should be firm and worked only with the hands.

Add the yeast to the flour and gradually add the eggs and warm water with the salt. Knead as for bread. Line a buttered tin well dredged with flour, with half the dough. Fill with chopped smoked ham and chopped chicken; cover with the rest of the dough and seal the edges. Put in a warm place to rise for 1 hour or so and bake with a few pieces of margarine or fine lard on top.

TRIPAS À MODA DO PORTO (OPORTO TRIPE)

The traditional local dish makes use of the strong flavouring of sausage and ham and spices. Beans and rice are added but only in small quantities.

FOR SIX TO EIGHT

$1\frac{1}{2}$ lb. calf's tripe
1 calf's foot (veal shank)
$\frac{1}{2}$ lb. *chouriço* (smoked sausage of the north) or continental sausage
$\frac{1}{4}$ lb. *toucinho* (streaky green bacon) or smoked ham
2 chicken joints
1 cup butter beans
3 onions
1 oz. lard
3 carrots
salt, black pepper, bay leaf, parsley, cummin seed
rice

Clean the tripe and calf's foot well, washing in water with lemon juice and salt. Cut into large cubes and cook together in water (enough to cover) with salt to taste. Simmer till tender – about 3 hours. Heat beans in water till boiling, leave to stand for an hour, then simmer in salted water till cooked. Simmer separately the chopped sausage, bacon and chicken covered with water for about 30 minutes. Add the carrots cut in rounds and one sliced onion. When all is tender, cut meats into small pieces, draining and keeping the broth. Meanwhile, in a large casserole, fry the chopped onions in lard. Add to this the meats, beans, vegetables, the tripe with finely chopped parsley, pepper, bay leaf and cummin seed and about 1 pint of broth from the meat. Cook gently for about ½ hour till blended, adding more broth if necessary. The final consistency should be that of a stew. Serve with a little rice.

VITELA ASSADA NO ESPETO
(*VEAL ROASTED ON A SPIT*)

In the Trás-os-Montes region the veal is spit-roasted over an open wood fire or in a fireplace. If you lack a spit roaster, the same mixture can be used to baste a piece of veal roasted in the oven in the normal way.

BASTING MIXTURE

3 soupspoons olive oil	1 bay leaf (broken up)
1 teaspoon vinegar	small pieces of hot chilli
1–2 cloves garlic (finely chopped)	(or pepper)

Use a boneless round veal joint and trim off any fat. Rub the meat with salt and place on a spit (or in the oven). The meat must be cooked slowly in order to avoid burning it. While the meat is cooking baste it with parsley which has been dipped in the basting mixture.

CARNEIRO À TRANSMONTANA
(MUTTON FROM TRÁS-OS-MONTES)
a cold dish

3 tablespoons white wine	2 eggs
1 leg of lamb or mutton	1 onion
3 tablespoons meat juices or stock	lard, butter, salt and breadcrumbs

Trim the fat off the meat, season and roll it in a fair quantity of lard. Place meat in an oven dish and pour white wine and meat juices or stock on it. Add sliced onion. Place dish in oven, and from time to time brush the meat with butter. When the meat is roasted, take it out of oven and roll it in the beaten eggs, spread breadcrumbs all over it and reheat. Leave to get cold and serve in slices.

COELHO EM VINHO VERDE
(RABBIT IN VINHO VERDE)

The slightly sparkling 'green' wine of the north – particularly round Amarante – is used to cook the wild rabbits of the mountains. Rub rabbit joints with a cut garlic clove, chopped parsley, salt, pepper and paprika. Melt a little lard and blend in a spoonful of cornflour in a casserole, preferably one that can also be used on top of the stove, such as Pyrosil ware or the Portuguese earthenware. When the flour becomes golden add the rabbit, browning it a little. Cover with dry white *vinho verde* and simmer slowly, adding a little water if necessary. (You can of course casserole this in the oven in the normal way.) Serve with fried potatoes or fried bread *croûtons*.

SWEETS

The north is particularly good for sweet items, both the creamy egg puddings and the shaped egg and sugar fabrications.

The *pudim creme* which Maria Henrietta de Gouvea made me was truly light and creamy and not so plastic smooth as some of the restaurant *pudim flan* creations. This version is traditionally served at country weddings in the Douro area. The pudding was finished with a thin translucent sheet of caramel. This is achieved in

Portugal by burning sugar scattered on the pudding with a heated heart-shaped iron gadget called a *torrador* (burner). A careful heating under the grill could achieve the same effect, but a cheat is to make a caramel by boiling sugar and water (see page 197) and scattering thin pieces over the pudding surface.

Mix together 4 egg yolks, 1 tablespoon cornflour and scant ⅓ pint milk. Strain to remove the skin of the egg yolks. Heat in a *bain-marie* or double boiler, stirring till thick, and continue to cook for 5 minutes. Pour into a serving dish. Scatter 3–4 spoonfuls of sugar on the surface and when cold burn the sugar on the surface.

Traditionally served at Christmas time in the Oporto and Douro areas are *rabanadas* and *sopa dourada*. Both these make use of a basis of bread, economical yet tasty, with the addition of syrup and eggs.

RABANADAS

Use up cold slices of toast which are soaked in a mixture of sugar, milk and beaten eggs. The slices are then fried in oil. A syrup is made from sugar and water (see page 197) and poured over them, and they are served hot or cold.

SOPA DOURADA (GOLDEN SOUP)

FOR FOUR TO FIVE

3½ oz. crumb part of bread
1¾ oz. butter for frying
8¾ oz. sugar
5 egg yolks
1¾ oz. chopped, peeled almonds
cinnamon powder

Cut bread in cubes and fry in butter. Add sugar and heat until hot enough to make a thread when dipped in cold water (*punto do fil*). Remove from heat and allow to cool a little. Then add beaten egg yolks and almonds and beat well. Return to the heat to thicken if necessary. Place in serving dish and scatter the surface with a little cinnamon.

This and the following recipe, ideal for tea parties or as a light sweet for buffet parties, were given me by the wife of Mr Brito e Cunha of the Port Wine Institute in Oporto.

TIJELINHAS DE NATA

Small puff pastry cases (these can be bought ready made from bakers) can be filled with a custard mixture made from:

$4\frac{1}{2}$ oz. cream 5 egg yolks
$4\frac{1}{2}$ oz. sugar

Mix the sugar and cream together and heat gently; when just hot add egg yolks and cook till mixture thickens. Pour into pastry cases and leave to set.

CREPES À ESCONDIDINHO
(ESCONDIDINHO PANCAKES)

FOR FOUR

$\frac{3}{4}$ pint milk 4 tablespoons flour
2 eggs grated lemon

SAUCE

1 oz. butter good tablespoonful
1 oz. sugar Bénédictine, Crème de
juice of 1 orange Cacão, cherry brandy,
Grand Marnier or Cointreau

Mix all the ingredients, beat and pass through a sieve. Pour a small quantity of this mixture into a frying-pan which is well greased with lard and previously placed on moderate heat. When pancakes are cooked fold in four and keep warm while preparing the sauce.

Heat all these ingredients together, add the pancakes, still folded, and place over a slow heat for 10 minutes; pour rum over and *flamber*.

CREME À MODA DA RÉGUA
(RÉGUA CREAM)

Mix together $8\frac{1}{4}$ oz. sugar, $\frac{3}{8}$ pint milk and 7 egg yolks. Heat gently till thick, stirring well. Serve hot sprinkled with grated chocolate.

DELICIA DE LARANJA
(ORANGE DELIGHT)

Beat 5¼ oz. sugar well with 5¼ oz. butter. Add the juice of ½ orange and the grated rind of a whole orange. Add the yolks of 3 eggs, one by one, beating all the time. Add 5¼ oz. flour and ½ teaspoon of baking powder and the whites of the eggs, stiffly beaten. Bake in a well-buttered mould in a moderate oven. When cold cover with a mixture of ½ orange and sufficient sugar to make a cream.

ROLO DE OVOS (EGG ROLL)

6 large eggs
12 oz. sugar (weight of sugar should be double that of the eggs)
1 teaspoon flour (optional; just to hold mixture together)
butter

Beat eggs, sugar and flour together. Spread on a well-buttered baking sheet. Bake in a moderate oven (325° F., Gas 6) till set and slightly browned. Turn out on to clean tea towel, greaseproof paper or kitchen foil dredged with icing sugar. Roll up gently like a swiss roll. The roll can be spread with a jam filling, but the recipe is traditionally served plain, usually with a glass of port after a meal.

TORTA À QUINTA DO PASSADOURO

an almond pudding named by Maria Gouvea after one of the family farms in the Douro

8¾ oz. ground almonds
8¾ oz. sugar
5 eggs
1 oz. butter

With a wooden spoon beat the almonds together with the sugar and add the yolks one at a time and then the butter, which should be softened. Then add the stiffly beaten whites of the eggs and mix well together. Butter a mould and dredge with flour, add the almond mixture and bake in a moderate oven for half an hour. Leave to cool, remove from the mould and dredge with fine sugar.

PAPOS DE ANJO (ANGEL'S BREASTS)

5 egg yolks   1 lemon rind
1 egg white   1 pint water
8 oz. sugar for the syrup

Beat the yolks until thick and creamy. Add to them the beaten egg white and pour the mixture into small cake moulds, well buttered. Cook these in a medium oven for 10 minutes or until the egg is set.

Meanwhile make a syrup with the sugar and water and boil until transparent. Remove set egg mixture from the cake moulds. Add a little lemon rind to flavour and immerse in the syrup the *papos de anjo* one by one and place them on a serving dish. Pour over them the rest of the syrup.

TRÁS-OS-MONTES CRISTAS

a jam pastry from the mountains

1 lb. flour   salt and scant $\frac{1}{2}$ pint tepid
4 oz. butter   water
1 egg   jam

Put the sifted flour in a bowl with the butter and a pinch of salt. Add the beaten egg and some tepid water. Mix all the ingredients well into a dough and let it rest for $\frac{1}{2}$ hour. Roll the dough on a floured board, cut into rectangles, spread with jam, but not too much. Join the dough into envelopes firmly and make small cuts with a knife. Bake on a floured tray in a hot oven till golden.

BISCOITOS DE LAMEGO
(LAMEGO BISCUITS)

$4\frac{1}{2}$ oz. butter $8\frac{3}{4}$ oz. sugar
5 egg yolks   1 lb. flour
2 egg whites

Beat the eggs with the sugar very well. Add the butter little by little, and the flour, and knead into a dough. Shape biscuits and cook on baking sheets greased with olive oil.

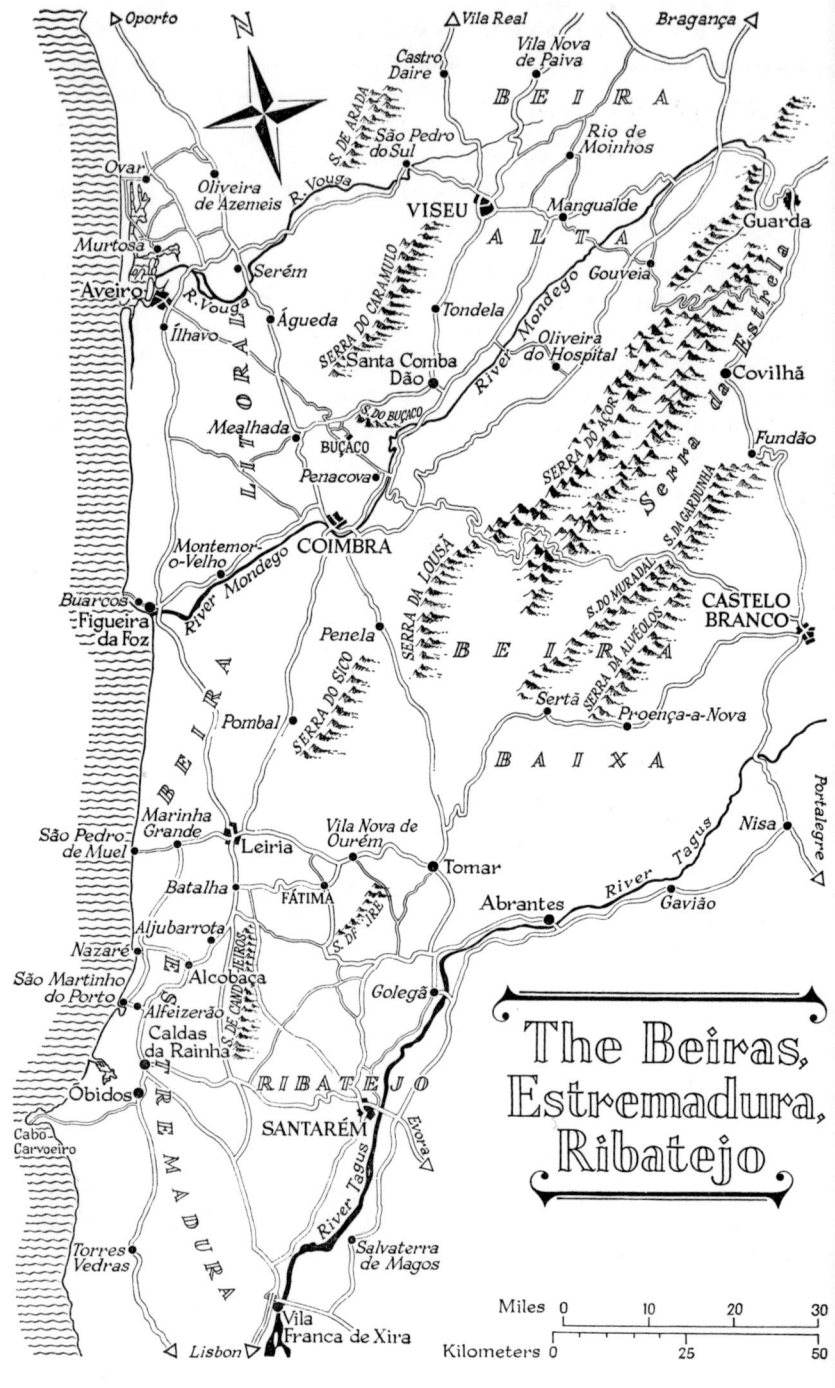

4

THE BEIRAS

The three Beira provinces – Alta, Baixa and Litoral, high, low and coastal – spread across the centre of Portugal, with an excellent wide road connecting Lisbon with Coimbra and the north, or a coastal road, die-straight like the coastline, hacked through the pinewoods and soaring over the dunes and river estuaries. It is possible to motor the whole width of the area, pushing on steadily, in three to four hours. There are, however, some pockets of great interest, principally round the towns like Viseu and Covilhã, which give the visitor an insight into the Higher and Lower Beiras less acclaimed than the better-known coast. The area is so diverse in character, yet without the sharply defined natural boundaries of the north, that generalization is dangerous; it is better to discuss the places as they occur along the road maps.

BEIRA ALTA

The capital of the province is Viseu, a town which for me epitomizes the grace and dignity of historic Portugal. This always seems a green and pleasant town, with its delightful camping ground – the Fontelo camp in the park of the former bishop's palace, with those fairy-tale-like, pointed bungalows the Portuguese rent, and which are so much more comfortable than a tent – and its gardens around the hem of the hill town.

The road to the town coming from Oporto and the north is one of the most delightful drives in Portugal. The pace is slow, the road well surfaced but narrow and for ever twisting and turning along the banks of the gentle Vouga River or up and over the valleys on its far side through the thick forests rising to São Pedro do Sul, a tiny spa resort hanging over the river banks.

All around in the extraordinary clear mountain light are superb views towards the higher mountains of the east. These can also be enjoyed from the stone terrace of Viseu's cathedral square; the Misericordia church's exterior, whitewashed and edged in chocolate-baroque, facing the two-towered cathedral alongside. The Palace of the Three Steps (Paço de Três Escalões), a sixteenth-century palace now a museum of works of the local painter Vasco Fernandes, whose greatest work of St Peter is best known as a wine-bottle label on the Dão bottles. The walled buildings of the hill-top cathedral square look like the backdrop for some elegant eighteenth-century comedy of manners. Down from this pinnacle of the town run narrow cobbled streets – the Rua Direita is full of stalls and small shops and has no traffic. Inexpensive woven bread-baskets and tableware can be bought at the small souvenir shop in the cathedral square. From the surrounding area the shiny black pottery from Molelos, the woven rugs and blankets from Vil de Moinhos, embroidery and carpets from Tibaldinho and lace from Torredeita can be purchased.

The narrow streets lead down past elegant corners of ancient noble houses and the Manueline window of the room where Henry the Navigator was born, to the newer part of the town near the river. Here there is an excellent hotel, the Grão Vasco, which serves good meals. Specialities include *caldo verde*, with local sausage in it and served with maize bread; black pudding; a white haricot bean stew; chicken with rice; river trout; pork sautéed with potatoes and served with *morcela* and *bacalhau Hotel Grão Vasco* (see page 75). The bread rolls served with the meal, baked in thin ridges like a terracing map of the Douro, are particularly good.

Other restaurants in the town in which to try the regional specialities of *serra* cheese, roast veal, kid, the 'dry' *sopas secas* thick with meat or fish or *empadinhas* (meat patties), all accompanied by a dry white Dão of the region – red if you prefer – are the

Restaurante Bocage at the second-class pension, Restaurante Alvorada and Restaurante Avenida. Just outside Viseu (not quite 4½ miles on the road to Mangualde) is the Estalagem Viriato, which has superb views over the river, a good restaurant and a natural swimming-pool in the river.   *Tourist office in Viseu*

GUARDA, SERRA DA ESTRELA AND COVILHÃ

This same road leads around the huge bend of the Mondego River connecting Viseu with Guarda and on south to Covilhã, two towns rarely featured on tourist tracks.

Guarda is one of the highest towns in Europe, a tough, historic stronghold city surrounded by a wall. Its history as a health resort has ensured that it has several hotels such as the first-class Hotel de Turismo and exclusive Pensão Filipe; the local speciality here is roast kid, and the local handicraft wrought iron.

Tourist office in Guarda

Guarda overlooks the Serra da Estrela, which can be more easily reached from Covilhã, a town known for its manufacture of woollen goods from the herds of sheep which abound in the area. Local cheeses are of course abundant, the shepherds making the tiny white cream cheese *requeijão*. The cheese market is held every Thursday at Gouveia between Viseu and Guarda on a secondary road. In Covilhã another speciality is trout. The town's annual fair is held in the second half of July.

The Serra da Estrela, which rises to around 6,600 feet, is becoming developed as a ski resort. There is a *Pousada* of thirteen rooms in the Serra, the Pousada de São Lourenço, and comfortable accommodation in less bleak surroundings can be found at the Estalagem da Neve (Inn of the Snow) at Fundao, 12½ miles south of Covilhã, in an orchard-filled river valley.

BEIRA BAIXA

Continuing south on this main road the motorist comes to Castelo Branco in the Beira Baixa, where the mountains gradually give way to huge open plains along the River Tagus's upper tributaries; plains which sweep southwards into the Alentejo area. Huge herds of sheep and pigs are reared here among the olive trees on lands once owned by Knights Templars.

The Tagus was once a good invasion route from the east, and the heavily fortified castles of the area bear witness to its defensive nature, where the native avoidance of any ostentation which might tempt an enemy is compensated for in the bright colours of the bedspreads based on designs, originally Moorish, made by the countrywomen for their weddings. A fine collection of these is on show in the museum at Castelo Branco.

In food, the area is rich with abundant olive oil, honey, cheese, goats' milk and the luscious *pão de ló* (see page 76). This light sponge-like cake is found only in certain parts of Portugal and is superb, if fattening.

In Castelo Branco *pão de ló* and *cavacas* are found as well as the locally made *frouxe*, single-silk-thread embroidered bedspreads. Cork articles and ceramics are good souvenir buys. The Episcopal Court here, with the park full of flights of steps, statuary and limpid pools, sculpted with inset flower beds, should be seen. The Hotel de Turismo provides comfortable accommodation and a restaurant for meals. *Tourist office in Castelo Branco*

BEIRA LITORAL

The coastal Beira is one of the best known areas of Portugal internationally. It has a pictorial publicity out of proportion to its actual number of visitors. The fisherman of Nazaré, their women in the seven petticoats, and the Coimbra students, black-cloaked with fringes, the cuts of which signify love affairs, are seen in Portuguese posters and tourist calendars the world over.

The coastal Beira is a seaward-looking area, the mountains giving way to a wide, rich, coastal plain. The coastline itself can almost be traced with a rule; its wide flat sands, Atlantic-lashed, are screened by sand dunes and thick pine forests through which the cobbled road north passes, dipping in and out of the morning sea mist. The straight line from Cabo Carvoeiro is indented in the centre by the wide mouth of the Mondego River on which Coimbra stands, and in the north at the mouth of the Vouga River at Aveiro where silting has drawn the town inland upon lagoons. Here fresh and sea waters are mingled and the eels and lampreys are a speciality. In this area rice is grown, and on the marshes there is wild duck shooting; a fine place to taste the popular Portuguese duck and rice dish.

Further south round Leiria the wide wheatlands give way to the spurs of the mountains of the Serra de Candieiros and the Serra de Aire backing round the town of Fátima; a harder rocky area of windswept plateau and shepherds. But this isn't the general character of the land, which is serene, the rich valleys fingering the mountains whose thick forests protect and beautify them.

The food – the *chanfana* (kid or lamb stewed in red wine) and veal or chicken in the pot – speaks of a richness and contentment of life. The beauty of the inland Beira Litoral is best seen from the road that curves down into the coastal plain from Viseu, tempting the tourist away from the harsher east of the Castelo Branco area.

SERRA DO BUÇACO

After a good meal or tiring shopping in Viseu, the slow curves down through the pinewoods are easy on the driver, with haziness through the trees across to the Serra de Caramulo. At Santa Comba Dão bear right towards Mealhada, making your way westward behind Serra do Buçaco. This is one of the loveliest and lushest of the Portuguese hill ranges, the most tranquil and calming spot to take a bottle of cool *vinho verde* or white Dão, some smoked ham, fresh salad, local bread (Portuguese butter is excellent – golden and salty) and an armful of oranges, and laze away the noon under the stately trees planted by monks who came to Buçaco for peace and contemplation isolated from the world. Ancient cedars, cypresses, oak, cork, and trees brought back from the voyages of discovery, compete for the 'fattest tree of all' title.

As in many other places of beauty, what the monks found and cherished was later seized upon by kings who built hunting lodges here, and a nineteenth-century one built by King Carlos at Buçaco itself has survived to become one of the loveliest hotels in the country. The Palace Hotel, at 1,807 feet, now acts as a *de luxe* spa hotel of seventy-six rooms open only in summer, but retaining the spacious regal dimensions of old-time pleasure that is more soothing to the traveller than the most modern concrete battery box. The saintly souls of the seventeenth-century hermits must have been disturbed by Wellington's troops in 1810, when they defeated Massena at the battle of Buçaco. A military museum containing souvenirs of the encounter is located in the Carmelite monastery near the Palace Hotel.

MEALHADA, HOME OF THE SUCKING PIG

On the main road the little town of Luso (Luso-Buçaco tourist office in Luso), which produces another popular brand of table water, lies just before Mealhada, which has produced an unusual contribution to Portuguese gastronomy. Its number one product – roast sucking pig – is famous enough to be exported to restaurants in other countries.

A little nucleus of restaurants specializing in sucking pig is situated on the roadside slightly more than half a mile outside Mealhada (turn right when you get to the Mealhada crossroads from the Viseu Buçaco direction). There are several restaurants, but Pedros dos Leitões (Peter of the Sucking Pig) is the original and uncrowned king of sucking pig producers, though the Rei dos Leitões opposite is also worth sampling. In summer you can eat sitting out under the trees, or year round in the spacious halls inside. A snack will cost about 2s 6d (30 cents) for a light, fresh roll with a thick slice of warm sucking pig inside and a glass of the cool white wine of the area. This pork is superb, with the skin crisp and salty; the meat younger (about $1\frac{1}{2}$ months) and tenderer than you would get anywhere else. There is no cheating about the freshness and age of piglet used. I was taken round to the back of the restaurant and shown the pig sty – probably 'Peter's' is not a place to eat if you are too sentimental about animals.

The piglets are roasted whole on wooden poles in huge outside ovens. Before cooking they are covered inside and out with a mixture of lard, crushed garlic, bay leaf, parsley, salt and pepper which looks like grey cement. During cooking the pig is occasionally 'watered' with white wine. The drippings are caught and made into a local Bairrada dish called *cabidela*.

Roast sucking pig is also sold to take away if you plan the picnic *de luxe* in the Buçaco woods or elsewhere. Cost is about 32s to 35s ($3.84 to $4.20) for a little over $2\frac{1}{4}$ lb. A full meal can of course be taken at the restaurant, and other specialities costing around 5s

(60 cents) a dish are *iscas de figado à regional* (regional style liver steaks), *febras de porco à Montejo* (lean pork in the Montejo way) and *sopa de massa fria* (cold soup made from fancy macaroni).

COIMBRA

From Mealhada the drive on the fine straight road takes about twenty minutes into Coimbra. Coimbra is the expression of romantic Portugal. Set on the side of a mountain, its back is firmly to the hills and its face open to the Mondego River and the west. With its special brand of *fado* singing, its university and connection with Portuguese poets such as Camões, it is associated in Portuguese hearts with youth and *saudade* (yearning).

It has a character reminiscent of every university town. Its hotels are old-fashioned yet comfortable, like those of Oxford. The restaurants have an almost cafeteria-like appearance; overgrown coffee-shops where students can eat cheaply and linger long over formica-topped tables in their discussions. The high, cobbled streets, twisting upwards round the cathedral, are film consuming, while the small shops with well-decorated windows in boutique style beguile the visitor to buy locally made textiles or the famous blue decorated Coimbra ware.

This pottery is made by hand and often copied from seventeenth- and eighteenth-century patterns. Examples can be seen at the Sociedade Ceramica Antiga de Coimbra, Quinto do Prior, 2–4. Wrought iron, another local craft, can be bought from Pompeu Aroso, Rua Nogeira, 8–10, or Lusa Mecanica de Coimbra, Rua João Cabreira, 20. The Coimbra fair day is the 23rd of the month and in May there is the students' festival, the Queima das Fitas.

Another unique local souvenir is the carved willow toothpicks made by the women of Penacova (about 15 miles outside Coimbra) who use leather pads as a work surface.

Sightseeing round the cathedral, university and city museums – the Machado de Castro Museum contains beautiful collections of jewellery, sculpture, embroidery and pottery – is tiring on a hot day. The municipal swimming-pool is a boon; but most charming is a visit to the Portugal dos Pequeninos, a children's garden which contains scaled-down buildings (but not fiddly miniatures – children can actually get inside). Demanding the minimum of effort, these most charmingly show the visitor of any age the regional architectural styles of Portugal, its overseas provinces, with reproductions of national monuments, and include a children's museum containing dolls and toys.

A full list of local restaurants is available in literature from the tourist office in the Avenida Navarro; but recommended for typical local food are the Nicola in Rua Ferreira Borges, the Imperio, Rua da Sofia, the International, Avenida Navarro alongside the river and the Texas Parque, Avenida Navarro, and sister restaurant, Texas Bar in the Rua Adelina Veiga. In spite of its unregional name, the Texas Parque is a charming little coffee-shop/restaurant near the river bridge in Coimbra, serving local dishes at reasonable prices. Although few restaurants in Coimbra seem to have English-speaking staff their helpfulness makes up for this. In the Texas Parque menus are available in French, and there is a speciality of salads with cold meats and also hot sandwiches. A unique speciality of this restaurant is fresh local strawberries in December. I had these served with a little port and sugar, and though they looked green, and were only tipped with pale rose, the flavour was delicious and summerlike in contrast to the chill winds outside. The *caldo verde* is served here at 10*d* (10 cents) a bowl and they do a kind of local hamburger. More localized is the *açorda de mariscos*, shellfish bread soup, Beira sausages, roast veal or chicken with *piri-piri* (see page 194).

But Coimbra specialities are *chanfana* (see page 63), roast meat, lampreys with rice, and roast kid. There are a number of local sweets sold at the many coffee-shops such as *pasteis de Santa Clara*, *manjar branco*, *bolos de Coroa*, *arrufadas*, and there are also the *queijadas de Coimbra* and, from near by, *queijadas de Pereira*, cream cheeses. Another delight is the *pasteis de Tentugal* from the nearby town of that name but sold in Coimbra. This is similar to *mille feuilles* with an egg-based flavouring.

Coimbra is within easy reach for a day's visit to Figueira da Foz, a popular seaside resort, but it also makes a convenient overnight stop on a drive between Lisbon and Oporto. The fairly new Hotel Bragança would be my choice rather than the Hotel Astoria, comfortable but with a depressingly dark and old-fashioned *décor*. Both hotels are on the riverside roads with parking opposite.

DIVERSION TO THE RIBATEJO

From Coimbra south to Lisbon you can travel fast on a wide road, and make few detours. The road passes through rolling hills, pines and heath down to Leira. South of this the only distractions are Ruinas de Conimbriga, $9\frac{1}{2}$ miles south of Coimbra, a very rich find of Roman city remains. (There is a tearoom here.) As an alternative to this main road, branch off at Ruinas de Conimbriga and travel through Tomar into the Ribatejo. Tomar, the old Knights Templar town, where an excellent meal may be had at the Hotel des Templarios or at the Estalagem de Santa Iria, was considered by Somerset Maugham to be the finest city in Portugal. The annual fairs are held 9th–13th September and 20th–22nd October; sweetmeats made here are called *doces de carna* and *fatias de Tomar*.

The Ribatejo, which runs along the wide, flat banks of the Tagus, is a land of rich wheat, salt production, rice, bull- and horse-rearing. The dances are fiercely male, the proud fandangos; the sport bullfighting, in which tourists are occasionally allowed to 'try' young bulls. There are bullrings in Tomar, which gastronomically is famous for its cheese and for the unusual Tray Festival, held every few years, when the women parade to the Templars building carrying on their heads trays with loaves and sausages threaded on reeds, and decorated with flowers and ears of wheat.

Tourist office at Tomar

Continuing southwards the motorist will pass through Santarém, the bullfighting centre for the country and famous for its sweet 'heavenly delights' (*celestes*), its early June two-week-long Ribatejo Festival, when bulls are let loose in the street and there is dancing till dawn, and its views across the flat river country from the hill to which this provincial capital clings. Before speeding along the new motorway into Lisbon it is worth pausing at Vila Franca de Xira for a meal at one of the inns for which the area is famous. Try the Estalagem do Gado Bravo or the Estalagem da Leziria, where the river fish is often made into soup and Tagus eels and local sweetmeats are served. The Ribatejano at Salvaterra de Magos (on the south bank of the Tagus) has folklore displays. Vila Franca is in the heart of the bull-breeding country and is the site of the Festival of the Red Waistcoat (the dancers hook their fingers into their waistcoats when performing the fandangos), held on the second Saturday and Sunday of July. Its food specialities are *caldeirada* (made from river fish), fried shad and sweetmeats – *campinos* and *marujinhos*.

BACK TO THE BEIRA LITORAL

This diversion into the picturesque, but neglected, Ribatejo area seems a natural follow-on for the tourist motoring through the country from Coimbra to Lisbon. But the more frequented road is the coastal road which enters Beira past Alcobaça. For the purposes of this book I shall deal with the coast from São Martinho do Porto north to Ovar and south of São Martinho in Chapter 6.

SÃO MARTINHO DO PORTO (tourist office) is one of the many so-called 'typical' fishing villages along this coast, which is a coast of fishermen; the tourist can go camera crazy picturing the tough, barefoot fisherman mending his nets while his wife spreads her laundry to dry on the beach; though on the more popular beaches the presence of beach huts leaves her space only behind the dunes. São Martinho, with its long cobbled streets bordered by single-storey colour-washed houses, is charming and unpretentious in a *M. Hulot's Holiday* way, as is São Pedro de Muel farther up the coast, which is also just beginning to make its mark on the international travel agents' books. Both these would make excellent and economical bases for visiting the surrounding area. São Martinho is set on an almost circular bay, with sheltered swimming. Its Hotel Parque has British/Portuguese management and is a charming example of Portuguese architecture. Its rooms are comfortable if not over-elaborate or luxurious. São Martinho has good bus and railway services for the tourist without a car who wants to make visits to Lisbon, Nazaré, Caldas da Rainha, Óbidos or Coimbra.

Just over 3 miles from São Martinho is the Pousada de São Martinho. This has only five rooms, and since São Martinho is so popular in the summer the earliest possible booking is recommended. One of the richest *pão de ló* (see page 76) recipes is produced at Alfeizerão, about 3 miles from São Martinho.

NAZARÉ, ALCOBAÇA AND LEIRIA

Nazaré, a favourite subject on Portuguese posters, is only 10 miles from São Martinho. Set in a cliff fault, the narrow cobbled streets run down to the crescent-shaped sand beach, with its high-prowed, eye-painted boats. It is a fishing village and, not surprisingly, its gastronomic specialities are *caldeirada* and shellfish. In spite of the immense publicity for its picturesque folklore the Nazaré fishermen remain natural, working on the beach or in their small cliff-top houses from which there is a superb view of the bay.

The Hotel Nazaré is situated at the upper end of the town and in addition to a dance floor has a roof-top restaurant with large open-air terrace and views over the town. Here they will serve the typical fish stew, made with sliced tomato, onion, pepper, vegetables, sardines, whiting, shrimps, lobster and pieces of toast. Among their other specialities, which include attentive service, is Nazaré chicken casserole, in which the chicken is first boiled with Portuguese ham in brandy and wine and seasoned with *piri-piri* and grilled sardines. More easily translated to the home table are their tuna fish pâté and orange salad recipes (see pages 71, 79), which were invented by the restaurant and whose secret they gave me. The tuna fish pâté is served with the aperitif and is superb with crispy toast and local olives.

Inland from Nazaré is Alcobaça, a town which was created by the monks and which is centred round the twelfth-century Cistercian monastery of decorated Gothic grandeur founded by the first King of Portugal. It contains the tombs of King Pedro and Inês de Castro. It was in this monastery that the macabre coronation of the body of Inês, murdered five years earlier, took place.

The abbey's great kitchens should be seen. Since the monastery became the most important in the kingdom it did a lot of entertaining. Uniquely, the kitchens have a stream running through their centre, which supplied fresh fish and eels for the Friday observances. The feasts must have been prodigious, even allowing for Portuguese appetites, for it was possible to roast six oxen at a time here. Today appetites can be satisfied at Pensão Coracões Unidos, Montero or Bau.

Try to visit Alcobaça on market day (Friday) when its narrow streets are crowded with stalls selling local produce such as fruits,

PORTUGUESE FOOD

cheese, wine, brass objects, cotton cloths and local earthenware pottery; little pig-shaped money boxes, plates decorated with flowers, and wickerwork. *Tourist office in Alcobaça*

About $3\frac{3}{4}$ miles away at Aljubarrota, where the English archers helped the Portuguese to beat the Spanish in 1385 and sealed the record-breaking alliance, is an excellent inn – the Estalagem do Cruzerio. Here you should ask for the local almond paste sweetmeat which is a reminder of an old score settled with the Spaniards. The sweetmeat is made in the shape of a baker's wife who killed six Spaniards with a shovel when she found them hiding in her bread oven. An excursion to be made from the inn is to Batalha, where the monastery, considered to be a perfect example of Manueline architecture, commemorates the 1385 battle.

From Batalha to Leiria (tourist board) is only 7 miles, and pottery can be seen and bought at roadside displays in this area. Leiria is a castle-dominated, agricultural centre with an inn, the Estalagem Claras. At the first-class Hotel Euro-Sol there is a swimming-pool. It is a town where bricks are made and pilgrims pass by on the way to Fátima. A diversion from the main coast road leads to Marinha Grande, a glass-making centre, and at the end of the road São Pedro de Muel, a tiny resort surrounded by pinewoods. It is a quiet artists' colony in spite of its new bungalows, and it has a choice of five beaches. The Hotel Mar e Sol is clean and well kept, with good food including many local specialities.

FIGUEIRA DA FOZ

From Leiria to Figueira da Foz the road is straight and has a cobbled surface; it runs through sun shafts shining through the pine forests which screen views of the shore. Figueira combines the activities of fishing and tourism; its food specialities are fish soup, mussels and particularly roast sardines. The hotels are mostly in the new quarter of Figueira with a choice of several, including the Grande Hotel da Figueira and Hotel da Praia, first class, and the Estalagem da Piscina, with swimming-pool as its name suggests. The fishing village of Buarcos, near Figueira, is full of character.

Tourist office in Figueira

THE LAGOONS

The lagoon area between Aveiro and Ovar in the north of the Beira Litoral is by-passed by the main road, but the Ria de Aveiro is a calm, sun-filled and reflective place for a holiday. The lagoon produces fish and mussels to eat, salt to put on them and, above all, to preserve the fish as *bacalhau*. This is an important centre for *bacalhau* drying. The cod is brought back in the fishing boats from Newfoundland and in summer lies drying near the cod factories. Boats are built on the lagoon and, as in the Venetian area, fishing and farming are almost interchangeable.

Aveiro itself is not only a beach resort. It is set on many canals and is a lively place to visit for a fish meal in one of the pensions like the Imperial, Europa or Palmeira, or just to wander along the quaysides. As one approaches from the south there is a superb view of the town beyond a long, narrow stone bridge, with the high sails of the boats and coloured buildings beyond.

Some of the local products are canned for the tourist to take away: eels or lampreys in sauce or a small cask of sweetmeats – the famous *ovos moles* (soft eggs) renowned all over the country (see page 78). Eels, lamprey and fish soup can be eaten in this area, which has established itself firmly on the country's gastronomic map.

One of the loveliest of the *Pousadas*, the Pousada da Ria, is situated within the embrace of the lagoon near Murtosa. Its ten modern, balconied rooms sweep out over the lagoon. Another *Pousada* in calming surroundings is situated in the hills of the Vouga valley near by at Serém. The Pousada do Santo Antonio is an old house, furnished in local traditional style, and its gardens, filled with lemon trees, give wonderful views over the Vouga's valley.

A glimpse of the character of under-water life in the lagoon can be seen in the museum at Ílhavo, south of Aveiro, which is devoted to lagoon fishing. *Tourist office in Aveiro*

RECIPES FROM THE THREE BEIRAS

As an introduction to the fish foods of the coast a *tuna fish pâté* (*empadinha*) from the Hotel Nazaré can be made with tinned tunny fish. Equal amounts of tuna fish and butter are blended together and seasoned to taste with *piri-piri* sauce (a hot sauce made from peppers and popular in the Algarve – see page 194), salt, pepper, Worcester sauce, mustard and ½ liqueur glass of port and of brandy. Chill slightly before serving.

SOPA DE FEIJÃO VERDE À MODA DA BEIRA (BEIRA RUNNER BEAN SOUP)

FOR TWO TO THREE

2 pints water
5½ tablespoons olive oil
1 lb. potatoes
1 lb. runner beans
½ lb. tomatoes
1 onion
salt

Boil the potatoes gently with the chopped onion, olive oil, tomatoes (peeled and seeded) and salt, adding more water if necessary. Blend till smooth. Reheat and as soon as the mixture starts boiling, add the beans. These should be cut very thin and diagonally. Simmer till beans are tender.

TRUTAS DE ESCABECHE MANTEIGAS (TROUT IN ESCABECHE SAUCE FROM MANTEIGAS)

Prepare trout without opening them and cook in a saucepan, covering with 2 parts olive oil to 3 of vinegar. Add pepper, garlic cloves, ½ bay leaf, salt and parsley to taste. Cook gently and serve cold with sauté potatoes.

GALINHA DE FRICASSÉ À MODA DA BEIRA (BEIRA CHICKEN FRICASSÉE)

1 chicken (or 4 chicken joints)
1 oz. butter
2 oz. cooking fat
12 small onions
2 egg yolks
5½ tablespoons white wine
1 sprig parsley
1 lemon
1 cup meat stock
pepper and salt

Trim the chicken, cut in pieces and fry them lightly in the butter and cooking fat in a deep pan. When the chicken is golden brown add the wine, stock, pepper and salt and onions. When the chicken is cooked drain off the gravy and add the beaten egg yolks, chopped parsley and lemon juice to it. Pour this sauce on the chicken and serve it with fried potatoes.

LINGUA À BEIROA
(OX TONGUE FROM BEIRA)

1 ox tongue
1 oz. butter
2 oz. cooking fat
⅓ pint white wine
1 onion
2 carrots
1 sprig parsley
1 teaspoon flour
salt and pepper

Wash the tongue well, cook in water till the skin can be removed easily. Leave for 24 hours sprinkled with salt. Fry the onion in the butter and the fat and, when it is golden, put the tongue, cut in large pieces, in the pan, adding the wine, chopped parsley and chopped carrots. Cover the pan and fry the ingredients slowly. Then add enough water to cook the tongue. When it is cooked blend the sauce to a *purée* and add the flour to thicken it. Serve with buttered peas.

FRANGO À MODA DA BEIRA
(BEIRA CHICKEN)

FOR FOUR

1 chicken
2 small fresh cream cheeses
(locally ewes' milk cheeses –
queijinhos de ovelha – are used,
but a cottage cheese would
do instead, about 4 oz.)
2 oz. butter
½ carton cream
1 oz. ham (smoked)
salt and pepper

Cream 1 oz. butter, salt and pepper and place inside chicken. Place a slice of ham on each side of the chicken breast and spread the chicken with the rest of the butter, and place in a fireproof dish. Cook gently in a moderate oven. Half an hour before serving spread the blended cheese and cream over the chicken and return to the oven until the chicken is tender. Serve with game chips.

ARROZ DE FRANGO À PORTUGUESA
(PORTUGUESE CHICKEN RICE)

FOR FOUR

Slice 1 large onion and cook in oil in a large pan till golden. Add 4 good chicken joints and season. Add a glass of white wine and chopped garlic, sausage or ham to taste. Simmer on a low heat, adding water gradually to cover. When ingredients are cooked add about 8 oz. rice making sure there is about twice the amount of liquid as rice. Boil for about 5 minutes. Then place in a casserole in the oven, cooking for a further ½ hour or till cooked through.

EMPADINHAS DE CASTELO BRANCO
(CASTELO BRANCO MEAT PIES)

A prize winner in a regional cookery competition organized to keep alive traditional Portuguese cookery.

2 lb. veal, pork or other meat	white wine
1 lb. flour	clove
2 eggs	dash of nutmeg
5 tablespoons warm olive oil	1 onion
a little cold olive oil	garlic (chopped)
2 oz. lard or margarine	bay leaf
tepid water	parsley
salt to taste	

Meats can be mixed, but should be free of bones, fat or sinew. Veal or fillet of pork are the best.

Cook the onion, herbs, margarine, olive oil, salt and white wine together with the meat, cut in smallish pieces, in a deep pan. When the meat is cooked remove from the heat and leave to cool.

In an earthenware ovenproof dish, mix the flour and the eggs, the warm olive oil, lard, salt with sufficient tepid water. The resultant dough should not be too hard. Let the dough stand for 1 hour wrapped in a cloth. Thoroughly butter some pie tins. Fill with meat mixture, cover with a lid of pastry and brush the top of each pie with beaten egg. Place pies on a baking tray and cook in a moderate oven till golden brown.

BACALHAU HOTEL GRÃO VASCO

A simple but delicious dish which could be served in small portions as an hors d'œuvres course

Prepare cod as on page 189, cutting into small fillets. Fry gently in fat – the hotel uses small individual earthenware dishes for this. When the fish is half fried cover with a *béchamel* sauce (see page 30) and put in a medium oven for 15 minutes. Serve very hot.

BROAS DE MEL DE CASTELO BRANCO
(LEMON FLAVOURED HONEY CAKES FROM CASTELO BRANCO)

1 teacup sugar	1 lemon
½ pint honey (16 tablespoons)	6 eggs
¼ pint olive oil	2 teaspoons baking powder
½ pint milk	1 lb. 2 oz. flour

Beat the egg yolks very well with the sugar. Put the milk, oil, honey and grated lemon peel in a saucepan. Bring to the boil, stirring well, then leave to get cold. Then add the yolks mixed with the sugar, the whites beaten stiffly and finally the flour sieved with the baking powder. Shape the *broas* into oblong small cakes and place them on baking sheets covered with flour. Brush them with egg and some sugar mixed with cinnamon. Cook in a fairly hot oven.

ESQUECIDOS (FROM BEIRA)

('Esquecidos' means 'Forgotten'. These tiny puffy mouthfuls are indeed quickly forgotten.) The amount for this recipe makes several dozen but can always be halved.

1 lb. sugar	4 egg whites
1 lb. flour	1 lemon
6 egg yolks	

Beat the egg yolks together well with the sugar and add, while still beating, the grated peel of the lemon and the flour. Fold in the stiffly beaten egg whites. With a small teaspoon put small quantities of this pastry on greased and floured baking trays. Don't put them very near each other because they swell a great deal. Cook in a hot oven till golden.

BOLO DE MEL DE CASTELO BRANCO (CASTELO BRANCO HONEY CAKE)

1 teacup sugar	½ pint honey
3 teacups flour	(about 16 tablespoons)
7 eggs	1 teaspoon baking powder
½ pint olive oil	

Beat the egg yolks well with the sugar. Heat the olive oil in a saucepan with the honey to boiling point, then let it get cold. When it is cool mix with the eggs and sugar. Add the flour and baking powder sieved together and finally add the egg whites stiffly beaten. Pour this mixture on to a baking tray greased with butter and sprinkled with flour and cook in a moderately hot oven. When cool cut it into small squares.

PÃO DE LÓ

Is found in many places in Portugal. Its main characteristic is its rich yellow softness – it practically collapses into a custard. It is sold wrapped in the paper in which it is baked, tied gently to keep its shape. It should go slightly soggy when taken from the oven and can be pressed down to almost nothing.

6 eggs (2 extra yolks can be added for the initial blending)	½ lb. self-raising flour
	¾ lb. sugar

Beat the egg yolks with the sugar and then the flour. Fold in the well-beaten whites of the eggs and when stiff turn into a well-buttered cake tin. Bake in a slow oven for 20 minutes till the top is just golden but not quite firm in the centre. The best way is to line the tin with buttered greaseproof paper by which it can be lifted from the tin.

DELICIAS (DELIGHTS)

4½ oz. butter 2½ teacups flour
9 oz. sugar 1 dessertspoon baking powder
3 egg yolks 1 lemon
2 teacups milk salt

Cream the butter and sugar together and then beat in well the egg yolks and grated lemon rind. Sift together the flour, salt and baking powder and fold this into the creamed mixture alternately with the milk. Put the mixture into small greased cake tins and bake for about 15–20 minutes in a fairly hot oven (400° F., Gas 6).

BATATADA

a Beira sweet made with potatoes instead of flour

5 oz. boiled potatoes sugar for syrup
10 egg yolks cinnamon

Cook potatoes and then mash them. Put sugar and half its weight in water in a saucepan and cook till it starts thickening into a syrup (see page 197). Then mix in the mashed potatoes and let the mixture boil for a while. Take the saucepan off the heat and let contents cool. Add beaten egg yolks and cinnamon to taste. Stir continuously while cooking the egg yolks. Pour into small dishes and sprinkle with cinnamon.

PUDIM DE OVOS DE COIMBRA (COIMBRA EGG PUDDING)

9 oz. sugar ½ oz. butter
8 egg yolks

Put the sugar in a saucepan with some water and let it cook for a while till it becomes a thick syrup. Then leave to get cold. Add the yolks beaten with melted butter. Blend well and put in a greased cake tin and bake in a moderate to hot oven.

BISCOITOS DE COIMBRA
(COIMBRA BISCUITS)

    1 teacup milk 3½ oz. butter
1 teaspoon baking powder 9 oz. sugar
     cinnamon flour

Mix together in a bowl the milk, baking powder, cinnamon (about 1 tablespoon is used in Portugal), butter and sugar; blend well. Add flour little by little until you get a firm dough. Shape into biscuits and cook in a moderate oven on greased trays.

OVOS MOLES (SOFT EGGS)

This is a very sweet egg dish found in many parts of Portugal but particularly in Aveiro. Sue Pereira, who cooked Portuguese food in a London restaurant, suggested allowing about 3 egg yolks and 3 oz. sugar per person (an ounce per egg seems the Portuguese measure). Beat these together into a thick paste with two tablespoons sweet white wine (this is not the most traditional way but is simple). Beat well while cooking over a gentle heat till it thickens somewhat but does not boil. Judging the thickness takes practice.

  Another method is to blend sugar with water and blend the thin syrup with the egg yolks. In Aveiro rice is boiled and the water used to make the syrup; it is said to give the right smoothness to the mixture, served there on its own in tiny dishes. It is better to chill before serving and to serve on a base of Chantilly cream topped with finely chopped almonds cooked in caramel sauce, as does Sue Pereira in London. Or the mixture can be used as a sauce or to fill a tart, a *mille feuilles* pastry or – most delicious – with the tang of raspberries and cream the way Mrs Brito e Cunha serves it at home in Oporto. A charming old Portuguese custom was to decorate the dish of Ovos Moles with cinnamon in the guest's initial.

  After all that sweetness and lightness of egg, the tourist palate turns gratefully to the superb Portuguese oranges. The chef at the Hotel Nazaré suggested a simple but effective orange salad, which is pleasant for a dinner party, particularly after a greasy dish such as roast pork, and was an interesting combination of spirit flavours.

SALADA DE LARANJAS NAZARÉ
(NAZARÉ ORANGE SALAD)

Thinly slice 5 peeled oranges – allow at least one large one per person. Place in a dish with plenty of sugar and any juice. Add ½ liqueur glass (for 5 people) of each of the following: brandy, port and whisky. Stir round and chill well.

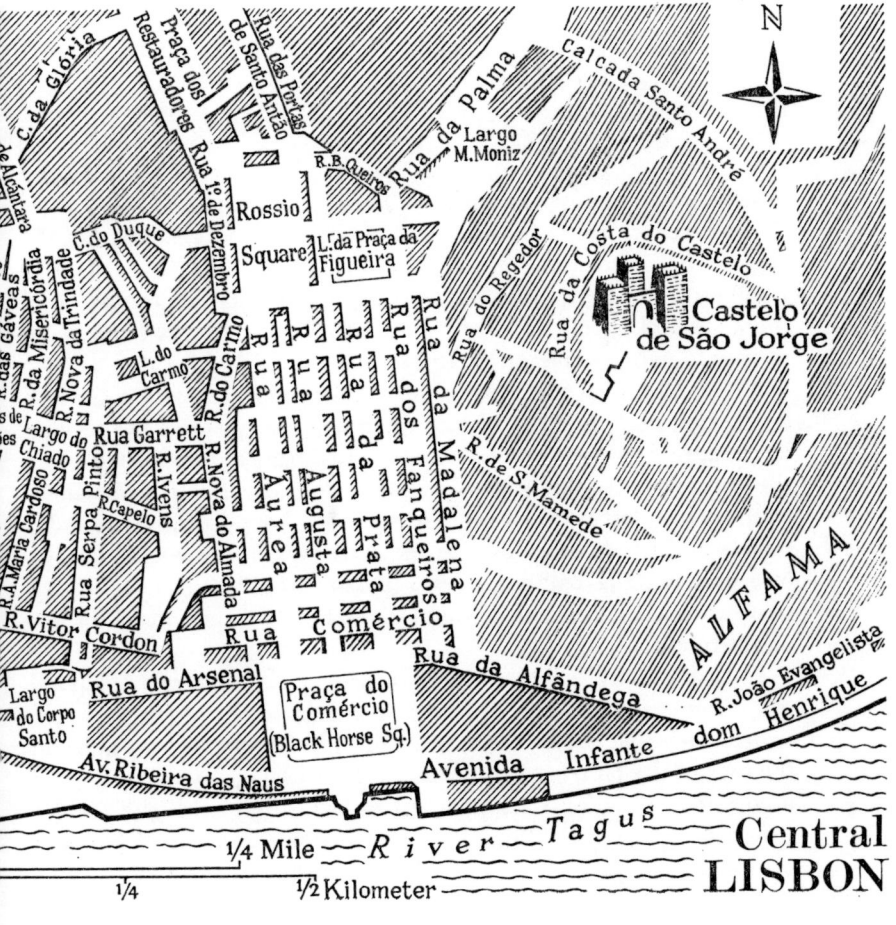

5

LISBON

A capital city's cooking is always influenced by its foreign visitors. For a city such as Lisbon, with its importance as a shipping and air centre, the character of its cuisine has remained remarkably unsullied. True, there is the usual crop of international and overseas speciality restaurants, but there are still excellent local restaurants which do not bend their recipes to pamper the visitor and so end by boring him.

The Lisboan is, like most of his countrymen, a hearty eater but he is often hampered by lack of time, and the speed of the service in restaurants patronized by working Lisboans at lunch time or in the evening is something to be marvelled at; young boys whisk round with platters piled high. Service is a keynote of restaurants, expressed in such attentions as the ceremony of the peeled orange (see page 6), the willingness to serve at virtually any time, to try to please the customer if he wants something a little unusual or not on the menu.

In Lisbon too the larger tourist hotels can be relied on to provide good international and Portuguese meals. The restaurants are situated with an eye to the view of the seven-hilled city. Those on the tops of the Hotels Mundial and Edward VII provide both good food and a view, and are pleasant on a hot day with the terrace windows open; the Mundial has a small open-air roof bar and provides a magnificent cold table, beautifully garnished.

Staying in Lisbon, I would recommend of the Grade A hotels the Mundial, which has friendly service and is most centrally placed for shopping and sightseeing round the Rossio Square area, although I find its *décor* shabby with the dark wood and drapes of a city hotel. It has a spacious private car park – no charge – at the back. In general it's better not to try to park in Lisbon (disk parking meters) because the traffic *mêlée* is bad enough without attempting such manœuvres. Taxis are cheap and horrifyingly swift, costing only a few shillings for a journey right across the centre.

A good recommended second-class hotel is the Flamingo, Rua Castilho, 41; but there are a great number of good, clean, if unpretentious, pensions where charges can be as little as 5*s* (60 cents) for bed and breakfast, though more usually around 10*s* ($1.20), and full pension around £1–25*s* ($2.40–$3), hardly budget-breaking for an elegant capital city. Many of these pensions are centrally placed, and Lisbon is a comparatively compact city, so that using local (double-decker) buses or the clanking yellow-peril trams makes getting around quick and cheap.

Nor need eating be expensive; there are dozens of restaurants where a three-course meal with local wine costs around 10*s* ($1.20). 'Tearooms' have a nasty connotation in English minds with quaint down-at-heel waitresses in crumpled caps serving congealing eggs on toast. In Lisbon they are superbly old-fashioned and in some, like the Caravela, the waitresses do indeed wear white caps and frilly aprons, but the service is excellent. It is a haven for the person who likes his tea abroad even if it is made with tea bags. These tearooms, their polished dark wood, white tablecloths, mostly with long-aproned servitors (male) and marble-topped serving counters, recall an old pharmacy rather than an eating-house. But each meal is individually made up with the care that old-fashioned chemists used in prescriptions. The tearooms are perfect for the tourist. Many are situated in the shopping area round the Rua Garrett. Among my favourites are the Ferrari in Rua Nova do Almada, 91–93, and the Pastelaria Marques, Rua Garrett, 70. You can stop for what you will; when you will too – till around seven at night when the shops close. It's enough to revive you while sightseeing or shopping without the tiring, time-consuming formal meal routine.

When shopping the visitor should take advantage of the rearguard fight 'service' and 'made to measure' is making in Lisbon against the modern pressures of mass production and self-service. Shopping in Lisbon is a relaxed potter of elegantly dressed women (high heels are not for comfort on the cobbled or patterned mosaic streets) who rarely tote the huge dress bags or parcels as women often do in Britain. Shops will deliver to hotels and actually go out of their way to oblige. In the dress boutiques, if you can find Portuguese styles and fabrics amongst the big selection of English ready-mades that are becoming fashionable in Portugal, and then find the garment doesn't fit or is the wrong colour, the shop will make up for you to your size in another fabric, or alter the garment at no extra cost. A dress shop I'd recommend for extremely helpful service is Boutique Jo on the first floor in the Rua Serpa Pinto, 14, next door to the Aviz restaurant (see below). The manageress speaks excellent English. They have another branch in the Rua Nova de São Mamede, 38, in the university quarter, where there are some inexpensive ready-to-wear shops.

Shoes are another excellent fashion buy in Lisbon. Here again they are practically made to the customers' requests. In the Rua Augusta there are many shoe shops, and in the Rua dos Sapateiros (literally Road of Shoemakers); both run from the south end of the Rossio Square. Typical of Lisbon service was this experience; in one shop I liked a style but not the thick heel. This they replaced with a thinner one, and another pair was made up for me overnight with the heel of one, the decoration of another and the body colour of a third – again for no extra cost.

Gold and silver jewellery, particularly the elaborate filigree work, can be found in the Rua Áurea; the shop of the same name at No. 89 is reliable. Eduardo Martins, Rua Garrett, is a good departmental store. Goatskins, attractive as rugs with their white, auburn and black markings, can be bought at the little household stores in the Rossio Square and cost about £1 ($2.40) each. They are also sold on the main roads on the way to Guincho beach, but cost more than in the city. Pottery and porcelain are other delightful souvenirs from Viúva Lamego, Largo do Intendente, 25, or Vista Alegre, Largo do Chiado, 18. Madeiran handicrafts are sold at Madeira Supérbia, Avenida Duque de Loulé, 75 and the Madeira House,

Rua Augusta, 131. Azores merchandise is displayed at the Casa Regional da Ilha Verde, Rua Paiva de Andrada, 4, where hand-carved and painted candles make acceptable souvenirs. Embroidered linen is one of Portugal's most pleasing handicrafts (with the accent in this machine-made world on handwork). An inexpensive selection from napkins to sheets is sold on the second floor of the old-fashioned Ramiro Leão store in the Rua Garrett.

FOODS OF LISBON

Lisboans offer in their restaurants most of the main national Portuguese dishes; the tomato soups, fish soups (though there is a local variety known as *caldeirada à fragateira de Lisboa*), the roast pork dishes, particularly with clams, fish and sweet egg puddings. Local partiality is for the excellent local seafood, soles, boiled hake (*pescada cozida de Lisboa*), the langoustines from around Cascais and the sardines from the Arrabida town of Setúbal. Crab meat is served deliciously as *santola à moda de Lisboa* mixed with egg yolks, mustard, seasoning and lemon. *Escabeche* sauce (see page 90) is used with cold fish such as *carapau* (mackerel).

The rich market garden area to the north-east of Lisbon, where the Tagus irrigates the soil, produces the basics for good vegetable soups and the fresh green beans beloved in many dishes, and particularly pleasant batter-coated as 'garden fish' (*peixinhos da horta* see page 88). Broad beans *à Saloia* (see page 89) is named after the quick-tongued inhabitants of the market garden suburbs: the Saloios.

Peas – *ervilhas* – are cooked with sausage slices and often include poached eggs. The Lisboans also have a passion for lettuce salads.

Of meats, *bife na frigideira* is a beef steak, usually cooked and served with an onion sauce in a small earthenware platter – the *frigideira*, see page 36. *Churrascaria* is the equivalent of steak house in Portugal. Liver (*fígado*) is most popular in Lisbon. Termed *iscas* it is in fact cut into very small pieces, unlike the relatively thick liver used in Britain. Tripe is often found, but termed *dobrada* in this area. The game found on the heather lands backing the beaches round Guincho is much used in season. *Guisado de coelho à amadora* is stewed rabbit. Partridge turns up roast *à Lisboa*, or *à moda de Alcantara*, stuffed with *foie gras* and truffles, cooked in port and perched on slices of bread.

There is a plentiful choice of restaurants in Lisbon. There are, of course, the tourist-orientated restaurants, mostly in the large hotels, which I have noted above. In addition there are the more expensive places round the Avenida da Liberdade along the pavements of which it is pleasant to sit after dinner and sip a coffee and *constantino* (Portuguese brandy). Of these good value, service and polished *décor* of a slightly pre-war gilded kind is offered by Vera Cruz, Avenida da Liberdade, 12, where steak *flambé* is the speciality. The Aviz, Rua Serpa Pinto, 12, is also luxurious.

Another elegant, but newer, restaurant on the expensive side is the Varanda do Chanceler, Largo do Chanceler, 7a. This is built out over the red-roofed clustered dwellings of the old Alfama district and, by day, its huge picture windows edged with geraniums look down over the riverside cranes and ships in the docks and across the river to the misty outlines of the Arrábida hills. By night there is dancing here; meals are international style with a few national Portuguese dishes included. The average price of a main dish is 12s to 15s ($1.40 to $1.80). If you are in the Alfama district during the saints' festivals of 12th, 24th and 29th June you can eat fresh-grilled sardines off street stalls with the local crowds and help them down with young red *vinho verde*.

Of the Portuguese dishes served, there is *lagosta à Dom Marolo* cooked at the table; *mariscos na Poca*, shellfish well cooked with onions and olive oil; and *cherne à moda do Minho*, a halibut grouper variety of fish cooked in the Minho way.

FADO HOUSES

In most cities I would not like to recommend the food served at nightspots. In Lisbon the *fado* night-clubs serve good typical Portuguese food as well as simple international dishes. There are, of course, cabaret-style night-clubs in the international sense listed in tourist board publications. *Fado* I find very relaxing and pleasant to listen to, rather like Arab music. It is soothing to watch singers whose appeal is in their voices and not primarily their clothes or sexy appearance. They don't stamp up and down, clutching a microphone and waving their arms. Instead the women wrap a thick fringed shawl round their shoulders, lean back against a wall partly in shadow and sing plaintively as the original *fado* women sang under the lamps of the Alfama streets.

Even more musical and attractive is the less-heard Coimbra *fado*. This is the young, more romantic singing stemming from the university students' lore. The male singer is cloaked from head to foot in deep black and accompanied by the lone guitar.

Fado houses in Lisbon, where a good meal can also be obtained, are A Severa, Rua das Gáveas, 55; A Tipóia, Rua do Norte, 102; Lisboa à Noite, Rua das Gáveas, 69; and O Faia, Rua da Barroca, 48, where regional folklore dances are included between the *fados*.

As a travel writer I have been subjected to dreary evenings of folkloristic dancing all over the world, and as a whole abhor them. Basically there are only two dance routines: the kicking type and the arm scarf-waving type. But in Portugal I can enjoy their regional dances, which are not forced or coy revivals to amuse the tourists, but a natural expression of pride in a way of life that still exists. In Lisbon there is none of the giggling, awkward, peasant lass feeling about folklore; it is put on by professional or well-practised teams with great verve. A production and entertainment is made out of it. I never believed I would be able to stomach a whole dinner cabaret of folklore, but the Folclore, Rua Nova da Trinidade, 22a, is fascinating.

The tables are grouped below a large theatre stage, and music and dances are given more impact by being backed with a screen projection of colour slides of various parts of Portugal; dances are broken up with singing and the show ends with a carnival style parade in which the audience join. (The Portuguese, after all, created Rio and the greatest carnival in the world.) If it sounds corny, it is infectiously magnetic. The food, on a limited menu, consists of Portuguese national style dishes. In all these *fado* houses it is refreshing to see Portuguese, both with tourist friends and by themselves, obviously enjoying the food and dancing.

EATING NATIVE IN LISBON

The restaurants noted below are all in the medium or cheap range; they all have typical Portuguese food, though, being Portuguese, they will always try to oblige with something designed for international stomachs if necessary, with egg and omelettes or steaks cooked to order. Lisbon restaurants are often closed on Mondays; it is wise to check in advance.

A Quinta, Passarela do Elevador de Santa Justa, is at the top of the quaint old-fashioned wrought-iron and glass lift structure that raises Lisboans from one level to another of their hilly city. It is considered by some to be the best Portuguese cooking in Lisbon and has excellent views of the city.

Cozinha Alentejana, Avenida Almirante Gago Coutinho, 66, is on the way to the airport. It is closed on Mondays. This restaurant specializes in recipes from the Alentejo area of Portugal (see Chapter 8), and offers an excellent way to sample the original and tasty recipes from this area little known by tourists.

Lisboa Parque, Solar dos Vinhos, Restaurante Bucelas are all in Parque Mayer, where open-air eating is pleasant on a hot night. The Policia, Rua Marques Sá da Bandeira, 112, is not on regular tourist tracks. It gets its name from the fact the police frequent it – for eating – as it is near a police station. Don't be put off by the garage entrance, basic bar of huge barrels and wine-scented air; dive past these and the kitchens to the bustling restaurant, where white-aproned boys whisk round the tables at speed, serving very regional dishes. There are many pork recipes – the pork and clams (the equivalent of English cockles), called in Portuguese *carne de porco con amêijoas*, is good. Cheap and cheerful.

Telheiro, Rua Latino Coelho, 10b, like the Policia, has swift service and is a noisy, throbbing place. It is not the spot for a *dîner intime*. The name means 'tiled roof', and this decorates the long, marble-topped bar displaying meats and fruits like a shop, which it isn't. You pass this on the way to the crowded back room. The Telheiro presents specialities from all over Portugal; a good place to 'table travel' without leaving Lisbon. Soups, from 1s to 1s 6d–12 to 18 cents, include *creme de marisco* (shellfish cream soup), *sopa Alentejana* and the *gaspacho à Alentejana* (see page 138). There are various baked sausages, roast tongue (*linguica*) and roast sausage and rice from Tomar; shrimp *açorda*; eels with *escabeche* sauce, Aveiro style; various *bacalhau*; roast kid in Beira Alta style, sucking pig (see page 64); steaks done in the Viana do Castelo way; roast veal *à Lafões, lombinhos de porco à Angolana*; Chaves ham; cheeses and sweet rice (see page 197); *Dom Rodrigo* (see page 159); *farofias* (see page 98); and *ovos moles* (see page 78) are all available. Main courses here cost about 6s to 10s (72 cents to $1.20), with half portions listed and priced.

Solmar, Rua das Portas de Santo Antão, 108, is considered to serve the best shellfish in town. Beer (*Sagres* is the national Portuguese beer name) is served with it. Vicente, Largo da Trinidade, 15, is another restaurant off the tourist track. White-shuttered, rather Left Bank French look from the outside – indeed many artists eat there. Otherwise it is patronized mostly by professional Lisboans for lunch. Clean and centrally situated. Good for fish, cost of three-course lunch around 9s ($1.08). Porto d'Abrigo, Rua do Remolanes, 16, is down in the docks. For those who like getting right away from tourism. It is considered by Maria Modesto, Portugal's television food expert, to produce excellent Portuguese cooking almost on a domestic level.

THE APRIL MARKET

To promote an 'April in Portugal' tourist theme, a market is held at Belém near Lisbon for two weeks in late April. Like the regional fairs all over the country the April Market enables a leisurely inspection of handicrafts, and many artisans attend the fair and demonstrate the making of their wares.

A rich selection of local sweets is on sale and freshly baked bread. A restaurant is set up in the Nautical Sports Pavilion at Belém, next to the market, serving only regional Portuguese dishes, and alongside a bar where a Portuguese aperitif can be taken. Lisbon and Coimbra *fado* evenings are given as well as displays of folk dancing.

Main tourist office in Lisbon: Comissariado do Turismo, Palacio Foz, Praça dos Restauradores.

RECIPES FROM LISBON

CALDEIRADA À FRAGATEIRA DO LISBOA

(LOCAL VARIATIONS ON A NATIONAL THEME)

fish fillets (mullet, bass, hake, cod, plaice, whitebait, skate, shrimps, cockles, mussels or lobster are suitable)
olive oil
coriander (see *cuentros*, page 186)
onions
1 garlic clove (crushed)
2 tomatoes

STOCK

bones and heads of fish
onions (finely minced)
parsley
bay leaves
lemon juice
1 tablespoon dry port wine
seasoning

Fillet the selected fish. Make a stock with the above ingredients and boil for ½ hour, stirring and skimming off the foam occasionally. Pour through a fine sieve into a pot. Add sliced onions, olive oil, coriander, garlic, and tomatoes from which the seeds have been removed, and let it boil for a further 10 minutes. Then add the fish and boil again for ¼ hour. Serve hot with bread *croûtons* fried in olive oil.

PEIXHINOS DA HORTA

(GARDEN FISH)

This is a charming name for the batter-coated whole French beans grown and served round Lisbon – usually eaten with the fingers.

1 lb. French or runner beans

BATTER

4 oz. self-raising flour
½ teaspoon salt
1 egg
¼ pint white wine

String the beans and cook whole till almost tender. Drain and sprinkle with flour before dipping in batter, so that beans will remain crisp after frying. Sift the flour and salt into a bowl, make a well in centre, add the egg, then mix to a thick batter with the wine. Beat thoroughly. Coat beans with batter, drop into hot fat and fry 1-2 minutes or till crisp and golden. Drain on kitchen paper. Serve sprinkled with plain or flavoured salt.

FAVAS À SALOIA
(SALOIA BROAD BEANS)

The Saloios are the country people living in the area surrounding Lisbon.

FOR FOUR

1 lb. broad beans — meat broth
2½ oz. lard — 8 oz. bacon
1 oz. pork fat — 8 oz. garlic sausage
1 onion — 1 dessertspoon sugar
1 clove garlic — salt
1 sprig coriander (see page 186) — olive oil

Melt lard in a pan with fat and a little olive oil. Add finely sliced onion and chopped garlic. Cook gently. Add coriander, chopped bacon, sliced sausage, sugar, salt, washed broad beans and meat broth to cover. Cook in a covered pot till tender. The Portuguese way is to cover with an enamelled plate filled with water. Never allow this to become dry, and shake the pot occasionally to prevent contents sticking to the bottom.

ERVILHAS COM PAIO
(PEAS AND PORK SAUSAGE)

Around Lisbon *ervilhas* are cooked long and slowly with *paio*, which is a smoked pork, salami style sausage; any smoked meat or garlic sausage can be substituted, or lean boiling bacon can be used. With the addition of a poached egg local style this makes a fine supper dish.

FOR FOUR

1 lb. peas   2 onions
seasoning   1 clove garlic
8 oz. smoked pork or bacon   oil for frying
8 oz. garlic sausage   4 eggs

Start cooking the meat first as it will take longer than the peas. Dice the pork or bacon and the garlic sausage and chop onions and garlic. Fry in oil until onions are soft then cover with water and simmer for 30 minutes. Simmer the peas in salted water until soft, then strain and put a layer into a greased casserole. Put over them the bacon, sausage, onion and garlic and cover with peas. Make four hollows in the peas and put an egg in each. Reheat in a moderate oven for about 30 minutes.

PEIXE CREME (CREAMED FISH)

FOR FOUR

1 lb. cod   4 oz. grated cheese
1 onion (chopped) $\frac{1}{2}$ pint milk
1 sprig parsley   1 oz. butter
1 lb. french beans (fresh or frozen)   1 tablespoon flour
breadcrumbs   seasoning

Simmer the cod, onion and parsley in boiling water (enough to cover fish) till just cooked (about 10 minutes). Drain and flake fish, reserving liquid for sauce. Cook beans in boiling, salted water. Drain, spread beans in the bottom of an ovenproof dish and cover with a layer of flaked cod and onion. Make the sauce with butter, milk and flour to blend, adding 3 oz. grated cheese and seasoning, and pour over the fish. Sprinkle breadcrumbs and rest of cheese over the top. Brown in a moderately hot oven.

MOLHO ESCABECHE
(ESCABECHE SAUCE FOR FISH)

A popular summer *hors d'œuvre* is cold cooked fish covered with *escabeche* sauce. Mackerel fillets are usually used, but other varieties of fish can be treated in the same way.

3 sliced onions 2 tablespoons white vinegar
garlic to taste (finely chopped) bay leaf
olive oil

Fry the onions till dark golden colour in olive oil with garlic and the bay leaf. Fry fish separately. When onions are ready, remove from heat and add vinegar. Cover the pan and leave to get cold. The fish can be kept for a week in the *escabeche* sauce; and in any case the sauce should not be served before it has been kept in a cool place for at least two days.

SOPA DE PURÉ DE GRÃO COM ESPINAFRES

(CREAM OF CHICK-PEAS WITH SPINACH)

from the Varanda do Chanceler restaurant

FOR FOUR TO SIX

½ pint chick-peas 2 soupspoons olive oil
3½ oz. green bacon 1 onion
3½ oz. *chouriço* (see page 186) 1 lb. spinach
salt

Soak peas for 12 hours, then cover with about 3 pints of water. Add onion, bacon, sausage, oil and salt to taste. Bring to boil and cook gently until peas are well done. Rub through a sieve or use a liquidizer to make a *purée*. Bring to boil again and add carefully washed spinach. Adjust seasoning and boil for a further 5 minutes.

AMÊIJOAS À BULHÃO PATO

(BULHÃO PATO COCKLES)

The nineteenth-century poet Bulhão Pato was also a gourmet; alas for his poetry, he is better remembered for a sauce in which to cook cockles.

FOR FOUR MAIN PORTIONS

(this could also be served as a first course)

3 lb. cockles with shells (or equivalent without shells, though the Portuguese flavour is then lost)
3 crushed garlic cloves
1¼ pints water

salt, black pepper
6 tablespoons olive oil
chopped bunch parsley and equal amount coriander (or basil)

If shelled cockles are used add straight to the water and all other ingredients, bring to the boil and simmer while heating through; adjust seasoning if necessary. Serve in soup plates. With cockles in their shells, wash thoroughly and soak in cold water for an hour or so. Cook as above until shells open. (Throw away any that do not.)

LINGUADO À LISBOA (LISBON SOLE)

Linguado, easily confused in the English-speaking tourist's mind with 'tongue' (ox tongue is *lingua*), is in fact sole and a popular Lisboan fish. It turns up in a variety of delicious ways, including *linguado recheado* (stuffed sole). A large cooked sole is filled with a sauce mixture of chopped onions, left-over chopped chicken, chopped bacon or ham; fried gently in olive oil and the yolks of 2 eggs beaten in and heated gently. Breadcrumbs and chopped parsley are used to sprinkle on the fish, which is finally browned in the oven.

At the Porto de Abrigo restaurant (see page 87) sole is served with a crispy cheese finish. Dot butter over the bottom of an ovenproof dish, sprinkle with grated cheese (parmesan is fine). Allow about 6 oz. of sole fillets per person and put them on top of the butter, coated with more butter and cheese. Bake in a hot oven till golden and the cheese is a crisp coating.

Another idea for sole, which was actually given me by the chef of the Escondidinho in Oporto, but is in the Lisbon vein, is to fry sole coated with seasoned flour in oil. When cooked serve with a thick meat sauce poured over it.

AMÊIJOAS À MARINHEIRA

This way of cooking cockles without the shells is used as a garnish sauce to serve with the favourite fried pork fillet of Lisboans and all other Portuguese (see page 195); the cockles can also be served with an omelette.

2 tablespoons mashed potato
4 large tomatoes
2 small bottles cockles or about 4 pints fresh cockles (clean and boil to open shells, remove from shells)
¼ pint olive oil
2 large sliced onions
1–2 cloves garlic
finely chopped parsley
1 tablespoon flour
1 pinch ground pepper

Cook the onions and garlic with the olive oil. When browned remove the garlic and add tomatoes (skinned and seeded), the flour and the pepper. When tomatoes and onions are cooked add the potato, cockles and parsley. Cook for 2 minutes and serve.

BACALHAU À CHANCELER

from the Varanda do Chanceler restaurant

FOR SIX TO EIGHT

3 lb. salt cod
6 lb. potatoes
3 pints white sauce (a plain roux)
several onions
olive oil
1 carton fresh cream
2 teaspoons made mustard
4–5 egg yolks
breadcrumbs

Prepare cod as on page 189. Simmer in water till cooked, then shred as finely as possible. Cut parboiled potatoes into small cubes and fry. Chop onions finely and fry in oil until golden. Add to this the cod and fried potatoes. Mix well. Then add the white sauce, egg yolks, half the cream and the mustard, and stir very thoroughly.

Pour it all into a shallow fireproof dish and coat with the remaining cream and sprinkle with breadcrumbs. Place in hot oven until crumbs are golden, or brown under a grill. Serve very hot.

ROBALO NO FORNO À PORTUGUESA
(PORTUGUESE BASS)
from the Hotel Mundial

FOR FOUR TO SIX

2 lb. bass	cup of white wine
2 medium onions finely chopped	2 skinned tomatoes
	1 oz. tomato juice
1 clove garlic	parsley
½ gill olive oil	2 lb. potatoes
1 oz. butter	juice of 1 lemon

Place in a baking dish half the quantity of oil and some sliced onion and chopped parsley. Place the whole fish on top then pour over it the lemon and tomato juice, chopped garlic, rest of the oil and onion, butter, wine, chopped tomatoes and other seasoning. Bake in a medium oven until cooked, with diced potatoes.

DELICIAS DE PEIXE ENVOLTAS
(WRAPPED FISH DELIGHTS)
from the Hotel Eduardo VII

Poach fish fillets (preferably hake or bass) in milk. Drain, coat lightly with breadcrumbs and fry in butter. Wrap them in slices of ham which have also been poached in milk. Cover with mayonnaise, sprinkle with grated cheese and brown under the grill. Serve with plain rice or plain boiled potatoes.

PEITOS DE FRANGO À VARANDA
(VARANDA BREAST OF CHICKEN)
from the Varanda Restaurant of the Hotel Eduardo VII

Season boned chicken breasts with salt and fry lightly in butter. Mix together a little melted butter, mustard, tomato sauce and 2 tablespoons consommé (or good stock). Add this to the juice from the fried chicken. Season, and add a little dry white wine. Simmer gently. Just before serving add a small glass of brandy and one of dry port or madeira. Serve with rice.

ISCAS À PORTUGUESA
(PORTUGUESE LIVER)

Iscas are thin slices of liver, unlike the thick pieces we use. Pig's or lamb's liver can be used to make this typically Lisboan dish.

Marinate the small liver pieces in white wine, with bay leaf, cloves, crushed garlic, peppercorns, salt to taste. Leave at least 4 hours, preferably overnight.

Dry the liver with a clean cloth. Sauté gently in a frying-pan with bacon or smoked ham and chopped boiled potatoes for about 5 minutes. The marinade liquid can be added to the pan to provide a sauce.

BIFES DE CEBOLADA
(ONION-SMOTHERED STEAKS)

Bife means 'steak' in Portugal. As the steak meat is often tough, though meat is improving now, recipes have been developed which by slow casseroling with vegetables soften the meat. *Bifes de cebolada* with the nationally loved soft onion *purée*, is widely found.

Fry thinnish steaks and about twice as much sliced onion in butter for about 5 minutes. Cover or move to a casserole dish and cook in a low oven for 1-2 hours. This results in a stringy onion *purée* in a gravy produced from the steam in the casserole (make the lid fit as tightly as possible – a pressure cooker could be used for this recipe). Season before cooking is finished. A very little port or sherry can be added. Serve with plain boiled potatoes.

BIFE À FRIGIDEIRA
(FRIGIDEIRA STEAK)

FOR EACH PERSON

piece of rump steak
garlic (chopped)
½ tablespoon white wine
(or wine vinegar)
bay leaf
thick slice gammon ham
slice bread
seasoning

This is not, as the title suggests, frozen beef. *Frigideira* is the oval earthenware dish in which the meat is cooked and served. The meat is fried in the dish on top of the stove and distinguished by the slice of ham added and the lemon juice customarily sprinkled over meats in Portugal.

Slowly fry the steak (usually medium rare) in butter with garlic, wine and bay leaf. Fry in the sauce the ham and the bread. Adjust seasoning to taste and serve in the dish (the Scandinavian fireproof china dishes are ideal for this) with the ham on the steak and the steak on the bread slice.

This was described to me by Sue Pereira, who used to prepare it at the Arabelle restaurant in London. She also prepared, as variations on this Portuguese steak theme, *bife Chave Douro* – the same as above but a fried egg substituted for the ham slice; *bife Nicola*, steak fried in butter with peeled chopped tomatoes, onions, garlic, bay leaf and seasoning. The steak is served with this sauce on top.

PENTEOLAS À PORTUGUESA
(SCALLOPS PORTUGUESE STYLE)

FOR SIX

6 scallops
½ lb. lean cooked pork
1 onion (finely chopped)
2 tablespoons olive oil
2 tomatoes
chopped parsley

2 tablespoons flour
salt and pepper
milk
1 tablespoon butter
breadcrumbs

Wash scallops and remove hard skin (some fishmongers supply scallops already prepared). Remove from shell (keeping the shells) and chop into small pieces. Put the pork through mincer. Fry the onion in the olive oil. When golden add the tomatoes and chopped parsley. Simmer uncovered for about ½ hour. Put through wire sieve and add pork, stirring well. Add the flour. When flour has become golden, slowly add enough milk to make a creamy consistency. Add chopped scallops, salt and papper to taste and butter and cook gently. Place mixture in washed shells, cover with breadcrumbs and put in the oven to brown.

PERDIZES CONVENTO DE ALCANTARA
(ALCANTARA PARTRIDGE)

FOR EACH PARTRIDGE

7 tablespoons port wine
7 tablespoons white wine
liver pâté (*foie gras*)
slice of bread (or breadcrumbs)
salt and pepper
pickled cucumbers (gherkins)
milk

This hundred-year-old recipe was originally invented at the convent of Alcantara near Lisbon. It is an extremely rich and 'dinner-party-to-impress' kind of recipe.

Prepare the partridge for cooking. Stuff with a mixture of the pâté, breadcrumbs soaked in oil and chopped pickled cucumbers. Sew up the opening with thread and marinate in the mixed wine for 24 hours. Bring to the boil in the wine seasoned with salt and pepper. Leave to simmer for about $1\frac{1}{2}$ hours in a well-covered pan. Remove the thread; cut into slices and serve with the wine sauce *reduced* in amount.

DOBRADA COM GRÃO
(TRIPE WITH CHICK-PEAS)

In the Lisbon area tripe is known as *dobrada*; in Oporto as *tripas*. In the south it is commonly cooked with chick-peas.

FOR FOUR

1 lb. tripe
1 lb. chick-peas or haricot beans
2 onions
2 tomatoes
2 carrots
bay leaf
$\frac{1}{2}$ lb. bacon or smoked sausage
olive oil
salt, pepper

Boil the previously soaked chick-peas or beans with the tripe and then cut the tripe into little pieces. Heat some olive oil in a pan and fry the chopped onions till golden with tomatoes, carrots and bay leaf. Add salt and pepper. Add the bacon or sausage cut in squares. When these are all soft remove the bay leaf, add the tripe and the peas or beans and heat together adding, if necessary, a little of the liquid in which the peas and tripe were boiled.

BIFINHOS DE VITELA (VEAL STEAKS)

A braising method of tenderizing veal.

FOR FOUR

Slice into 2-inch long strips 2 lb. best rump of veal and soak in lemon juice. Melt a dessertspoon of butter in a pan. When hot add the meat and fry until golden brown. Remove the fat and flour the meat, and continue to fry until brown. Add ¾ pint hot water. Season and simmer for 1 hour. Half an hour before serving add ½ glass of tawny port. Make certain that the gravy is not too thick.

FAROFIAS (SNOW PANCAKES)

just over 1 pint milk   grated rind of 1 lemon
8 tablespoons sugar   6 eggs
2 teaspoons flour   cinnamon

Mix flour with a little cold milk. Add the other ingredients (beaten egg yolks only) and most of the rest of milk. Heat gently, stirring continuously till custard thickens. Let it cool. Beat egg whites stiffly. Boil a little more sweetened milk and drop large spoonfuls of beaten egg-white into it and cook till the whites are firm without losing their shape. Remove from the milk and put in a serving dish. Pour the custard over them and sprinkle with cinnamon.

6

NORTH-WEST OF LISBON

Lisboans are most fortunate in having such accessible seaside resorts so near them, both to the south of the city across the Tagus in the Arrábida district and, more frequented both by them and the tourist, the resorts to the west and north-west. Estoril and Cascais are well established, the Guincho beach is a week-end playground and, further north, Ericeira, more newly discovered, is a possible day visit. Past that the coastal resorts of Peniche and the inland towns of Óbidos and Caldas da Rainha are more for visiting while touring north. Sintra, with its palaces and spires, reminiscent of an illustration for a child's fairy-tale book, is a famed inland relaxation spot easily reached from Lisbon.

Gastronomically, the area is famous for its sea food: the lobsters of the Guincho restaurants; the famous steamed lobster dish from Peniche, the sardines which Cascais boasts as the best in the world – plainly grilled with lemon and parsley; the *cherne*, or halibut, with its thick meaty flesh; partridges from the heath shores behind Guincho (in the autumn); the *caldeirada* fish soups; and grilled shrimps and *camarão* (scampi).

THE ROAD TO ESTORIL

Moving round the coast from Lisbon along the easy-drive Marginal road past the barley-sugar Manueline of Belém's

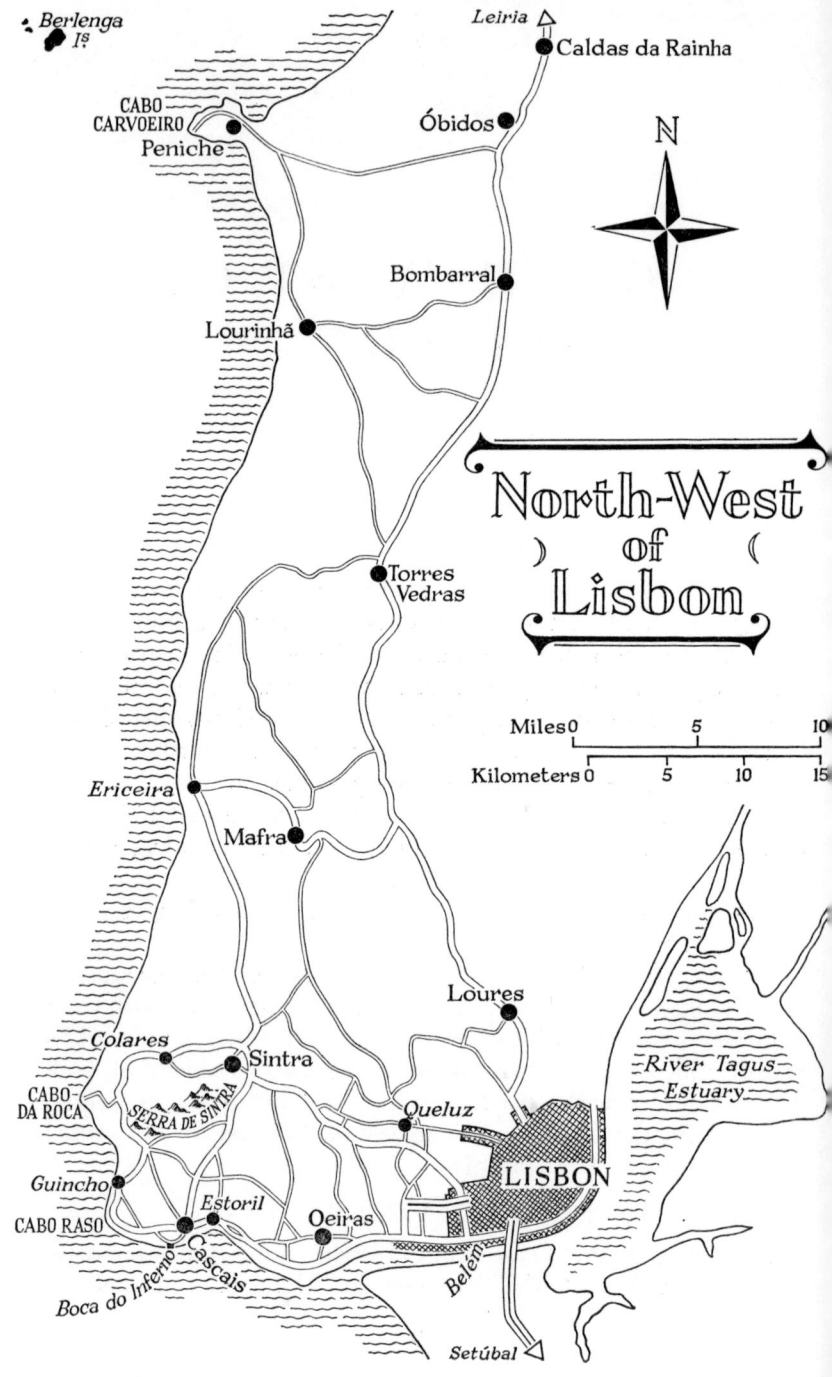

Jeronimos monastery, the tiny Tower of Belém and the streamlined modern monument to Henry the Navigator, Estoril is reached in 20 minutes. Although the journey is swift (there are good train connections too) and built-up till way past Cascais, the atmosphere of a capital city is soon left behind and the ambience is one of seaside and holidays. However, this is very much the route the Lisboans take in search of good eating-out at week-ends and the area is rich in good Portuguese restaurants. Recommended names to watch for on the Lisbon–Cascais road are Choupana near Estoril, well sited overlooking the sea, where there is dancing (the name means 'little house of the poor'); the Mónaco (with dancing) at Caxias; and the Pérgula at Santo Amaro, Oeiras; or there is the Saísa on the Santo Amaro–Oeiras beach.

MONTE ESTORIL

Just before Estoril is the twin resort of Monte, which I consider has more charm and character than Estoril. It was an area much favoured by English people before the war, though the English colony has now shifted to Cascais, which has begun to ape the swinging Britain image and is a great draw with young Lisboans who consider this currently smart.

In Monte Estoril the English-Bar is an excellent restaurant, set in a private house style building in its own small garden masked by a petrol station from the main Lisbon approach. The name belies the good Portuguese cooking it serves, and comes from the heavy mock-Tudor wood panelling, big fireplaces and a bar with oak trestles as tables. This might be a little oppressive on a hot day, but the restaurant has a built-out terrace window with good views over the mouth of the Tagus. Main courses cost around 7s 6d (90 cents) and specialities include *cherne na canoa* (halibut) with a clam sauce; roasted and stuffed partridge (see page 97); *toucinho do céu* (see page 118); mixed shellfish; *lulas fritas* (fried squid); and lobster.

ESTORIL

The road past Estoril is marred by the hideous monster block of the Estoril Sol *de luxe* hotel, topped with a huge chimney – one of the relatively few blots on the copybook of Portuguese tourist development. The hotel does, however, have a restaurant with a fine view (the one place where you can't see the darned hotel), and serves mainly an international cuisine. More regionally charming to visit in Estoril is the Tamariz restaurant, producing excellent sea food. *Tourist office in Estoril*

CASCAIS

Cascais is now turning itself into a mini St Tropez, fashionable with the smart younger set. Yet its innate character of a fishing village where Columbus once lived is still very much alive. The gaudy, poster-famed painted boats are hauled up on the beach, nets mended around them; the fish market – worth a visit – reflects the essential steady basis of prosperity of this little town. Its tiny cobbled streets are beautified with old tiled fronts; vines; gaslit lamps still glow at corners; and pastel-shaded washed houses back up against the deep blue sky. Although a lot of restoration work has been done, and many of the houses are now owned by foreigners, Cascais has luckily escaped being 'twee' and, so far, is unselfconscious. Once there were many small fishermen's cafés and bars where the husband served the drink and the wife did the cooking; these are slowly changing in favour of much smarter restaurants and discothèques. One such fishermen's drinking bar which changed recently is now the John Bull, an English pub right in the middle of the town where the main road turns up towards the beach.

The John Bull's interior, perfect in its traditional fumed oak *décor*, was literally shipped out lock, stock and English beer barrel from Britain, and folkloristic Victorian pub songs on tape provide a background to the drinking. On Sunday mornings it is home from home, with English voices and people in riding clothes. In the afternoon young Lisboans come for the smart drink of English beer at a premium (local wines and ports are inexpensive here). Upstairs there is a small restaurant seating about forty-five people, serving an English-Portuguese menu. For the English abroad with a sudden craving for a home-style sausage, the John Bull have their sausages made to English specifications by a local butcher, and they are delicious. The proprietors are a young Anglo-Portuguese couple: Philippa Couto is a good cook herself and gave me several excellent ideas for adapting Portuguese foodstuffs to a more Anglicized stomach.

When I visited Cascais last winter the chef at the John Bull was Clotilde, a renowned cook who has worked in restaurants in the Lisbon area all her life, including running the kitchens at the royal palace of Queluz (see page 9). Clotilde is a great natural expert on Portuguese cookery, adores her work, and once started on her theme wanted to deluge me with her treasured recipes. These included recipes garnered from the convents and from the recipe books of the Portuguese queens who became absorbed in food preparation. Wherever Clotilde has worked her recipes remain a memorial to her work as a chef; the refreshing thing about Portuguese cuisine is that there are many enthusiastic women like Clotilde. At the John Bull the Portuguese items to try are rabbit stew, partridge stew brought *flambé* to the table, *pato Português* (duck in the Portuguese style), grilled fillets of pork, tuna rice, orange pudding, pressed tongue and chestnut pudding.

More in the old-style Cascais is the Retiro restaurant which is in the same street as the back entrance to the John Bull. This is small and modest, with a definite fishermen's flavour. Lobster for four people costs about £2 10s ($6), but other Portuguese dishes are cheaper: *carne de porco à Alentejana* (see page 141) with cockles is 13s ($1.56), a shellfish omelette (*omelette marisco*) 6s (72 cents), and grilled *camarão* (scampi) 14s 6d ($1.74). There is *pudim flan* and chocolate mousse, a popular sweet in this part of Portugal.

The famous Fim do Mundo restaurant is situated near the railway station, so that it is easy to visit from Lisbon, and is open from midday to midnight. Prices are more expensive than the other restaurants below. The menu is available complete in English translation, and Portuguese specialities to try include tomato soup with eggs (see page 177); grilled sea bass (*robalo*); lobster curry and other lobster dishes; steak with onions (see page 195); duck with rice; *caldeirada*, fillets of sole served with banana in the Madeira manner; calf's kidney with bacon as kebabs; Portuguese style liver (see page 95). Non-regional dishes include steak and kidney pie, American style tournedos steaks and hamburger steak – a selection to satisfy many tastes.

Other Cascais restaurants of note are O Túnel, O Pescador near the fish market; Aos 3 Porquinhos, also a boarding-house (French food); the Gil Vicente (also French); the Snobissimo, a rather young style bar and restaurant; and the Frango Real in the Avenida José Frederico Ulrich. The English Tea Room in the main shopping street running down towards the John Bull entrance serves tea and scones – good but pricey. O Batel, opposite the *lota*, a fish auction market, serves, not surprisingly, good sea food.

Beyond Cascais the buildings give way gradually to the open, windswept sand dunes interspread with copses of pine trees. Before turning the corner of the Tagus estuary and heading north up the Atlantic coast you come to the fascinatingly fearful Boca do Inferno, the 'mouth of hell'. This is a formation of rock through which the Atlantic rollers burst in a freak explosion of spray many feet high. By the Boca is a small café.

GUINCHO

Six and a quarter miles from Cascais is Guincho beach. Although a very popular week-end spot with Lisboans it has retained its majestic spaciousness and the rule of the sea rather than of man, which adds splendour to the scene of huge sweep of smooth sand to a headland lunged out into the sea. This headland – Cabo da Roca – was the Fim do Mundo of the ancient medieval world before Columbus. Here the Europeans believed the earth ended; nothing lay to the west except sea and then a ledge over which ships and sailors would disappear to their destruction.

Portuguese headlands have an historical fascination for me, they so vividly evoke the tiny Spanish and Portuguese caravel ships setting off into the unknown and, more miraculous, coming back with their tales of land on the 'other side'. Cabo Espichel (see page 122), and, most enthralling of all, Cabo San Vincente (see page 147) are the places to take a picnic and sit above the sea, watching the shipping on the greatest sea lanes of the world.

At Guincho, however, to picnic would be a shame with the cluster of good restaurants crouched, some seemingly buried, in the sand at the southern end of the beach. There is the Hotel do Guincho in a strange, yellow-washed, Moorish style castle. The restaurant Do Mestre Ze (meaning 'the respected fisherman') and a little way apart, towards Cascais, O Faroleiro, 'lighthouse keeper'.

Best known of the group is the Estalagem Muchaxo, a small inn and restaurant. A charming place to stay, with fifteen country style rooms that have thick whitewashed walls, narrow balconies, dark wood fittings, beds with heads made from the carved ox yokes of the Minho and poetic views of the seascape. As for most of the hotels in this area, bookings should be made a very long way in advance. This delightful, rambling place has grown piecemeal from a wooden shack restaurant, which has always attracted crowds to its food.

Lisboans come out to eat lobster at Muchaxo, its veranda restaurant, decorated with tree trunk and sacking, curved out over the beach. In the hollow in the centre of the circular room is a menagerie of birds, foxes and dogs. After a meal there is the comfort of the wooden panelled lounge with log fire or the patio corridors with black and white patterned cobbles and intimate seats set into arched stone alcoves. Muchaxo's also has a huge sea-water swimming-pool set among the rocks, and sheltered courtyard sun areas.

The food is superb. Meat and game – partridge in autumn – are served as well as the supreme speciality, the lobsters. Muchaxo keeps pens of live lobsters near by and even has a kind of lobster hospital to treat any that don't feel too strong. Cookery experts in Portugal insist that lobsters must be cooked alive and sauces made from their 'blood'. Certainly this seems to add flavour; at Muchaxo lobsters are served Barraca style with cognac and a sauce of tomatoes (see page 114). Lobster *à Muchaxo* (see page 114) is another chef's speciality and so, for *hors d'œuvres*, are *perceves* (literal translation, 'thou understandeth'). These are tiny barnacles which are described as being like mini-elephant's feet, about a quarter of an inch across and purplish and tasty under their shells. Another rare find is the *bruxas* (witches), tiny prawn-sized lobsters.

SINTRA

From Guincho a direct road twists and turns up over the Serra de Sintra to the extraordinary village cluster of Sintra. (There is also a good main road connection from Lisbon via Queluz – see below).

Half way between Guincho and Sintra is Colares, the small town which produces such excellent red wine. There are two good restaurants here, both of which also have tearooms for light refreshments on the journey. The Recreio da Várzea is near the lake and the O Moinho on the Cascais road.

Once over the ridge of the Serra de Sintra, the blustery sea coast gives way to rich lush verdant growth and narrow, stone-walled, corkscrew lanes (maximum concentration needed for driving) which are a little reminiscent of England. Sintra was the favourite country retreat of the Portuguese royal family, and is distinguished by its collection of six architectural oddities: one, a Moorish style royal palace, is dominated by huge, oast-house-like chimneys of the royal kitchens. This palace is now a museum and has beautiful gardens.

Near by is the Estalagem dos Cavaleros, where Byron stayed; he adored Sintra and called it an Eden on earth. Nowadays the Estalagem da Reposa and Sintra Sol provide first classification comfort.

The bizarre Palace of Pena is situated on the tallest of the peaky hills. This looks as if the Disneyland castle in California had mated with Edinburgh Castle to produce a setting for Camelot. The grey stone spires, gargoyle-blobbed bridges over nothing and turrets are in keeping with the hideous plush and plaster work inside; one is thankful plastic hadn't been invented in the time of the Braganças. The effect has a certain enchantment amidst the thick forest growth containing hundreds of rare trees and shrubs, one of the foremost arboreal collections in Europe. Another monument to view in the area is the São Pedro Capuchinhos convent, with its tiny cells, cork-lined as an insulation against the cold. Near the church in the São Pedro village is a square where markets are held on the second and fourth Sundays of each month. The antique stalls here are well worth a visitor's viewing.

To stay in a royal palace which retains its regal air is always satisfying for the tourist to boast of on his return home. At Seteais the eighteenth-century palace is now a luxury hotel, costing £4 to £6 ($9.60 to $14.40) per day full pension; hardly a princely sum for kingly comfort in superb grounds, a dramatic central archway approach to the gardens and dignified furnishing in period backed by many original frescoes. The restaurant is excellent and worth a visit on its own. *Tourist office at Sintra*

QUELUZ

Queluz is another palace that can be visited for food, served more humbly here in the royal kitchens which are yet grand enough by today's building standards. Motoring from Lisbon the main road suddenly changes into a sea of cobble waves and one is surrounded by eighteenth-century buildings on both sides of the road. Apart from cars and coaches, usually packed alongside, it is a surprising step back two hundred years. The palace itself has spread-out low buildings, with pink-washed walls surrounding a large formal garden, cooled with fishponds and fountains.

Queluz has an air of happiness and gaiety not often found in royal palaces. *Décor* is light and feminine, the rooms sunny and airy, the furniture touchingly worn with human contact; it has a strange warm non-museum feeling as if the owners had just left. This particularly applies to the ballroom; it is not really big enough to be dignified by that title, yet I could sense the mood of happiness and movement in this room, and I have seen too many evocative places to be easily moved by them.

The Queluz Cozinha Velha restaurant is in the royal kitchens just across the drive from the main palace. The high-ceilinged rooms, with their huge fireplaces, have simple, wooden-backed chairs, and there is a countrified air, with huge pots of flowers and displays of fruit, *pâtisseries* and *hors d'œuvres*. It is a perfect place to rest over a cup of tea or coffee and a superb pastry after sightseeing, or to lunch or have dinner by candlelight.

ERICEIRA

The Sintra road from Lisbon continues north to Ericeira, across to Torres Vedras and then northwards to Óbidos and Caldas da Rainha. This area is worth while making the effort of a long day's visit from Lisbon if the driver is prepared for at least five to six hours' driving. Usually one makes a first-night stop on a tour north at Ericeira or Peniche, charming places to pass a summer seaside holiday. At Ericeira the cliff-top village peers down at a sandy beach on which there are lobster tanks for the Hotel de Turismo, where the gourmet can pick his own meal. Shellfish of all kinds are the specialities here, in soup form as well, and the local sweet dish is *pasteis de feijão*. The Ericeira annual fair is held on 25th July. The Hotel do Turismo has a fine drinks terrace overlooking the bay, backed by a huge dining-room with beamed ceiling, blue and white half-tiled walls, and high, ladder-backed chairs. The *estalagem* Pedro O Pescador has a high reputation for good sea food; to stay here very early booking is necessary.

Tourist office in Ericeira

PENICHE AND BERLENGA ISLANDS

Peniche near Cabo Carvoeiro, reached by turning off the main road just before Óbidos, is another fishing port also famous for its lobster dishes. The supreme local recipe, copied in many parts of the coast, is steamed lobster (see page 113). Sardines are canned here and local women make lace. Peniche is on a peninsula surrounded by water at high tide, but has two first-class pensions, the Casa Pim and Félita, both very inexpensive. From the harbour daily boats run to the Berlenga Islands, on which there is nothing but some fishermen's houses and a lighthouse and a *Pousada* – just the place for 'get-away-from-it-all' types. The Pousada Abrigo de Pescadores ('fishermen's shelter') has fourteen rooms built within the walls of an old fortress jutting out into the sea. It is only open from June to September. Lobster is again the local speciality (see page 114), though there is wild-duck shooting available on the island, and duck and rice dishes are often prepared.

Tourist office in Peniche

ÓBIDOS

Another characterful *Pousada* in the area is the one at Óbidos about $1\frac{1}{4}$ miles inland from Peniche, set near a small lagoon (fishing is possible). Óbidos is a perfect example of a walled city, its toothlike Moorish ramparts against the invader unbroken. Inside, the churches and fluted roofs piled high peer down on the passer-by. The streets of this market town are blessedly free of traffic. The Pousada do Castelo is one of the oldest *Pousadas* and has only six rooms created in Óbidos castle itself. The views are superb, and a *Pousada* speciality is squid cooked with onion, tomato and pepper.

NORTH-WEST OF LISBON

Three and a half miles from Óbidos, Caldas da Rainha is an old market town and has a spa. Monday market day brings displays of local fruit – huge peaches a speciality – and of the locally produced unusual pottery. Its local sweetmeats are *cavacas* biscuits and *trouxas de ovas*.

Tourist office in Óbidos

RECIPES FROM NORTH-WEST OF LISBON

TOMATES RECHEADOS
(STUFFED TOMATOES)

from Philippa Couto at the John Bull, Cascais

Scoop out tomatoes and fill with stale bread mixed with parmesan cheese (or other strong grated cheese). Mix half and half with scooped out chopped tomato and a little salt and pepper. Put a dab of butter on top, replace top of tomato. Bake in oven with 2 tablespoons olive oil till tender.

ARROZ DE TUNA (TUNA FISH RICE)

A popular summer dish which can be made with tinned tuna, though in Portugal fresh tuna fish would be used.

Wash cooked cold rice, mix with mayonnaise, tuna and chopped lettuce and tomato to taste in a large pudding basin. Press down hard and turn out. Decorate with olives and chopped, hard-boiled eggs. Keep in fridge till used.

RISSÓIS (RISSOLES)
a grim name for a delightful dish

Boil 1 cup water with 1 oz. butter. Mix 1 cup cold water with 1 cup flour, add to the rest of the water in a pan and stir all the time over a medium heat till the mixture thickens. When the bottom of the pot just begins to burn (careful!) and the pastry comes away from the pan sides cleanly, remove from heat, cool and knead a lot. Roll out very thinly. Place spoonfuls of a chosen filling – anything cooked and mixed with a sauce; shrimps or *bacalhau* in a cream sauce are perfect – on the pastry. Place an upturned cup over each spoonful of filling and cut pastry. Fold pastry over to make a half-moon-shaped package, cover with beaten egg and breadcrumbs and drop in hot deep fat; turn once, remove and drain.

CANJA (CHICKEN BROTH)

Canja is the generic word used in Portugal for all chicken broth soups. Rice and ham are common ingredients, but chopped roast chestnuts, lemon juice, egg yolks, onion and even nutmeg may be added. In some parts of Portugal fresh mint is added and this is delightful, combined with a little lemon juice flavouring. Allow about ¾ tablespoon fresh chopped mint per person and add just before serving or it will quickly lose its effect.

FOR FOUR

3 cups chicken stock ½ cup rice
¼ lb. fat bacon or ham, chopped seasoning

Cook bacon in chicken stock gently. Add seasoning and rice; serve when rice is cooked.

SARDINHAS DE CASCAIS
(CASCAIS SARDINES)

FOR FOUR

12 sardines breadcrumbs
6 onions olive oil
1 glass white wine salt, pepper
5 tomatoes

Chop the onions and fry till golden brown in olive oil. Add the wine, simmering until it reduces in quantity. Skin tomatoes, cut into small pieces and add to rest with salt and pepper. When the tomatoes have softened, transfer everything to an ovenproof dish. Clean sardines and roll in breadcrumbs. Place sardines on top of the tomato and onion and pour a little olive oil on each fish. Cook in a moderate oven till the sardines are done.

CALDEIRADA À PESCADOR
(FISHERMAN'S STEW)

Popular all over Portugal (composition depends on local varieties), particularly round Cascais, and similar to a bouillabaisse. In Portugal little bags of fish pieces ready to make the *caldeirada* are sold in fish markets; at home select fish pieces and varieties according to taste and pocket – since removal of the bones is a messy business use fish fillets or steaks and chop into small pieces. Squid can be optionally added.

FOR FOUR

1½ lb. mixed fish
½ lb. cockles in their shells
2 onions
3 garlic cloves
salt and pepper
paprika to taste
olive oil
hard bread
1 sprig parsley

Slice onions in a large saucepan, add chopped garlic, salt, pepper, paprika, chopped parsley and oil. Fry for a few minutes. Add some water, the fish cut in pieces and cockles. Tomatoes can be added with the onions. Serve on fried bread slices.

LULAS À POUSADA
(SQUID FROM THE POUSADA DO CASTELO, ÓBIDOS)

FOR EACH PERSON

1–2 squid
1 medium onion
4 oz. lard
olive oil
pepper, deseeded, sliced and cooked
tomato *purée*
seasoning

Heat a little olive oil with sliced onions. Add pepper and lard. Cut the squid into rings, put in a casserole together with the onions, oil and add salt to taste. Cook in the steam of the squid without adding water. When tender add tomato *purée* to taste and the pepper. Cook a little longer and serve with small potatoes and chopped parsley.

SALMI DE PERDIZ
(SALMI OF PARTRIDGE)

A rich quality recipe I can imagine being made in the stately kitchens of the Queluz or Seteias palaces.

partridge	leeks
onion	carrots
celery	stock

Boil partridge lightly. Place in the oven and surround with chopped vegetables. When browned, cover with a good stock and simmer together on top of the stove till tender. When the partridge is tender cut in two and remove bones. (In Portugal the bones are roasted, pounded in a mortar and added to the stock.) At home I feel it is more likely that the meat only will be replaced in the stock with seasoning. Serve with fried bread slices, potatoes and, ideally, asparagus and also *foie gras*.

PERDIZ ASSADO (ROAST PARTRIDGE)

from the English-Bar, Monte Estoril

FOR EACH PARTRIDGE

6 small onions	carrots (chopped)
a little butter	mushrooms
4 thin slices bacon	seasoning
a little white wine	a little cream
fried potatoes	demi-glace and madeira
peas	

Roast each partridge in the oven with onions, butter and bacon wrapped round the bird. Add a little white wine. Remove from oven and fry the bird, surrounded with previously fried potatoes, vegetables and seasoning till everything is heated through. Pour cream on the vegetables and a little demi-glace. Heat gently to boiling point. Add a little madeira just before serving.

SANTOLA NO CARRO
(CRAB IN A CARRIAGE)

This delightful dish, which would make a good *hors d'œuvre*, is prepared on the coast, particularly in the north round Oporto. The Portuguese crab is the spider crab less frequently available in England, thrown away as considered too small when caught. (The tinned Japanese crab is usually the leg meat of spider crabs.) Fresh, frozen or tinned crab can be used in this recipe.

The 'carriage' in Portugal is the crab's small but deeply coloured shell, which is used to serve the meat. In its absence small ramekin dishes can be used.

FOR FOUR

2 medium tins crab meat, or equivalent in fresh or frozen
1 large, finely chopped onion
5 oz. butter
1 oz. soft fresh breadcrumbs
2 oz. olives
freshly ground black pepper
parsley
lemon
few drops hot pepper sauce (*piri-piri*, see page 194); Worcester sauce could be substituted

Fry onion in 1 oz. butter till golden. Add breadcrumbs then, off the stove, crab, olives, the rest of the butter and seasoning to taste. Put into serving dishes and bake in a hot oven till golden (about 10 minutes). Serve topped with parsley sprigs and lemon pieces.

LAGOSTA SUADA
(STEAMED LOBSTER)

a speciality from Peniche

1 lobster
4 onions
5 or 6 tomatoes
4 cloves garlic
1 oz. butter
1 bay leaf
parsley
pepper, paprika, salt
2 glasses madeira or port wine

Put sliced onions, crushed garlic, chopped tomatoes (peeled and the pips removed) and the seasonings together into an earthenware or ovenproof dish and bake in the oven with the butter. Do not remove the lobster from its shell, but chop into small pieces, put in a saucepan with any liquid from the lobster, add a *little* water. Bring to boil quickly. Once boiling, turn the heat down and cook very slowly for about an hour. Keep the lid on the pan so as to allow the lobster to 'sweat'. Shake the saucepan from time to time. After 1 hour remove the lid, add salt to taste and pour in the wine. Cover and cook for some minutes. Serve on a base of the tomato and onions.

LAGOSTA À MUCHAXO
(MUCHAXO LOBSTER)
from Guincho

Remove lobster from shell and cut up into small pieces. Use 5 onions for 4 people, slice and cook with ½ wineglass olive oil (4 tablespoons), a little chopped garlic, bay leaf, a dash of *piri-piri* sauce (see page 194). Fry till the onions are golden. Add a *purée* of 5 tomatoes; bring to boil. When boiling add lobster and cook till tender. Serve with white rice.

LAGOSTA BARRACA
(LOBSTER BARRACA)
from the Muchaxo Restaurant

FOR FOUR TO SIX

3 lobsters
2 medium onions (peeled and chopped)
2 tablespoons olive oil
3 cups tomato sauce (see *Lagosta à Portuguesa* recipe below for making this sauce)
4 oz. butter
1 cup cognac

Remove lobster meat from its shell and cut in thick pieces. Fry the onions in olive oil until well browned. Add tomato sauce and allow to simmer 10 minutes. Fry lobster in the butter for about 5 minutes. Place on a fireproof dish, pour the warmed cognac over and *flamber* until the flames go out. Place lobster pieces in tomato sauce and simmer gently for 15 minutes. Serve with rice.

LAGOSTA À PORTUGUESA
(PORTUGUESE LOBSTER)

1 lobster
1 medium onion (sliced)
parsley and thyme
peppercorns to taste
1 bay leaf, salt
2 tablespoons brandy

SAUCE

1 lb. tomatoes
2–3 oz. butter
4 onions (finely chopped)
salt and ground pepper
1 wineglass dry white wine
1 clove garlic
1 tablespoon flour

Place chopped lobster meat in water to cover in which the onion, parsley, thyme, bay leaf, peppercorns and salt have already been boiled. Simmer gently till tender. Make the sauce by cooking together the tomatoes (sieved), onions, salt, wine, ground pepper and garlic in butter. In another saucepan melt 1 oz. butter, remove from the heat and mix with the flour. Return to the stove, gently adding the tomato sauce mixture and stirring till smooth. Cool well, blend until smooth. Place the lobster meat on a baking-dish, pour over the sauce, add 2 tablespoons brandy, allow to simmer for 8 minutes. Serve with boiled potatoes or boiled rice.

The delicious scampi-sized prawns found round the coast to the north-west of Lisbon are often cooked on kebabs and served with a sauce made with tomatoes, onion, olives and white wine and rice.

CAMARÃO À PORTUGUESA
(PORTUGUESE SCAMPI)

FOR FOUR

1½ lb. scampi
olive oil
2 oz. butter
1 chopped onion
3½ cups rice
7 cups stock
seasoning

SAUCE

1 lb. tomatoes	½ glass dry white wine
1 tablespoon oil	12 stoned olives
1 chopped onion	seasoning
1 crushed garlic clove	

Heat butter in a large pan, add onion and rice. Fry gently till golden brown, stirring all the time. Add stock, season to taste. Bring to the boil, stirring well. Cover pan and simmer gently for 20 minutes. To make the sauce, fry onion and garlic in oil for a few minutes. Add tomatoes, peeled and chopped, and the rest of the sauce ingredients. Simmer gently for about ½ hour.

Put scampi on skewers, brush with oil and grill for 7–8 minutes. Place on top of rice in serving dish. Serve sauce separately.

BACALHAU ASSADO À PORTUGUESA
(PORTUGUESE FRIED COD)

Occasionally the Portuguese do eat unsalted the cod they bring back from Newfoundland and other places. This is one of the classic ways, using the national tomato- and onion-based sauce.

FOR FOUR

SAUCE

1 lb. cod fillets	4 medium tomatoes
oil	about 12 stuffed olives
butter for frying	1–2 tablespoons seasoned flour
½ oz. lard	¼ green pepper
1 medium onion, finely chopped	½ pint dry white wine

Melt the lard in a small saucepan. Cook the finely chopped onion till golden and tender. Remove pips from green pepper, slice and add to onion; cook lightly for a few minutes. Skin tomatoes, quarter and shake out the pips. Tip into the onion mixture and keep warm. Put flour and plenty of salt and pepper in a good-sized paper or polythene bag. Cut the cod fillets (across the fish) into pieces about 2 inches wide and put in the bag. Shake till the fish is well coated. Heat a good-sized frying-pan and cover the bottom with ½ inch oil and add about 2 oz. butter for flavour and browning quality. When fat is hot lay the fish in the pan and let it cook briskly but not too violently. As soon as one side is browned, turn and cook the other side of each piece. Add the wine and olives to the tomato mixture and bring to the boil. Pour a little over the fish and serve the rest in a sauceboat.

FRANGO NA PUCARA

(chicken cooked in a deep earthenware pot)

In Portugal chicken and seasonings steam together. The strong mustard and brandy ingredients impart an extremely pungent flavour to the usually somewhat characterless taste of chicken, and is marvellous for pepping up frozen chicken. In Portugal the chicken goes in whole, but chicken joints can equally well be used.

FOR FOUR

1 small chicken (or 4 good chicken joints)	2 garlic cloves (crushed or chopped fine)
2 medium tomatoes (chopped)	1 wineglass port
2 oz. butter	1 wineglass brandy
3 oz. smoked ham (chopped)	1 tablespoon mustard
6 small onions (chopped)	white wine to taste
	salt, pepper

Put everything into a large casserole, cover and cook slowly till chicken is done. Remove lid and let the top become golden. Serve with fried potatoes and mixed salad.

QUEIJADAS DE SINTRA

MAKES ABOUT TWELVE

These are popular Portuguese sweet pastries. Little pastry cases, made traditionally of a flour and water dough, almost box-shaped, are filled with a cream cheese, almond and coconut mixture and baked.

Make ½ lb. short crust pastry dough. Knead and roll out thinly. Cut circles, 4½ inches in diameter, out of the dough with a pastry cutter. Cut the edges of the circles in 4 places, then fold up on the cuts to form little boxes. Fill them with the following mixture:

½ lb. cottage cheese (unsalted)   ½ oz. ground coconut
            3 egg yolks   pinch of cinnamon
            3½ oz. sugar   ½ oz. ground almonds
            1 oz. flour

Sieve the cheese and mix with egg yolks and sugar. After mixing well add flour, coconut, cinnamon and almonds. Blend all ingredients well and fill the pastry cases with the mixture. Bake in a fairly hot oven (400° F., Gas 6) for 15–20 minutes.

BISCOITOS DE SINTRA
(BISCUITS FROM SINTRA)

     4 oz. sugar   ½ tablespoon cinnamon
     8 oz. flour   1 oz. butter
     3 eggs

Blend together all the ingredients well. Roll the dough and shape into biscuits. Cook in an oven 350° F., Gas 3 or 4 on greased baking sheets.

TOUCINHO DO CÉU
(HEAVENLY BACON)

This is a dish originally from the north of Portugal, but served at the English-Bar in Monte Estoril. It is a sweet and, despite its name, has nothing to do with the bacon *toucinho*. In Portugal it is often served decorated with paper cut-outs.

     9 oz. almonds   8 egg yolks
     9 oz. sugar

Cook sugar with ⅓ its weight of water and boil until sugar dissolves. Skin and grate the almonds. Add to sugar and boil for about 5 minutes until you can see the bottom of the pan and the mixture is slightly clear. Remove the pan from the heat and add the egg yolks. Cook the yolks lightly, stirring until the mixture slightly thickens. Do not boil. Butter a 7 in. sponge tin with a removable base, pour in the sweet; sprinkle with granulated sugar and cook in a hot oven till set – about 15 minutes. This will make a tart giving 10–12 slices.

PUDIM DE NOZES
(NUT PUDDING)

prepared for the Casa de Portugal, London, by Chef Anthony Bell, Cross Catering Group of Companies

FOR FOUR TO SIX

4 oz. shelled walnuts
8 oz. ground walnuts
8 oz. castor sugar
¼ teaspoon mixed spice
6 eggs
kirsch
2–3 oz. butter for frying

Mix ground walnuts with the spice. Beat the egg yolks and castor sugar until well blended. Add the walnut-spice mixture gradually and beat well. Whisk three of the egg whites and fold into the mixture. Pour mixture into a buttered mould leaving space at the top for the pudding to rise. Cover the top of the mould with greaseproof paper and place in a large saucepan of water to steam for about 1 hour. Keep the water simmering until the pudding is set, adding more water as necessary. When cooked turn out of the mould to set. Fry the shelled walnuts with plenty of butter and when almost cooked add a teaspoonful of kirsch. Allow to cool and use to decorate the outside of the pudding. Serve with whipped cream.

7

THE ARRÁBIDA

The Arrábida is the name given to the large peninsula of land formed by the indentations of the estuaries of the rivers Tagus to its north and Sado to the south. Its sandy flat surface is covered with pine trees and agricultural lands rising to the protective cliff hills of the Serra da Arrábida in the south centre.

As a Londoner who finds it hardly worth it to struggle out of town for a day in summer, I deeply envy the Lisboans their unspoilt retreat south of the river only half an hour's easy drive away. At week-ends in summer the beaches are crowded, but otherwise the place is sleepy and charming, peopled only by fishermen, farm workers, tourists in the few new hotels and lately a few Lisboans building villas there. Even the completion of the magnificent Salazar toll bridge and fast road across the Tagus (lowest single fare 3s – 36 cents – per car) hasn't choked the area with crowds.

Inland the area produces good light wines like Palmela from the town of that name, rice, fruit and cheeses and vegetables, but, above all, fish. The sardine is the big local industry, with huge canning factories at Setúbal; the *cherne* or halibut, swordfish, whiting, red and grey mullet (*salmonetes*) and hake are caught off the coast. Near Setúbal the sandy island of Troia produces oysters – a rare find in Portugal in spite of the name association. Oranges

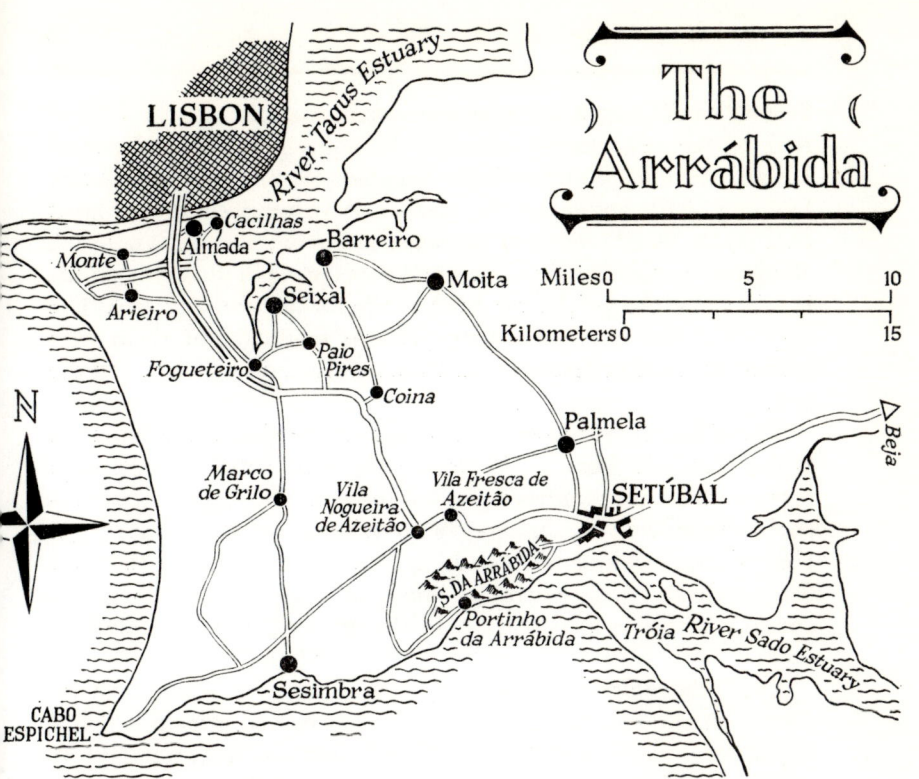

from around Setúbal are famed and mainly made into a smooth orange preserve sold in the streets from boys who hopefully follow the tourist with their baskets.

CACILHAS

The peninsula has always been popular with Lisboans for the view it affords them from across the river of their beloved Lisbon piled from the Tagus shores on its seven hills. The ferry (which takes cars) leaves Black Horse Square for this Arrábida port, where there are a number of good fish restaurants overlooking the river. The Floresta is a good one to make for.

SESIMBRA

The main road slices across the Arrábida centre to Azeitão with a choice of turn to Cape Espichel at the most westerly end or

Setúbal to the east. Cape Espichel, where there is a graceful fall of rock to the sea, affords views of the ships going in and out of Lisbon beyond a mysterious deserted church and monastery building. Near by is the tiny fishing town of Sesimbra of great charm; its streets wind to its heart and soul, the narrow beach alongside the fish market. The small boats bring in the catch, which is laid along the wall of the promenade for auction and sale. The display of fish is enhanced by patterns made round them with stones, or small pedestals of sand are moulded on which to rest the fish.

The village is set in a sea valley, and on one side of the cliff arms is the Hotel do Mar, set in terrace strata into the cliffside, each room with a private, flower-planted terrace. The interior design is cool and modern; the dining-room overlooks the bay, terrace style. Here are served tuna fish salads, grilled halibut (*cherne*), the local fish, or hake. A three-course lunch or dinner costs about 22s ($2.64). There is a night-club in the grounds and a swimming-pool.

The local *caldeirada*, fish stew, in Sesimbra contains swordfish, for which the area is famed. One hotel is named after this fish – Espadarte – which prepares *caldeirada* containing it on Sundays. It is also served at the Náutico restaurant looking high over the sea. *Zimbros* is the local Sesimbra sweet.

At the back of Sesimbra is one of the chain of huge castles protecting the Arrábida. Fortresses have been used to less pugnacious effect at Portinho da Arrábida and Setúbal, where cliff-top forts have been turned into inns.

PORTINHO DA ARRÁBIDA

The road along the top of the Arrábida hills has magnificent views over the steep cliffs to the sea. There is no coast road beneath the Serra to mar the seaside. But a road turns down to Portinho itself and the Estalagem Santa Maria, open only in summer. The hotel itself consists of a few rooms built into the towers and turrets of a seventeenth-century castle overlooking the sea. There is a modern annexe up the road, and the thickly starred sky and scent of wild herbs on the walk back after dinner are worth

THE ARRÁBIDA

the exercise. The inn has a veranda terrace covered with vines on which to eat in summer after a swim off the rock-studded beach and a drink at one of the wooden shack bars standing on stilts in the sea. Food is simple but good, excellent *salade niçoise* style *hors d'œuvres*, fish dishes and fruit.

SETÚBAL

Setúbal is an industrialized fishing port with extensive sardine and tunny fish canning works; it has not developed as a tourist resort, but the opening, three years ago, of the Estalagem de São Filipe and plans for development of the River Sado island of Tróia, with its Roman remains and marvellous extensive sandy beach, as a tourist area may well bring it more into prominence. It already has bullring, theatre, sailing and tennis facilities.

The Castelo de São Filipe is reached after a steep climb through narrow streets on the outskirts of Setúbal. The drive-in and car park are inside the ruined walls, and one enters the castle through the original worn rock steps of the keep. Above there is a spacious sun terrace on the ramparts, with wonderful views over the bay of Setúbal. Alongside the castle chapel contains perfect blue *azulejos* tiles telling St Philip's life story. The *estalagem* has lounges and the bar in the old dungeons; potted plants grow everywhere on the grey stone walls; there are sixteen comfortable double bedrooms and the prices are in the *de luxe* category.

Food here is excellent and the chef is a vivacious young girl from Lisbon called Maria da Encarnacão Ferreira Borrego – 'Zita' for short. Her creations, served in a traditionally furnished dining-room overlooking the bay, make use of the local oranges for the popular orange pudding (see page 132); *caldeirada*; squid São Filipe, with a special cream sauce; duck and rice; *bacalhau* with a toasted-cheese finish; shellfish *açorda* made from clam water boiled with garlic, olive oil and sliced bread and clams. 'Zita' had vast pots of clams steaming on her stoves. A four-course lunch here costs about 17s 6d ($2.10). Drink as an aperitif a slightly sweet wine from Palmela, the wine town which overlooks Setúbal. Along with the meal there is local mineral water (non-sparkling) called Agua de Bela Vista. After a meal the local brandy. There is also a very sweet muscatel wine which can be tried as an aperitif. Sometimes you may be lucky enough to have the oysters from Tróia, which are exceptionally big. These are fried, grilled, served au gratin or served with cheese and spinach at the São Felipe. Other of 'Zita's' recipes are on pages 128 and 132.

In Setúbal itself there are a couple of restaurants worth visiting. The premier is the Restaurante Naval Setubalense in the main through street. The *décor* of the first-floor restaurant is unpretentious, a plain room with wooden chairs, seascape paintings on the wall, but a charming tree-lined window view. The *hors d'œuvres* is famed for its array of around twenty little dishes, including many sorts of local shellfish; oysters, clams, mussels, squids, fried sardines – the latter served with an *escabeche* sauce (see page 90). For 14s 6d ($1.74) you can start with the *acepipes muito variados* (*hors d'œuvres* much varied), an understatement, considering the boast that never less than eighteen varieties are served.

Fish includes the locally plenteous *salmonetes* (red mullet served with butter and parsley sauce), *filetes* (see page 130), a nationally popular dish, and grilled *cherne* (halibut). Pork turns up in the meat dishes, and for dessert there is the inevitable *pudim flan* (see page 198) and *leite creme queimado*.

A most delicious way of serving oysters – *ostras recheadas* – (see page 125) is offered here, and the visitor can also purchase the local *doce de laranja*, an orange jam made in Setúbal.

The Restaurante O Pescador, Avenida 5 Outubro, the next large street parallel to the main street, is modest in *décor* but charming in welcome and extremely swift in service; each dish is cooked to order. Here the chef is Spanish – Rodriguo Dias Alonço – and he has a special sauce of his own for serving with the fish *filetes* (see page 130); red mullet are grilled here and the meat speciality is the *bife à pescador*, steak served on fried bread with a slice of cold ham and fried egg on top, garnished with pickles and olives and served with fried potatoes.   *Tourist office in Setúbal*

AZEITÃO

Just over 8 miles inland from Setúbal is the wine- and cheese-making village of Azeitão. Here the Estalagem Quinta das Torres provides some of the most romantic accommodation in Portugal, with ten rooms and two bungalows in the grounds. A sixteenth-century family estate house, still partly inhabited by its owners, provides suites and a few rooms furnished in period fashion and heated by cosy wood stoves; the huge tree-lined grounds and vast ornamental pool, now used for swimming, are graceful and charming. Non-residents can dine by soft candlelight (there is no electricity used in the *estalagem*) in the high, panelled dining-room or outside on the terrace in summer. Broad beans *à la Portugaise* in season, *cataplana* (the Algarve dish – see page 149) and duck and rice are served. Produce comes fresh from a farm on the estate.

RECIPES FROM THE ARRÁBIDA

OSTRAS RECHEADAS
(STUFFED OYSTERS)

from the Clube Naval, Setúbal

FOR SIX

12 oysters pepper, salt
2 medium onions olive oil to taste

CREAM SAUCE

¾ pint milk   2 egg yolks (to give colour)
1½ tablespoons flour

Cook shelled oysters in a little water with onions, seasoning and olive oil. When oysters and onions are cooked, replace in the shells or in an ovenproof dish and cover with cream sauce. This is made by mixing the flour in a little cold milk and blending it gently in the rest as it heats. Add the beaten egg yolks but do not allow to reboil. Season to taste. Bake in a medium oven until top is golden. Serve hot. Crisped breadcrumbs can be added to the top if wished.

SOPA DE AGRIÕES
(WATERCRESS SOUP)

Widely eaten in Portugal with the customary addition of beaten eggs.

FOR SIX

2 bunches watercress
12 medium potatoes
1 chopped onion
2 oz. butter
2 egg yolks
large cup milk
salt

Remove leaves of watercress from stalks, wash and put on one side. Boil potatoes with chopped watercress stalks, onion and salt. Blend or sieve to a *purée* when cooked. Melt butter, add chopped watercress leaves and cook gently in an uncovered pan for about 15 minutes. Add egg yolks beaten with milk. Reheat but do not boil. Serve at once. The consistency should be that of a thin cream and not porridgy.

RED BEAN SOUP

A cream consistency soup found in many parts of Portugal. Boil 1 lb. packet of red haricot beans (which have been soaked overnight) in a little salted water. Sieve or blend to a *purée*; add a little rice and simmer till cooked. Some Portuguese cooks add finely chopped *caldo verde* cabbage (see page 23). Adjust liquid to produce a creamy thickness.

SARDINHAS FRITAS
(SARDINES FRIED IN BATTER)

This is a way of using tinned Portuguese sardines, the majority of which are canned in Setúbal.

Drain oil from tinned sardines and remove the tails. Make a stiff frying batter, using lukewarm water and a teaspoon of olive oil instead of milk. Dip the sardines into the batter and drop into boiling olive oil. They should be served very hot and crisp, lightly sprinkled with cayenne pepper and garnished with slices of lemon.

OVOS VERDES (1)

A Portuguese *hors d' œuvre* filling for hard-boiled eggs well worth adopting.

FOR EVERY TWO LARGE EGGS

    1 teaspoon minced onion   1 heaped tablespoon parsley
1 teaspoon (scant) curry powder   (finely chopped)
    1 tablespoon mayonnaise   salt and pepper

Boil eggs for 10 minutes; plunge into cold water for 10 minutes. Remove shells, cut in half longways and ease out yolks. Mash yolks with all the other ingredients and pile back into the egg whites. Serve in a mixed *hors d' œuvre* or with black olives, radishes and spring onions.

OVOS VERDES (2)

This alternative uses tinned Portuguese sardines and deep frying.

Mix the yolks of hard-boiled eggs with a mixture of sardines, butter, lemon juice, salt, pepper, mixed herbs (such as parsley, chervil, chives and tarragon – a liberal amount). Fill the yolk cavities with this mixture. Place the halves of the egg together, dip in beaten egg and breadcrumbs and fry in oil in a deep pan.

Although the Portuguese seldom use their cheese in cookery the small round cheeses of the Azeitão area deserve a culinary compliment in the form of three recipes using cheese; if making them at home, cheeses more universally available can be used.

PUDIM DE QUEIJO (CHEESE PUDDING)

    2 tablespoons flour (heaped)   salt and pepper
                    ¾ pint milk   3 whole eggs
                3½ oz. butter   3 yolks
       7 oz. grated parmesan

Melt butter in a pan. Mix in flour and add milk. Bring to the boil slowly, stirring well until the mixture thickens. Add cheese and seasoning, cook gently, stirring till smoothly blended. Beat eggs and yolks slightly. Add to mixture, stirring slowly. Butter a mould, put mixture in and cover and cook in a *bain-marie*, or double boiler, over a low flame for an hour. Take off cover and put in medium hot oven for an hour. When cooked turn on to plate and cover liberally with tomato sauce (see page 195).

QUEIJO PHILLIPA (CHEESE PHILLIPA)

This recipe, although not in the least traditional in Portuguese cookery, was given me by Phillipa Couto of the John Bull in Cascais, and is delicious and simple enough to merit wider audience.

Small Gouda cheeses could be used in the absence of the small round Azeitão cheese. Slice the top off and scoop the cheese out of a small Azeitão or Gouda cheese. Fill with soft scrambled egg, which is still fairly sloppy, and replace cheese skin on top. Cook in a hot oven for 5–10 minutes. Serve cut in slices. The remains of the cheese on the inside of the skin should be soft and blended with the scrambled egg.

BACALHAU GRATINADO

FOR FOUR

1 lb. dried cod   1 lb. potatoes
8 oz. onions   2 oz. cheese
11 tablespoons olive oil

Soak cod for 12 hours or more (see page 189). Cut fish into small squares. Slice onions into the olive oil and fry gently till golden. Transfer to earthenware or ovenproof dish. Place cod on top mixed with pre-fried, diced potatoes. Make a cream *béchamel* sauce (see page 30) and mix in with the cod and potatoes. Bake in a medium oven till cooked. Grate cheese on top and brown under the grill.

BACALHAU COM NATAS (CREAMED COD)

Prepare cod as on page 189. Slice onions finely and fry in butter till golden (allow 1 large onion and 4 oz. cod per person). Fry flaked cod with onions till golden brown. Mix in diced boiled potatoes (4 oz. per person) and add to the cod mixture a plain white sauce. Season and add fresh cream, mix well. Cook till golden brown in a medium oven in a buttered fireproof dish.

TOMATADA À PORTUGUESA

It is popular in Portugal to serve vegetables with scrambled egg.

Boil 3 or 4 kinds of vegetables (selecting from potatoes, carrots, turnips, peas, green beans, cauliflower, broccoli, mushrooms, asparagus tips). When cooked, dice and mix together. Add 6 or 7 tablespoons of tomato sauce (see page 195). Serve hot with scrambled eggs.

FAVAS (BROAD BEANS)
from the Quinta das Torres

Chop onions finely and cook gently in olive oil and chopped coriander (*coentros*). Add beans, cover with water and cook in a covered pan on a gentle heat for 2 hours (or in a pressure-cooker for about 15 minutes).

FRANGO À CASTELO VIDE
(CASTELO VIDE CHICKEN)

FOR FOUR TO SIX

1 boiling chicken (4–6 lb.)
bouquet garni of onion, bay leaf, celery ends, carrot and parsley
4 oz. butter
3 egg yolks
4–6 large tomatoes (blanched and skinned)
4 oz. button mushrooms
8 oz. rice

Boil the chicken (with bouquet garni) until tender. Boil the rice in the chicken stock for 20 minutes and then strain. Take chicken meat off the bone while still warm and cut into small pieces. Place the tomatoes in base of casserole around the edge and put the chicken meat in the middle with raw sliced mushrooms on top. Cover with the rice and dot with butter. Beat the egg yolks and pour over the top of the rice. Cover with the lid and bake in a moderate oven until eggs are set.

FILETES À CLUBE NAVAL
(*WHITING FILLETS*)
from the Clube Naval, Setúbal

Filetes are a popular dish in the Arrábida area and in Lisbon.

FOR FOUR

8 whiting fillets (about 2 lb.)   ½ lemon
2 eggs   small wineglass milk
4 tablespoons flour   oil for cooking
3 cloves garlic

Fry fillets, sprinkled with lemon juice, gently in oil. Meanwhile make a sauce with the milk, in which the garlic cloves have been soaked for about ½ hour, and flour, stirring till thick. Add the beaten eggs and reheat but do not boil. Serve with the cooked fish; melted butter and lemon juice can be put on the fish before serving.

LULAS RECHEADAS (STUFFED SQUID)

FOR EACH PERSON

1–2 squid   1 tablespoon pork fat
a little smoked ham   3 egg yolks
parsley   seasoning
1 onion

SAUCE

5 tablespoons olive oil   ½ tablespoon tomato purée

Small squids should be used whole, removing only the tentacles and the wing flesh, which is minced with the ham, parsley, salt and pepper. Cook all this with the pork fat and onions. Add salt and pepper to taste. When cooked, add egg yolks, mix well and stuff squids, closing the opening with a cocktail stick. Prepare a sauce with the olive oil, tomato *purée*, a pinch of salt and ground pepper. When hot, place the squids in this sauce and cook until tender (½ to ¾ hour). Serve with boiled new potatoes or boiled peas.

FILETES PESCADOR

from the Restaurante O Pescador, Setúbal

4 fillets whiting or sole
flour
egg

SAUCE

1 oz. butter
1 tablespoon cornflour (or plain flour)
1 or 2 egg yolks
lemon juice
chopped pickle (piccalilli or gherkins)
cockles
parsley

Dip the fillets in flour and then in beaten egg. Fry till cooked and serve with the sauce made as follows: melt butter and mix in cornflour or plain flour and add gradually $\frac{1}{2}$–$\frac{1}{3}$ pint of water in which clams have been cooked (or the juice from a tin of mussels or cockles). Stir the sauce over heat until it thickens. Add salt, egg yolks, a squeeze of lemon juice, chopped pickle, cockles and a little chopped parsley fried in oil.

SALMONETES SETUBALENSE
(SETÚBAL RED MULLET)

Clean the mullet, removing and keeping the liver. Thoroughly clean any blood from the spine and sprinkle with salt. Let the fish stand for 2 or 3 hours, then wash and grill it till cooked. Serve with the following sauce: for 6 medium mullets, mash the 6 salted livers well. When reduced to a pulp, cook in a frying-pan with about $5\frac{1}{2}$ tablespoons water and $5\frac{1}{2}$ oz. butter. When the mixture has melted, but is not boiling, remove from the stove and add the juice of $\frac{1}{2}$ large lemon and chopped parsley. Place the mullet on a dish, pour the sauce over them and serve very hot.

DOCE RAPIDO (A QUICK SWEET)

This makes use of the oranges of Setúbal; the orange conserve made in the area can be used instead of bitter orange marmalade.

4 oranges
8 tablespoons bitter orange marmalade (¼ pint)
¼ pint unsweetened pineapple juice
desiccated coconut

Slice oranges thinly and marinate in a sauce made of the mixed juice and marmalade. Chill and sprinkle with coconut before serving.

MANJAR DE PRINCIPE

(PRINCE'S TITBIT)

This sweetmeat is found in most parts of the country.

5½ oz. sugar
4 oz. crumb part of very stale bread
9 egg yolks
5½ oz. almonds

Cook the sugar in water until dissolved and transparent. Meanwhile blanch and skin the almonds and put through a mincer. Crumble the bread finely. Add the almonds and the bread to the syrup; boil until it dries a little.

Remove from the stove and let cool. Mix the egg yolks in one after the other. Return once more to the heat for the yolks to thicken, being careful to remove as soon as the mixture begins to boil. Let it cool again and pour into serving dishes. Serve chilled.

PUDIM DE LARANJAS

(ORANGE PUDDING)
from 'Zita' at Estalagem Castelo São Filipe

FOR FOUR

8¾ oz. sugar
6 eggs
juice from 2 oranges

Beat all ingredients together for 5 minutes. Butter a round tin or Pyrex dish. Shake a fine coating of granulated or icing sugar over the butter and cook the mixture in a *bain-marie* or double boiler till it thickens.

8

THE ALENTEJO

The Alentejo, the largest province in Portugal – seemingly half the size of the country on the map – is the least known and is scarcely visited by the tourist. Its roads act as through routes from Lisbon to Seville and Madrid, or, for the English tourist, the route to the beloved Algarve, which takes about eight hours' hard driving to reach from Lisbon. (T.A.P. run flights from Lisbon to Faro in the Algarve which take about forty minutes.)

Although the Alentejo is wealthy in regional recipes which have spread their fame all over the country it has few tourist centres. The Alentejo has a gravity about it; a vastness that deters the imposition of outside influences. With its rich agricultural plains, the province has never developed a great fishing industry along the coast. There is a marked lack of the 'quaint little fishing villages' over which travel agents like to rhapsodize in their brochures, and which tourists love to patronize.

The Alentejo has a harsh climate, hot by day, cold by night. The heat rises off the huge undulating plain which produces the wheat for the country. With wheat the number one source of wealth it is hardly surprising that the *açorda* bread soups of Portugal originate here. *Açorda* is basically a kind of bread porridge to which fish, meat, eggs, bacon or other flavourings are added. It was a dish born of poverty; even stale, hard crusts were saved and used.

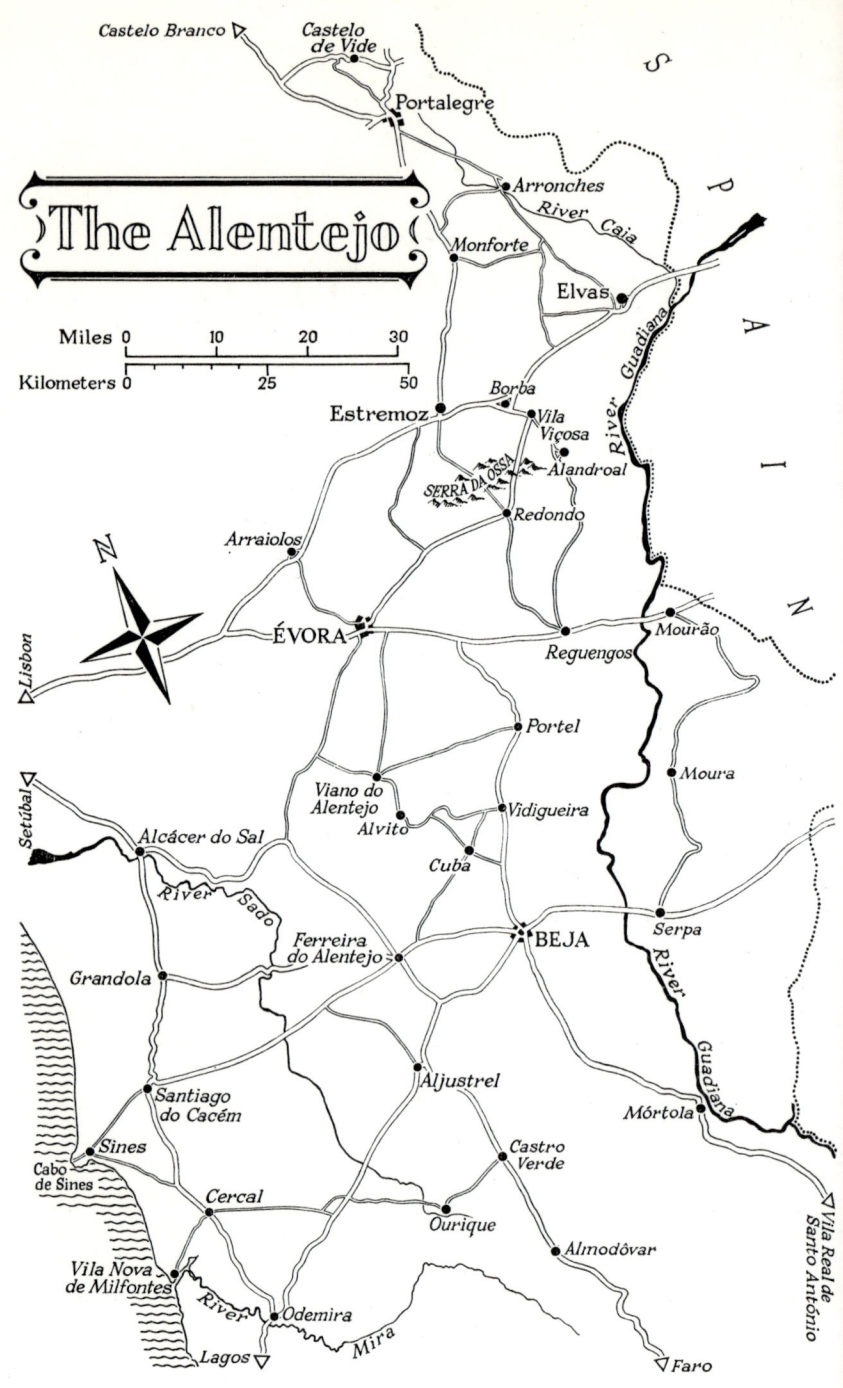

Beggars carried these in little bags. They were soaked in water, cooked to a smooth paste and whole cloves of garlic and olive oil, both easily obtainable, were added; the result, though perhaps unpalatable to our minds, was nourishing and good for the health.

After wheat the second most important activity is cork production and, thirdly, the rearing of pigs and sheep which wander the plains with their shepherds. The shepherd takes his cork bucket of soup with him for his lunch – the cork keeping the *açorda* hot in winter or the local *gaspacho* soups cold in summer.

As in other parts of Portugal the sheep are more prized for their wool and milk than for their meat, which is rarely eaten except spit-roast. The milk is used to make cheese, the best of which is that of the Serra d'Ossa, where excellent oranges are also grown. Pig is used with careful economy, lungs, trotters, brains (very popular) being incorporated in various recipes. Pork smoked and dipped in dried pimento is the favourite meat and, with chicken, provides the basis of many local recipes. Alentejo pork, renowned with clams, is said to have a special smell of its own, since the pigs dig up and eat white truffles.

Olives and plums are other important crops. The plums are made into the famed soft preserved fruits of Elvas, which are exported in boxes in time to make perfect Christmas presents.

The handicrafts are agricultural: spoons and boxes carved from willow by the shepherds, carpets from Arraiolos or from Portalegre, ice buckets and other cork articles; pottery, terracotta dolls and primitive ceramics of country figures are also found in the region.

ÉVORA, CASTELO DE VIDE, ESTREMOZ AND ELVAS

The tourist is most likely to tear down the main road parallel with the coast, but he could take a big loop inland to see Évora and Beja on his way to the south. To see all the most important towns of the Alentejo it would be necessary to start from the border town of Portalegre (tourist office) where the carpet factory can be seen and cork articles bought. Its culinary creations are marzipan and *cacholeiros* sweeatmeat. Good food can be obtained at the Quinta da Saude, Serra de São Mamede.

Nearby Castelo de Vide, set in a watered dip of land sprouting with flowers, roses and flowering shrubs, is a charming country town and spa surrounded by wooded hills. The Estalagem de São Paulo and pensions Casa do Parque and Sintra do Alentejo are all first class. The market day is the last Friday in the month.

South to Estremoz – a town characterized by its lack of windows (to keep cool) and women in masculine felt hats, where earthenware figures are produced – the road branches west to Lisbon, east to walled and fortified Elvas, where there is the charming five-roomed Pousada de Santa Luzia. As well as plums, garlic, sausages and olives are produced here, and handicrafts include copper goods and paper-cutting.

VILA VIÇOSA AND ÉVORA

Évora, the town of churches and a superb Roman temple of Diana, is fifty-five miles south-west of Elvas. On the way to Vila Viçosa (tourist office) the favourite palace of the Braganças can be seen. Cheese and oranges are locally produced and the Vila Viçosa sweet is *tibornes*. Pottery and wrought iron are the handicrafts.

Évora also has a *Pousada*, built in a convent; the Pousada dos Loibos is considered one of the loveliest, with its twenty-eight rooms furnished superbly, and situated behind the Loios church and valuable old library. The local specialities of *açorda Alentejana* (see page 138), *porco à Alentejana* (see page 141), *requeijão* and *queijadas* (sweets) can be sampled at the *Pousada*, the pension O Eborense or the restaurant Gião. *Tourist office at Évora*

BEJA

Beja, like Évora, produces brightly coloured woollen blankets and cork articles as well as wood carvings and earthenware. Its food contributions of smoked pork and *morgados* sweets can be sampled at the nearby Pousada de São Gens at Serpa just off the main road. This is a whitewashed building (the Alentejo is fanatical about painting and keeping its houses in camera-conscious order).

THE ALENTEJO COAST

On the coastal route to the Algarve, the stops are limited to Santiago do Cacém, Sines and Vila Nova de Milfontes. The last makes a fairly good half-way overnight stop if necessary. At Santiago do Cacém, there is the Pousada de São Tiago, a locally styled old house furnished in regional style, with seven rooms and a small swimming-pool in the garden. A special dish here is lamb cooked country style, fried in egg and breadcrumbs, cooked with vegetable sauce and served with rice. From Santiago, a secondary road leads down 10 miles to the seaside village of Sines, historically famed as the birthplace of Vasco da Gama. Again the national sea food dishes come back into favour, the *caldeirada* and lobster. Tuna and swordfish are also found here and it is a good place for fishing. There are five pensions in the village, of which the Pensão Malhada is rated *de luxe* and the pensions Clemente and Lar de São Rafael first class.

The Duke of Vila Nova de Milfontes has turned his country house into a charming small hotel and pampers his guests with marvellous food. The atmosphere is one of house rather than hotel; the only problem is to book far enough in advance to get in.

RECIPES FROM THE ALENTEJO

The Alentejo is a wonderful region for soups – a meal easily carried by shepherds guarding their flocks or farmers working on the undulating plains. The *açorda*, or bread-based soup, is the great Alentejo contribution to Portuguese cuisine; the cold summer *gaspacho* as much indigenous to the Alentejo and Algarve regions as to Spain. Nourishing soups based on tomatoes, beans and potatoes are also abundant.

SIMPLE AÇORDA
often also spelt in the old way, *Assorda*

FOR SIX TO EIGHT

3 pints water   salt and cayenne pepper
5 cloves garlic   1 egg per person
3 tablespoons olive oil   bread, bunch of thyme

Put the oil into the cold water and bring to the boil. Add garlic, thyme and seasonings. Simmer until the garlic is soft. Break in one egg per person and poach in simmering soup. When ready, pour into hot plates on top of sufficient pieces of bread to cover the bottom of the plate.

AÇORDA ALENTEJANA

A similar soup, made with typical coriander flavour, is served as an accompaniment to grilled sardines.

FOR SIX TO EIGHT

1 small sprig coriander	3½ pints water
3–4 cloves garlic	8¾ oz. hard bread
2¾ tablespoons olive oil	salt

Pound to a paste the coriander, salt and garlic. Put in a serving bowl, add the olive oil, stirring well, then pour in the boiling water and add the hard bread in small pieces. Mix well till smooth.

GASPACHO À ALENTEJANA

FOR FOUR

1 lb. tomatoes	1½ tablespoons vinegar
2 green peppers	3½ oz. bread
2 cloves garlic	half a cucumber
3 tablespoons olive oil	salt and pepper

Cut the bread in thin slices and small cubes and brown slightly in the oven. Skin the tomatoes, remove the pips and cut in small pieces. Cut the green peppers in slices. Crush the tomatoes, peppers, garlic, salt and the toasted bread together into a pulp. Add the olive oil, pepper and vinegar. Put in a large basin and soak, preferably for a day, in a cool place. Add sliced cucumber, some fresh sliced green pepper and tomato as decoration and cubed pieces of toasted bread before serving. In Portugal, sliced *chouriço* sausage (see page 185) and chopped gammon are also added.

SOPA DE TOMATE À ALENTEJANA
(ALENTEJO TOMATO SOUP)

FOR SIX TO EIGHT

1 lb. tomatoes	1 bay leaf
5½ oz. pure lard	3½ pints water
5½ oz. *linguica*	1 green pepper
(roast tongue)	hard bread
1 large onion	salt

Melt lard in a saucepan. Fry the sausage in slices, add the sliced onion and fry till golden brown. Then mix in the peeled and seeded tomatoes and fry a little longer. Add the boiling water, the bay leaf, salt, and the green pepper cut in pieces. Pour the soup on slices of bread to serve.

SOPA DE BATATA À ALENTEJANA
(ALENTEJO POTATO SOUP)

FOR FOUR

8¼ tablespoons olive oil	2 lb. potatoes
1 large onion	1¾ pints water
1 sprig parsley	1 teaspoon cayenne pepper
1 clove garlic	salt
1 bay leaf	bread

Chop the parsley together with the garlic and the onion and fry them in the oil till golden brown. Add the chopped, peeled potatoes, salt and bay leaf. Fry for a while and then add the water. Simmer till potatoes are cooked and then add the cayenne pepper. Make fried *croûtons* of bread to garnish the top of the soup before serving.

SOPA DE FEIJÃO FRADE À FERVIDA ALENTEJANA
(BOILED SOUP OF BLACK EYE BEANS)

These are small white haricot beans, each with a black 'eye'. In this country only the dried variety is obtainable.

FOR FOUR

½ lb. black eye beans   1 tablespoon vinegar
1 onion   pepper, green pepper and
2 cloves garlic   paprika
½ bay leaf   hard bread
small sprig parsley   small sprig mint
5½ tablespoons olive oil   3 pints water

Cook the beans (which have been soaked overnight) in enough water to cover well. Fry the chopped onion, cloves of garlic, parsley and bay leaf in the oil. Allow onion to get golden brown then add the beans (keeping aside the water in which they were cooked), the pepper and the paprika. When boiling, add the vinegar. Brown thin slices of bread in the oven with crushed mint leaves on top. Pour on the water in which the beans were cooked to make a soup. Strain the beans and serve as a separate dish.

SOPA DE ALHO (GARLIC SOUP)

This is also typical of the north of Portugal, and shows the national desire for 'eggs with everything' and the Alentejo characteristic of basing soups on garlic.

    Fry chopped cloves of garlic (to taste) in a little olive oil to which a pinch of paprika has been added. Add to water (1 cup per person) in which 1 garlic clove per person has been boiled. Simmer and add slices of fried bread and poach an egg per person in this. Serve immediately.

ENSOPADA DE BORREGO
(STEWED LAMB FROM ALENTEJO)

A spicy recipe which makes use of the lamb from the huge flocks of the Alentejo plains.

FOR FOUR

2 lb. lamb (from the saddle and ribs)	parsley
10½ oz. lard	1 tablespoon peppercorns
1 lb. onions	1 dessertspoon paprika
flour	a little chilli
5 cloves garlic	3–4 tablespoons vinegar
1 bay leaf	salt
	stale bread

Cut the lamb into pieces and coat with flour. Fry till golden in 5½ oz. lard. Meanwhile cut the onions in slices. Fry lightly with the chopped garlic, bay leaf and crushed peppercorns in the rest of the lard. Add this to the lamb; add salt and a little chopped chilli, the paprika and parsley, and enough water to soak the bread. Cut the bread in slices and place in a deep dish. To serve, pour the hot lamb broth with added vinegar over the bread. The meat is served separately.

Pork is the main meat of the Alentejo and the three following recipes show some of the major ways of preparation. The national love of cockles marries with pork as in the Algarve's *cataplana* to make:

CARNE DE PORCO Á ALENTEJANA (ALENTEJO PORK)

FOR FOUR

1 lb. pork	paprika
1 lb. mussels or cockles	lard
2 large onions	olive oil
2 large tomatoes	salt, pepper
1 bay leaf	

Cut the pork, which should be very tender, in small pieces and *sauter* them in lard until they are nearly cooked. Meanwhile heat a tablespoon of olive oil in a pan and in it cook the chopped onions and peeled chopped tomatoes, bay leaf, a little salt and pepper, and paprika, if liked. When these are well browned add the mussels in their shells (well washed) and part cooked in boiling water. Add the pieces of fried pork and cook all together for a few minutes. Remove the bay leaf before serving.

COSTELETAS DE PORCO À ALENTEJANA
(PORK CUTLETS FROM ALENTEJO)

FOR FOUR

8 pork cutlets
3 tablespoons white wine
2 cloves garlic
1 dessertspoon green pepper paste (see page 194)
2 eggs
pepper and salt
fat
breadcrumbs

Trim the fat from the cutlets, season with salt, pepper, garlic and add white wine and green pepper paste. Leave for 24 hours. Dip in the beaten eggs and breadcrumbs and fry in deep fat. Serve with slices of orange.

LOMBO ASSADO À ALENTEJANA
(ROAST LOIN OF PORK)

FOR FOUR

2 lb. loin of pork
3 cloves garlic
½ tablespoon green pepper paste (see page 194)
3 tablespoons water
3 tablespoons white wine
2 tablespoons margarine or butter
salt

Season the meat with salt and crushed garlic. Spread with green pepper paste, add water, wine, margarine and roast in the oven.

GALINHA COM VINHO DO PORTO À ALENTEJANA
(CHICKEN WITH PORT WINE)

FOR FOUR

1 chicken (or 4 chicken joints)
2 tablespoons fat
2 tablespoons olive oil
1 large onion
1 sprig parsley
1 small glass port wine
1 tablespoon plain flour
fried bread
water

Fry chicken with fat, oil, chopped parsley and onion in a deep saucepan. Add enough water to cover the chicken, and port wine. Cover pan well and simmer till cooked. Before serving, thicken sauce with flour mixed with a little cold water. Serve with fried bread triangles, small bunches of watercress and radishes.

ENSOPADA DE LEBRE À ALENTEJANA
(ALENTEJO HARE STEW)

FOR SIX TO EIGHT

1 hare
3 medium size onions
3 cloves garlic
parsley
2 tablespoons pork fat
3 tablespoons olive oil
14 oz. potatoes
3½ pints water
7 oz. hard bread
1 tablespoon vinegar
salt and pepper

Prepare the hare and cut it in pieces. Fry the chopped onions, garlic and parsley in the fat and olive oil. Place the meat in the same saucepan and fry it lightly till golden brown. Then add the water with the salt and let the whole simmer for a while. Finally, add the potatoes cut in thick slices, the pepper and vinegar. When everything is cooked place the meat on a serving dish with the potatoes. Pour the broth on bread slices in a soup tureen and serve separately.

FAISÃO ESTUFADO
(STEWED PHEASANT)

This recipe comes from the Alentejo town of Pinas; a good celebration dish after the harvest.

FOR FOUR

1 pheasant
5½ tablespoons cognac
5½ tablespoons port wine
2½ oz. butter
5 peeled almonds
salt and pepper

Prepare the pheasant, season with salt and pepper and soak it in the cognac and the port wine for 24 hours, turning occasionally.

Melt butter in a pan, fry the pheasant lightly in it together with the almonds. Now pour the wine in which the pheasant was soaked into the saucepan gradually, if necessary add some water. Cook the pheasant gently, keeping the pan covered.

CERICA

An Alentejo style soufflé, rich in eggs and spiced with lemon and cinnamon.

6 eggs	1 stick cinnamon
8¾ oz. sugar	grated rind ½ lemon
1 pint milk	powdered cinnamon
6 level tablespoons flour	

Beat the egg yolks with the sugar. Blend the flour with the milk, little by little, and mix in the yolks, the broken cinnamon stick and the grated lemon rind. Put on a medium heat and boil until a thick cream is formed. Remove from the heat and allow to cool. Remove the cinnamon stick and lemon rind. Beat the egg whites stiffly and add to the rest. Spoon into an ovenproof soufflé dish well buttered. Sprinkle with plenty of cinnamon and cook in a hot oven for 20–30 minutes, till it rises, splits and is golden brown on top.

QUEIJADAS DE ÉVORA
(ÉVORA CHEESECAKES)

Make ½ lb. short crust pastry, roll the dough out very thinly and line small patty tins. The tins must be greased with butter and sprinkled with flour. Fill with a mixture made from:

FILLING

½ lb. cottage cheese	2 oz. butter
6 egg yolks	4 oz. sugar
1 egg white	1 oz. flour

Blend the cheese with egg yolks, egg white, melted butter and sugar. Mix well, add the flour and fill the pastry cases. Bake in a moderate oven till pastry is cooked.

OURICOS ALENTEJANOS
(ALENTEJO HEDGEHOGS)

An 'ourico' is a hedgehog and in this recipe the almond slivers are used to represent the hedgehog's spines.

>   8 oz. sugar   pinch of cinnamon
>   8 oz. almonds wafer biscuits
>   2 whites of eggs

Well beat the sugar with the egg whites and a large pinch of cinnamon. Mix in the almonds, which should be left with their skin on and sliced thinly lengthwise. Take small portions of this mixture and put them on small pieces of wafer. Cook in a moderate oven.

BOLO DE OURO ALENTEJANO
(GOLD CAKE FROM ALENTEJO)

A rich, light, sponge cake, full of eggs.

>   8 oz. sugar   7 eggs, separated
>   10¾ oz. butter grated rind of a lemon
>   8 oz. flour

Beat the sugar and lemon rind well with the egg yolks. Melt and add the butter then the stiffly beaten egg whites and finally the flour. Cook it in a hot oven in a baking tin greased with butter and sprinkled with flour.

EMMANUELS

These sweets are similar to many Portuguese *doces* and come from Elvas.

>   8 oz. sugar   1 egg
>   8 oz. ground almonds flour

Beat the egg with the sugar and then the ground almonds and sufficient flour to make a firm paste. Shape the dough into a roll, cut it in little slices, flatten them with the hand and brush the top with egg yolk. Cook in a hot oven till golden.

PÃO CONSTIPADO
(BREAD WITH A COLD)
from the Algarve

A small child's teatime style of sweetened softened bread in the tradition of the *rabanadas* of the Douro.

Fry slices of bread in olive oil. Remove from the pan, dip the slices fairly quickly in cold water, drip off excess water and then coat with sugar and cinnamon.

9

THE ALGARVE

The hundred-mile coastline of the south of Portugal was for centuries so cut off from the rest of Portugal in thought and customs that it was known as the 'land beyond', and kings signed their titles 'King of Portugal and the Algarve'. The name means 'to the west'. The coast level rises from the flat, sandy valley of the Guadiana River in the east on the Spanish border, breaks into photogenic blocks around Praia da Rocha and sweeps on into the Atlantic with flat, broad headlands around Sagres and Cape St Vincent. This once useless central clifftop land is now a tourist mecca, largely developed and run by English settlers.

The gently rolling coastal plain which backs up to olive-coated hills produces such a superb array of vegetables and fruit crops that it has earned the area the name of the 'garden of Portugal'. The only snow the region boasts is the almond blossom in February. The almonds themselves turn up in a particularly wide variety of egg and sugar (sugar-cane is grown here) concoctions which can be seen displayed at shops in Portimão (see page 159). Bananas, grapefruit, pears, grapes, olives, figs, chestnuts, oranges, pomegranates, lemons, tangerines, apples and cherries are all grown in the Algarve. Rice, a long-grain patna variety good for curries, which needs no washing to prevent stickiness, is produced here and made into a sweet coupled with cinnamon; but basically it's

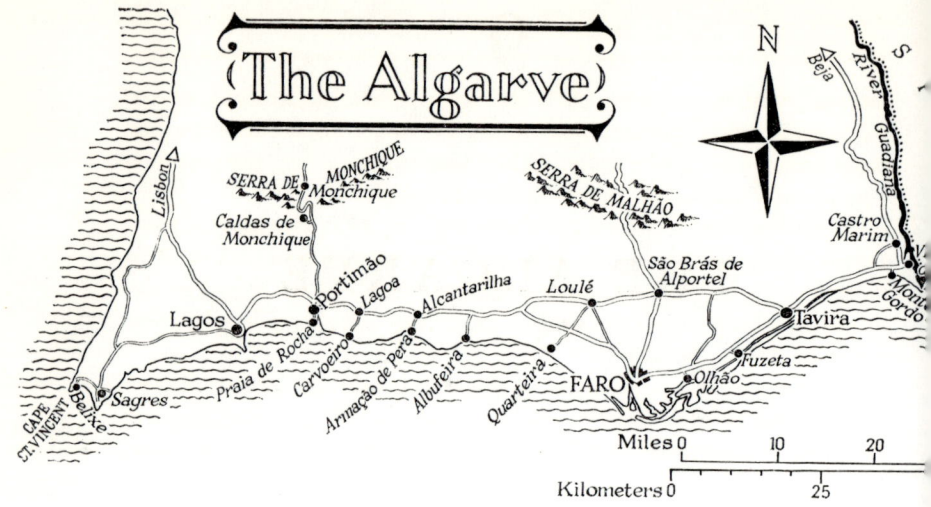

the vegetables that are the delight of the area. Tomatoes, large and slightly green, are superb. These are made into chutneys and *purées* by local factories. Onions, lettuce, huge cauliflowers enough for four meals, potatoes, sweet and ordinary, courgettes, melon, cabbage and asparagus are all plentiful. These find their way into the local casseroles; onions and tomatoes, as usual in Portugal, being showered into everything. Favourite flavourings of the area are fresh-ground black pepper and lots of chopped parsley and chervil.

Meat is poor, though the better hotels get well-butchered meat from Lisbon. Chickens are killed young and are good in flavour, though, like the big meaty turkeys that abound, care should be taken when buying one (usually from peasants by the roadside) that it hasn't been reared on fish – the smell alone tells. Chicken, partridge and pigeons are also sold along the roadside. But it is the fish that is the area's main industry and basic diet ingredient. Oysters, large and inexpensive, are found here. The sardines, large and fresh, are charcoal-grilled outside and served at the little beach restaurants with fresh parsley and rough salt. Tourists eat them from plates, locals serve them on slabs of bread. The juice of the fish drips on to their 'plate', which is then eaten. Traditionally they are served with 'Irish potatoes'.

Bread incidentally is good in the Algarve; there is the *pão integral*, which is served with the grilled sardines: round brown wholemeal loaves made with unrefined flour. Also there are the *papa seco*, small white rolls, rather like bridge rolls, and there is a good copy of British shortbread made locally.

Tuna fish are a speciality of the region. It is one of the great tourist sights of the area in May and June to watch from Vila Real de Santo António fishermen struggling with the death throes of the huge thrashing fish trapped in encircling nets, the bright blue water purple with blood.

In spite of the abundance of locally produced foodstuffs the Algarve has not the richly creative history of recipes that are, for example, found in the north. Life in the sun here is uncomplicated, almost a permanent holiday atmosphere; cuisine matches it. One tends to assume that the development of the few regional recipes has been enriched by the creative ideas of the chefs of the large tourist hotels along this coast. The exception is the elaborate variations on the egg, sugar and almond theme of sweetmeats, moulded into intricate shapes, delicately shaded. The complications of producing the *Dom Rodrigo* (see page 159) is witness of the skill of the Algarve cook.

Out beyond the tiny capital town of Faro, Faro beach forms a long sandy spit between the sea and a lagoon which becomes mud flats at low tide. The peasants from stilted huts round about can then be seen bent double like crows in their bunchy black clothes searching for clams, aided by their children and their dogs. Clams are eaten all over Portugal, but here in the Algarve they are served in the unique *cataplana*. The *cataplana* is a kind of primitive pressure-cooker. It is metal, usually aluminium, but copper is better – made by hand in the forges of the market town of Loulé – comprising two round shallow dishes with handles. The dishes, shaped rather like small dustbin lids, seal tightly together so that no steam escapes in cooking. If necessary the dish can be turned over so that the food on the top can be placed near the heat. In addition to clams *na cataplana* (cooked with sausages or pork pieces) other foods can be cooked this way (see pages 141, 163–4). Some towns along the coast have a fish specially 'theirs': at Fuzeta it is hake; at Quarteira red mullet; at Portimão clams; and at Sagres lobster.

As *cataplanas* are not available in Britain or the United States, a large frying-pan or top-of-stove casserole with tightly fitting lid can be used, or alternatively, one of those covered metal meat roasters.

The visitor will probably prefer fresh fruit and figs to the almond and egg concoctions. Chocolate mousse is popular here as in other areas; but most typical are the tiny, almond-based *petits fours*, each town having its own variation, many moulded into fruit and animal shapes. As a change from *pudim* there are two excellent local cheeses: the *serra*, a ball of red-skinned cheese; and *queijo de manha* (morning cheese), which is rather similar to *petit suisse*, and is made from goats' milk. It comes in various shapes in thin gauze bags and can be eaten with sugar. Insist that the cheeses were made freshly that morning.

Local people are, alas, turning towards plastic as a status symbol away from the traditional brown earthenware dishes, glazed inside and often simply decorated with a flower or fish design in yellow or pale opal shades. Some restaurants like Togis still serve all their dishes in and on these. To buy them from the potter himself costs only a few pence, and the agony is deciding how many one can safely take home. In towns like Lagoa, look round the quiet cobbled back streets for signs of pots drying in the sun outside a shed; pick out what you want from the piles of crocks stacked in the dim, dank sheds and discuss the price with the potter, but don't give away how cheap you think they are.

VILA REAL DE SANTO ANTÓNIO

The main road runs across the Algarve from east to west, cutting inland to conceal the many charming rock-strewn beaches west of Faro from the motorist's gaze. The road is good and gently rolling. It is possible to drive right across it and back within a day, though the area is far too charming to rush through in this way. The part from the Spanish border at Vila Real de Santo António to Faro is not my favourite. The fishing quays of Vila Real on the Guadiana river banks are fascinating, as are the tiny fishermen's bars along the straight criss-crossed streets. Restaurants include the A Chaminé Algarvia, Caves do Guadiana and Portugal. There is the night-club Boite Tareco and one or two discothèques on the quayside. A Arca, on the Avenida da Republica, sells regional handicrafts. Castro Marim, a mile or so north, is worth a detour to see the fine castle ruins.   *Tourist office in Vila Real*

MONTE GORDO

Monte Gordo has become rather a camping and a large hotel resort, less picturesque and characteristic than the resorts to the west. There are the restaurants Juli-Mar and Oceanos; and at night a *boite* in the large Vasco da Gama Hotel. Between Monte Gordo and Tavira are huge, open, sandy beaches backed by pine woods and scattered with small fishing villages. Tavira is a Moorish town and another tuna fishing centre, with a fair on 1st and 2nd August. From here a main road branches off inland to São Brás de Alportél and Loulé.

OLHÃO

Just over six miles outside Faro is the odd little tuna-fishing town of Olhão, in which the buildings are madly cubist, piled on each other like toy bricks in whites and pastel colours touched up by the sun – a lot of yellow is used. The Estalagem Caique has a restaurant on the beach and will arrange fishing tours. Ask to be allowed to photograph from its rooftop terrace. A meal here is around 14*s* 6*d* ($1.74). The town advertises its fish-canning and tuna-fishing industries in the perfumed air; but its autumn fair at the end of September is worth a visit, as are the fish market and *lota* (fish auction). Its local sweetmeat, *nogados*, should be tried. Typical restaurants are Chamine, Rua do Camerios; O Pescador, Rua Teofilo Braga, 42; and Tropical on the main coastal road. Chamine incidentally is a most common name for clubs and restaurants in the Algarve. It means 'chimney' and refers to the tall, ornate chimneys characteristic of the area.

FARO

Faro is the capital of the Algarve and the airport is just outside the town. Although a bustling marketing and fishing centre, it also makes a good central base for exploration of the area. Its narrow cobbled streets run down into a beflowered main 'place' round the harbour. There are two excellent tourist hotels on the square, the Eva and the Hotel Faro. The Eva, about two years old, is well run by a Savoy-trained Englishman, and the rooms are comfortable and well furnished. As Faro lacks a beach in the town itself – Faro beach is about 4 miles away but linked by regular ferry boat service from the harbour – the Eva has a large swimming-pool on its roof, with superb views of the flat coastline and hills behind. Non-residents can use the pool and have an excellent luncheon meal near the pool for around £1 ($2.40) a head with wine. In the main restaurant, which was awarded a star by the International Hotels Federation, cooking is a blend of international and Portuguese. The chef, Roguerio Alcaria Teodosio, although born in the Algarve, spent fifteen years working in Australia. His own invention is the *Tournedos Eva* (see page 167) and *Frangainho Hotel Eva* (see page 165). He cooks the superb broad beans of the Algarve in the local manner (see page 167), tuna fish steak (see page 165), the Portimão red mullet with clams, tomato and garlic; his fish soup (see page 161) is superb and he makes an Alentejo style *açorda*. Local mussels are used in another speciality: *sopa de conquilhas* (see page 161). Lamb and roast kid, principally from round the Sagres area, are popular Algarve meats. At the Eva the chef cooks baby kid in a regional style casserole (see page 166). As well as a meal with a view over the town and church spires from the top floor restaurant drinks can be taken on the charming terrace facing the sea. There is open dinner dancing and the Eva, like the Hotel Faro, has a small fishermen's bar style night-club on the ground floor.

The Hotel Faro's dining-room commands no view, but produces good regional cooking at a reasonable price. Lunch and dinner cost 19s ($2.28) with choice of four courses which can include the local huge oysters. The chef's clam *cataplana* (see page 163) is excellent and he also cooks rabbit or pigeons in the *cataplana* dish. *Pescada* (hake) is used in a special Pescada Hotel Faro dish (see page 163) and dessert may include the Algarvian regional almond and fig sweets (see page 168).

The Restaurant Al Faghar has recently been taken over by a

British/Portuguese company and is being run in conjunction with a small hotel and *residência* apartment building. The restaurant is in the Rua Tenente Valadim, 30, on the first floor and right in the centre of Faro's shopping area. (Faro produces cork articles; annual fair is 16th July.) Drinks can be taken on a sunny Moorish style patio and then local recipes eaten in the atmosphere of a private house. The Restaurant Arcadia, Travessa dos Arios, 7, will prepare *cataplana* if given advance warning.

Faro beach is a vast spit of land on which summer villas jostle fishermen's storage sheds. On the south side there is brisk Atlantic bathing, on the north side a calm arm of the lagoon for the less superb swimmer and also the learner water-skier. There is a small water-ski school run by two Englishmen, with a bar and a unique way of teaching water-skiing, particularly fine for the nervous beginner. The small but clean and modern Hotel Santa Maria has its own small beach restaurant on Faro beach, and the Eva have plans for one. The first-grade Estalagem Aeromar is also on Faro beach.

A few years ago a fisherman named José de Rosa Roque began to prepare meals for local fishermen and those who holidayed on the beach. His simple thatched patio restaurant on the beach has become famous as La Roque, and is now dignified with a government tourist sign. The place, luckily, remains unpretentious and the cooking cheap and local. It is certainly informal, the guests usually wear beach clothes and have a healthy appetite for the huge *cataplana* which usually forms the main dish, washed down with red wine, innocuously smooth like all Algarve wines but packing a punch. The *cataplana* is usually preceded by crispy sardines cooked in wire grills over charcoal at the side of the house while you watch. The cooking is usually supervised by one of José's children. A meal costs about 10*s* ($1.20) inclusive.

Tourist office in Faro

SÃO BRÁS DE ALPORTÉL

North from Faro the main road leads up to São Brás de Alportél 10 miles away and also, eventually, to Lisbon. For peace, quiet and charming views try to book one of its twelve rooms at the Pousada de São Brás. Its terraced gardens are full of flowers, birds and pools; its view gazes down through almond, cork and olive groves to the sea beyond the rich coastal plain. The rooms are small but countrified in *décor* and the food good and ample. If nothing more, it is worth dropping in for afternoon tea and some of the local sweets that the women cooks make so well. Particularly excellent are the *bolas de figo, toucinhos* and *doce de ovos* sweetmeats (see pages 168, 169) made by the sweet-cook María Graciett, who learnt her recipes from previous *Pousada* cooks. They also make a delicious milk pudding here, *pudim de leite* (see page 170). For *hors d'œuvre* there's *carapau com molho de escabeche*, the *Pousada*'s speciality. For this sardines are fried in butter, left to get cold and served with potato salad and *escabeche* sauce. A *cataplana of* pork and clams and *sopa de conquilhas* (clam soup) is often served. If you can, take a look at the charming kitchen of scrubbed wood and marble, a huge fireplace decorated with local platters and views over the almond orchards. The women cooking staff are as bright and clean as their kitchen, in blue-and-white gingham aprons over white overalls, and blue-and-white mob caps.

Near by São Brás there are some interesting Roman remains newly unearthed in a farmyard at Milréu, near Estoi.

LOULÉ

Loulé is just over 8 miles from São Brás on the inland road, or can be reached from the coast from Faro or Quarteira. The huge covered market in the centre is full of the superb fruit and vegetables from the surrounding countryside. As well as being a place to see the Algarve chimney at its best, Loulé is also the centre of the copper-beating industry and a good place to buy some of the copperware which Portugal exports widely. There are many good places to buy, but one to recommend is José de Brito Barracha, Rua 9 de Abril, 25–29. Here you can see the boys at work with bellows and hammers and choose a souvenir from a showroom crammed with dusty examples of their art. Some are over-ornate, but there are delightful, smooth cooking-pots with handles, about 26s ($3.12), or tiny jugs just right for spring flowers for around 7s 6d (90 cents).

QUARTEIRA

Travelling along the coast road westwards from Faro the main road by-passes Quarteira which is rapidly developing as a new tourist resort. The English-owned Dona Filipa Hotel, opened in February 1968, is a luxury hotel (with its own golf-course, swimming-pool, private beach and night-club in the grounds). The tiled dining-room is cool and spacious. Near by the Black Horse (O Cavalo Preto) is an English-style country club and pub with a bar open to non-residents, swimming-pool and local food with English overtones – e.g. butter for cooking, not oil.

ALBUFEIRA

Albufeira is the next resort along the coast and the smartest and most highly developed of them all. It appears rather like a Portuguese St Trop. full of tourists – principally English – all the year round; but luckily a lot of the local character has been preserved even if converted into delights for tourists. The charming, demure, lacy weaving of local women, for example, is turned into not so demure beach dresses at the local boutique (the Chaminé). Old fishermen's sheds are turned into night-clubs; their nets decorate the bar of O Pescador, the Rank Hotel Sol e Mar's night-club in the centre of the town, while they themselves carry on their work in the small harbour over a headland from the main town. There is an English pub (Sir Harry's Bar), a fish and chip bar on the beach terraces of the Sol e Mar and tearooms in the main street. The most popular bars are Jules Bar and Bailote, the artists' café, the top eating spots in the centre of town Alfredo's and the Cafe Oasis. It is very much a tourist town now, the best cooking being found at the restaurant Boa Vista owned by an Englishman, Alf Worth, who also owns and runs the apartments near. by. This restaurant is perched on the cliff top to the west of Albufeira and has a superb view over the town. Regional specialities are served here and the fish dishes are excellent. A meal costs around 46s ($5.50). Squid are cooked in the Albufeira manner; *bacalhau gomes de sá* (see page 190), casseroled chicken, lobsters, crab, clams *Bulhão Pato* (see page 91) are all served.

To stay in I would recommend the Estalagem do Cerro near by, which has typically Algarvian *décor* of whitewashed walls, dark wood fittings, goatskin rugs, sheepskin on deep window seats, tiny roof terraces and the tall slotted Algarve chimney. The do Cerro has a small bar with dancing. On a budget, the Pensão Vila Recife, set in charming gardens, is excellent value, particularly for families.

Travelling towards Lagoa there is a fairly new inn on the main road just as you get to Alcantarilha, where there is also a new restaurant – the Ribeiro – and a turning leading to the resort of Armação de Pera. The new inn is the Estalagem São Jorge, with tables and chairs outside, and inside a cool dining-room with high-backed, dark wood chairs and local pottery. The rooms are charming and inexpensive. Lunch here would cost about 14*s* 6*d* ($1.74), a room only (for two) about 38*s* ($4.50).

Tourist office in Albufeira

ARMAÇÃO DE PERA

Armação de Pera is a charming small resort with the sculpted beach rocks characteristic of the area, old arches and colourful fishing boats in which to visit the splendid sea caves near by. The Casino Restaurante (not a gambling casino) has a superb terrace overlooking the beach, and dancing at night. It is opposite the Pensão Atlantica, which is good value. There is the Restaurante Regional, Rua Gago Coutinho, 18, but for the summer visitor Fernando's Hideaway on the beach serves good food. It is closed from 6 p.m. to 9 p.m. but serves dinner after this. The Hotel Garbe to the west of Armação also has a reputation for good food served in a light and airy restaurant lit with golden globe lights and overlooking the sea. The hotel is charmingly set into the cliff side with lush gardens and a blend of modern and regional room *décor*. Meals here cost about 19*s* ($2.30). *Tourist office in Armação*

LAGOA

Lagoa is a market centre and also the centre of the Algarve wine trade, and the back streets contain many potteries which produce the huge brown plates decorated with opal-shaded fish and fruit. In the somewhat unprepossessing streets are one or two restaurants patronized by the local resident English from the colony round Carvoeiro under 3 miles away. Noite e Dia is the most popular, run by Manuel Fernanda, who does a good chicken *piri-piri*. He also does a superb *pudim* – caramel sauce topped with whipped white of egg and chocolate. Café Onda in Lagoa prepares excellent liver kebabs and a *ratatouille*.   *Tourist office in Lagoa*

CARVOEIRO

I am specially fond of the area round Carvoeiro with its smugglers' cave cliffs, where the active can clamber through sea-cut passages and arches to find a secluded beach. The area is, however, being developed with small cottages and villas. Togi's restaurant on top of the cliff above Carvoeiro village is well established. Its name is derived from 'Tom' and 'Gilda', the Dutch Portuguese couple who own it. They have plans to build a few bedrooms on to the restaurant, which is a simple thatched room. Specialities here include *bife à togi*, rumpsteak cooked in wine; *iscas portuguesas*, from Gilda's home area of Lisbon (see page 95); a pineapple cream pudding (see page 170), Gilda's invention; and a fish cocktail using sea trout in a sauce similar to that in a prawn cocktail. Stuffed squid – *lulas recheadas* – is excellent and typical of the Algarve. Chocolate mousse is made by Gilda (see page 170).

Near by is the Chaminé night-club and bar at Ferragudo, and down in Carvoeiro village, where the cluster of fishermen's houses slithers to a stop against the spur of beach between the squared-off cliffs, is O Patio, a delightful restaurant carved out of the cliff. Formerly a *taverna*, its wine casks remain embedded in the rock wall; chairs and tables are of dark Algarve wood. *Robalo* (sea bass) is popular here, *bacalhau* and steaks are always on the menu with ham from Monchique. *Caldeirada* (fish stew) can be ordered in advance. Lobster, crab and shrimps are available, the latter most popular with the English who make up 30 per cent of the Patio's clientèle. The average price of main dishes is 6s to 13s (72 cents to $1.56).

PORTIMÃO

An attractive fishing centre set across a wide bridge, Portimão's main streets look over broad quaysides and tiny, garden-filled squares. Portimão is the centre for rush and furniture work and has a big fair at the beginning of August. It is possible to eat remarkably cheaply in Portimão, where appetites are as sturdy as the people. The Caravela is good; the Seven Seas has a French-Spanish character, but at Sanches the doses (so 'portions' are described on the menu) are good value and meted out whole or half; at the Economica in Praça de Republica, one can have a whole meal for about 6*s* (72 cents) all in. Red mullet with butter sauce is a dish possible for this price. The Estalagems Miradoiro and Mira Foía are excellent. A discothèque bar is the Avozinha, Rua Capote, 7; the Dennis bar-boutique is opposite the Hotel Globo.

Portimão is the place to indulge any sweet-tooth craving and see or buy some of the wide variety of local concoctions. The place to go is the Pastelaria Almeida, Largo o Dezembro, 4, where you can also watch them being made. Seeing the intricate making of thread eggs set in bubbling syrup is fascinating. These are used to fill the famous 'thread eggs' (known as *Dom Rodrigo* in the Algarve). You will also find plenty of *morgados*, the local Portimão sweetmeat here (see also page 159 on Lagos sweet-seller).

The sweets are often sold in little baskets woven from esparto grass grown locally. Other articles made from this are mats of all sizes and slippers. *Tourist office in Portimão*

PRAIA DA ROCHA

Near by at Alvor, which has several new hotels opening up, there is a new 'thatched hut' style of restaurant. Also near Portimão is the more established resort of Praia da Rocha, its beach one of the most photographed in Portugal. This resort has somewhat spoilt its beauty with huge modern block hotels. Retaining its old-world Portuguese private house charm is the Bela Vista, always booked well in advance, but delightful to see and have a meal around 19*s* ($2.28). The Pensão Sol and Pinguin are other recommended places to stay; the Fortaleza de Santa Catarina for a meal. Just outside Portimão is the luxury Penina golf hotel, with huge swimming-pool and restaurant overlooking this and the golf-course. Worth while if you want to pay for a touch of high standard international cuisine, handy if you are driving along the main road.

MONCHIQUE

From Portimão the hill road winds inland to Monchique. The best drive, however, is to go from farther east through Silves. Coming over a hill crest the sight of this Moorish fortified town against a backdrop of hills is dramatically impressive. The road winds through the fruit orchards of the plain then climbs rapidly through thick lush forest growth, cool and thick after the coastal heat, to Caldas de Monchique, a tiny and old-fashioned spa which still produces mineral water for Algarve restaurant tables and has a first-grade pension, the Central. Monchique itself is coolly balanced at the height of the mountains, with hazy views. It has a small *estalagem* – Abrigo da Montanha – where you might try the local chestnut dishes or the fruit dish of oranges and cherries soaked in local Alphonso III (rather like a dry sherry, usually served chilled as an aperitif).

LAGOS

Back on the coast the next and last town of note is Lagos, much associated with Henry the Navigator's work (its name originally meaning 'town of the sea'), now a fishing port overlooking its large bay. As well as producing basketwork and copper goods, it is famed with visitors for the making of the *Dom Rodrigo* sweetmeats sold in foil wrappings. These are 'thread eggs' bound together with cinnamon syrup and browned sugar. Thread eggs, an important Portuguese sweet, are found all over the country and on their own often form a dish at a wedding feast, but they originated in Lagos. The thread eggs are made by straining eggs through a fine-holed container into bubbling syrup and then cooling. I feel it would tire the patience of non-Portuguese housewives to make these. They can be bought ready made, along with dozens of other Algarvian sweets, at Casa dos Doces Regionais, Rua da Porta de Portugal, 27, a modest place which inside is a child's paradise of tempting sweetmeats arrayed on beds of fluffy white paper.

In Lagos one may eat at the Os Arcos, the best-known restaurant, run by an English couple. The Estalagem São Cristovão serves a pleasant international style food overlooking glorious gardens going down to the wide sandy beach. The Pensão Costa D'Ouro serves good food and A Lagosteira specializes in shellfish.

SAGRES

From Lagos, on to the tiny fishing village of Sagres, the landscape becomes less lush and agricultural and gives way to wilder, more open rolling downs, the roads edged with bright hedges of geraniums bent with the wind. The cliffs lose their intriguing carved and statuesque sculpted appearance and become flat-topped, the ends neatly squared off into the sea. Towards the irresistible Cape St Vincent the narrow cliff-top peninsula is so flat that while driving along it is difficult to see below.

In this area sheep and goats are reared and make popular eating. Around the cape game is hunted on the cliffs. Sagres is the home of Henry the Navigator's school where the famous Compass Rose can still be seen. The village sleeps in its history 'where the land ends and the sea begins', the fishing boats riding at anchor in the deep bay. On the cliff top the Pousada do Infante makes a wonderful spot for a meal (where roast kid stew is a favourite dish). The Baleeira Hotel is another of those skilfully modern coastal hotel buildings the Portuguese specialize in, with its rooms tucked into the cliffs. This hotel has a splendid restaurant overlooking the sea, with lobster a speciality. They also frequently organize beach barbecues and picnics. Price of a meal is 17s 6d ($2.10). The Estalagem das Descobertas near the *Pousada* has a smart glassed-in restaurant with a sun terrace projecting over the bay, with simple but good cooking.

At Belixe, practically on the tip of the cape, there is a restaurant-café in a converted fort, the sort of place to stop for a drink – hot or cold – after a visit to this impressive cape with many ships, both big and small, making their way past. One feels here more strongly than at Guincho that one has reached the end of Europe.

RECIPES FROM THE ALGARVE
SOPA DE CONQUILHAS
(MUSSEL SOUP)

Conquilhas are local Algarve mussels but other kinds of mussels, shelled or bottled, can be used. If shelled, clean and beard before using and allow 8–10 mussels per person.

FOR FOUR

2 lb. mussels in their shells
1 onion
½ lb. potatoes
5 oz. rice
2 tablespoons olive oil
chopped parsley
seasoning

Put about 1½ pints boiling water in a big pan. Chop the onion, add olive oil, cubed potatoes and seasoning to taste, and when these are cooked add mussels in their shells and parsley to garnish. Cook for half an hour, adding rice after 15 minutes.

SOPA À PESCADOR
(FISHERMAN'S SOUP)

These soups are found all over the country. In this one a local Algarve touch, added by the Eva's chef, is the inclusion of almonds in the soup.

FOR FOUR

1 lb. crayfish (langoustines)
¼ lb. almonds
4 oz. rice
2 tomatoes
2 tablespoons olive oil
2 pints fish stock
1 large onion
garlic

Fry chopped onion in garlic till golden. Chop tomatoes and crayfish. Add fish stock and finely chopped garlic and grated almonds. Boil for about 45 minutes, adding rice after about 30 minutes. Add chopped parsley at the end.

SARDINHAS PORTIMÃO
(PORTIMÃO SARDINES)

This is an unusual *hors d'œuvres* idea using Portuguese sardines, tinned or fresh, but it would be equally suitable as a lunch or supper dish. Ready-made frozen puff pastry, rolled out very thin, can be used. Drain the sardines or if fresh split lengthways. Remove the bone and replace the two halves, head to tail, to make a neater shape. Between the two halves put some stoned and chopped black olives, some very thin slices of tomato cut in half and salt and pepper. A pinch of thyme may also be added. Fold each sardine in pastry as if making sausage rolls and bake in a hot oven. These rolls can be eaten hot but are equally delicious cold.

OSTRAS DO ALGARVE
(ALGARVE OYSTERS)

FOR FOUR

24 large oysters (fresh or bottled)
1 sprig parsley
2 soupspoons white wine
butter, salt and pepper
crumbled bread

Wash the oysters well. Place in a saucepan on the stove to make them open. Remove from their shell and allow them to soak in their own water. Bring to the boil for a very few minutes. Grease an ovenproof dish with butter and arrange the oysters there in layers with chopped parsley, white wine, salt and pepper. Add plenty of butter and spread crumbled bread on the top. Roast lightly in the oven.

COCKTAIL DE PEIXE
(FISH COCKTAIL)

Sea trout is used in a similar way to prawns to make a fish cocktail. The flaked cooked trout is mixed with chopped lettuce and tomato and a sauce added made by blending to taste whipped cream, Worcester (or *piri-piri*, see page 194) sauce, lemon juice, seasoning and brandy.

PESCADA HOTEL FARO
(HOTEL FARO HAKE)

FOR EACH PERSON

7 oz. cleaned hake 1¾ oz. small onions
3½ oz. cubed boiled potatoes

Cook chopped onion in fat or olive oil till golden. Place the fish on top of some of the potatoes in a baking dish and surround with the rest of the potatoes mixed with onions. Spread a sauce mayonnaise over the fish before cooking. Cook for ½ hour in a very hot oven. About 5½ tablespoons port wine can be added as well.

AMÊIJOAS NA CATAPLANA
(COCKLES, FROM THE HOTEL FARO)

Cataplana (see page 149) is a metal cooking-pot (now usually aluminium or copper) of two shallow dish-shaped parts rather like a double-sided shell, which fit closely together when cooking and act as a primitive kind of pressure-cooker.

Amêijoas are the favourite Algarve *cataplana* dish laced with smoked sausage and ham.

FOR TWO

32–40 cockles (1 lb.) onions
ham, Portuguese sausage and parsley
other cold meat ½ pint white wine

Butter the inside of cockle shells, add the chopped meats, plenty of chopped onion and chopped parsley. The meat should be placed at the bottom with the cockles on top and more meat and onions on top again. The dish is usually reversed for service when a proper *cataplana* dish is used. Add white wine and cook on top of the stove for about 15 minutes. I am assured by the chef that it won't burn. Turn over once during cooking or shake well.

AMÊIJOAS E PORCO NA CATAPLANA
(COCKLES AND PORK COOKED IN CATAPLANA)

FOR FOUR

Fry 1 lb. pork well, in lard, cut in large chunks with bay leaves, finely chopped garlic, half a glass white wine and cockles in their shells. (Allow about 16 each.) When fried put everything into the *cataplana* and cook for about 15 minutes. Of course onion can be added – as much as required – also chopped parsley.

COELHO NA CATAPLANA
(RABBIT IN CATAPLANA)
from the Hotel Faro

Game or pigeon can be prepared in the same way. The day before cooking, marinate the rabbit meat in just over ½ pint white wine, herbs to taste, a little vinegar and black pepper. Next day place plenty of finely chopped onion in the *cataplana* – having first cooked the onion in oil or butter. Sauté the rabbit lightly in olive oil or butter for about 5 minutes to give it some colour. Remove rabbit and cook marinade sauce in the butter in the same pan. Put rabbit and sauce in the *cataplana*, topped with some slices of smoked ham. Cook for 45 minutes to 1 hour. Serve with bread fried in thin strips.

SALMONTE VLADIMIRO
(RED MULLET HOTEL EVA)

A way of cooking local red mullet with cockles, created by the Hotel Eva's chef at Faro.

FOR FOUR

4 red mullet (about 3½ oz. each)
2 tablespoons olive oil
1 clove garlic
2 medium tomatoes
1 lb. cockles with shells (allow about 8–10 bottled cockles per person)
parsley
2 onions

Place prepared fish on a deep baking tray or oven dish with olive oil and finely chopped garlic, chopped tomatoes (skinned), chopped onions and cockles. Bake in a moderate oven for about 45 minutes. When cooked, scatter chopped parsley over the fish five minutes before serving.

BIFE DE ATUM À ALGARVIA
(ALGARVE TUNA STEAK)

FOR FOUR

1½ lb. tinned tuna   4 oz. fat bacon
2 onions   1 glass white wine

Fry sliced onions with the bacon then, when onions are soft and bacon almost cooked, add wine and the tuna and gently heat through for about 10 minutes.

SALADA DE TUNA E AMÊNDOAS
(TUNA AND ALMOND SALAD)

3 oz. blanched almonds cut into slivers   3 sticks celery
2 oz. black olives   7½ tablespoons mayonnaise (scant ¼ pint)
2 hard-boiled eggs   salt, black pepper, lemon juice

Tinned tuna can be used for this. Two 4-oz. cans will be enough. Drain the oil from the tuna and flake it with a fork. Fold in with the other ingredients into the mayonnaise and season with salt, pepper and lemon juice. Serve on a large cos lettuce leaf.

FRANGAINHO HOTEL EVA

Chicken done in a particularly delicious way.

FOR TWO TO THREE

1 oz. mushrooms   1¼ lb. boned chicken meat (a
chopped parsley   small chicken boned but left
rosemary   in one piece is the way the
4–6 oz. rice   chef does it at the Eva)

SAUCE

1 large onion   1 glass madeira wine
jelly from veal stock   rosemary

Cook rice separately, and when cooked mix cooked mushrooms, parsley and a little rosemary with the rice. The Eva chef stuffs the boned chicken with the rice, but the chicken meat can be laid on top of the rice in an oven dish (undercook the rice in this case and leave very moist). Wrap buttered foil over the top of the chicken and cook in a medium oven for 30 minutes. Alternatively cook and serve rice separately with cooked chicken and the rosemary sauce. For this sauce chop a large onion finely, add jelly from veal stock, 1 glass madeira wine, rosemary, and cook for about 20 minutes until reduced. Strain before serving.

CAÇAROLA DE CABRITO À REGIONAL
(BABY KID CASSEROLED IN REGIONAL STYLE)

Casseroled kid is popular all along the coast, particularly in the west. In this recipe the Eva's chef has substituted lamb for the kid meat. Chicken, duckling, veal, pork or – popular eating in the Algarve – pigeon, could be treated in the same manner.

FOR FOUR

2 lb. cooked lamb (or other meat as above)
2 tablespoons olive oil
2 cloves garlic
2 onions
2 bay leaves
2 tomatoes
¼ lb. carrots
¼ lb. mushrooms
¼ lb. green peas
½ lb. potatoes – in small balls (*noisettes*)
parsley

Fry in a casserole or frying-pan finely chopped onions, garlic, bay leaves, chopped, peeled tomatoes in olive oil for 5 minutes until browned. Chop the cooked lamb into small cubes, mix with other cooked ingredients, carrots cut into *juliennes* (small sticks), peas, chopped mushrooms and raw potatoes scooped into ball shapes (or small whole potatoes can be used). Mix all together. Add a little stock to moisten if necessary. Begin cooking on top of the stove for 10 minutes, then in a moderately hot oven for a further 20 minutes. Add chopped parsley when cooked.

TOURNEDOS HOTEL EVA

(An example of the Portuguese love of serving eggs with everything – particularly with beef steaks; a speciality of chef Roguerio Alcaria.)

Grill an 8-oz. lean fillet steak per person. Poach an egg and put it on top of the steak and cover with a classic *béarnaise* sauce to which some slivers of cooked mushroom and tongue have been added. Brown the sauce by flashing under the grill to give it colour.

FAVAS À ALGARVIA
(ALGARVE BROAD BEANS)

FOR FOUR

1 lb. broad beans
4 oz. salami
4 oz. smoked ham
1 onion
4 oz. carrots
½ tablespoon tomato *purée*
1 pint chicken stock
1 tablespoon olive oil
seasoning

In a frying-pan or casserole gently cook finely chopped onion, chopped salami and sliced smoked ham (parma is a suitable substitute) in the olive oil for about 5 minutes. Add chicken stock, beans, sliced carrots, tomato *purée* and seasoning. Cover and cook in a slow oven for about 1 hour until beans and carrots are tender.

FRUTAS REGIONAIS DE AMÊNDOA

from the Hotel Faro

This mixture is shaped into imitation fruit and in the Algarve so cleverly coloured that it looks completely realistic. The fruits are served with liqueurs after a meal.

1 lb. ground almonds
1 lb. sieved castor or
   icing sugar or
   ½ lb. of each
1–2 egg whites
juice of ½ lemon

2 teaspoons sherry or rum
1 teaspoon vanilla essence
1 teaspoon orange flower water
¼ teaspoon almond or ratafia
   essence

Mix ingredients together into a paste and form into fruit shapes.

FIGOS RECHEADOS À ALGARVIA
(STUFFED ALGARVE FIGS)

equal amounts of almonds   dried figs
and plain chocolate

Skin and grate almonds. Grate chocolate and mix with almonds. Widen the opening of the fig and fill the interior with the mixture and close the opening again. Place the figs on a tray in a very moderate oven, turning from time to time so as to brown them slowly.

DOCE DE OVOS (EGG SWEET)

from the Pousada São Brás

This sweet is served in small individual dishes, and these amounts will make enough for 4 large servings or 8 or so small servings.

3½ oz. sugar
3 egg yolks
1½ egg whites

2¾ tablespoons water
cinnamon

Bring sugar and water together to the boil, lower heat and simmer. Strain yolks into a basin so that the skins are removed – this is important. Beat the skinless yolks well and add the sugar and water slowly in small amounts. Stir all the time. Return to the heat for about 5 minutes, then leave to cool (but not in a fridge). About an hour before serving beat the egg white till frothy but not over stiff. Mix with the rest and place in individual dishes. Sprinkle with cinnamon.

TOUCINHOS

A typically Algarvian dessert which is set in mini-moulds – not more than two inches in diameter. Small cake patty tins can be used, partially filled. The amounts here from the Pousada de São Brás recipe make about 20 *toucinhos*. The finished texture should be yellow with a shiny surface.

14 oz. sugar
just over ½ pint water
7 egg yolks
2 egg whites
2 dessertspoons flour

Boil sugar and water together until sugar dissolves (stir for about 5 minutes). Pour into a *bain-marie* (or double boiler) surrounded by cold water to cool. Beat egg yolks and whites with the flour and, when sugar sauce is cool, mix with the eggs. Grease tiny moulds with butter and dust with flour. Pour mixture into moulds and cook in a *bain-marie* (with water half way up the moulds) for about ½ hour, adding more water to the saucepan if necessary.

BOLAS DE FIGO (FIG BALLS)
from the Pousada de São Brás

Typical of the Algarvian sweets, using locally grown figs and almonds. They are excellent served with after-dinner coffee. This recipe was taught to the *Pousada* manageress twenty-five years ago by two ladies who lived in Lagos and who were considered to make the best *bolas de figo* in the Algarve.

7 tablespoons water
8¾ oz. sugar
8¾ oz. dried figs (stalk bits removed)
8¾ oz. peeled, blanched almonds
1¾ oz. cooking chocolate
1 piece orange peel

These ingredients make about 1½ lb.

Heat the almonds in the oven until roasted and slightly brown. Put almonds, figs, orange peel and chocolate all together through a fine mincer or electric grinder. Boil the water and sugar until thick and mix in the ground ingredients. When cool form into little balls and roll in sugar.

PUDIM DE LEITE (MILK PUDDING)

FOR FOUR

4 eggs 1 tablespoon sugar
11 tablespoons milk piece lemon peel

Mix eggs and grated lemon peel in a basin. Add sugar and milk and mix well. Line a ring mould with caramel (see page 197). Pour egg mixture into the mould and cook in a *bain-marie* – or half fill a meat tin with water, place mould in it and bake in a moderate oven till set and the top just browned.

MOUSSE DE ANANÁS
(PINEAPPLE MOUSSE)

2 tablespoons cornflour medium tin chopped pineapple
¾ pint milk (sweeter than fresh)
4 egg yolks

Blend the cornflour with the milk and bring to the boil, stirring all the time. Cook till thick, stirring well. Blend in the beaten egg yolks and the finely chopped pineapple together with a little of the pineapple juice. Pour into a serving bowl and chill till served. Serve with fresh cream.

MOUSSE CHOCOLATE À TOGI
(TOGI CHOCOLATE MOUSSE)

Popular all over Portugal. Gilda the chef uses powdered chocolate for her recipe.

FOR FIVE TO SIX

6 eggs 2 tablespoons sugar
8 oz. chocolate butter

Melt butter in a *bain-marie* (or in a bowl over a pan of simmering water) and dissolve chocolate in it. Add sugar according to taste, and egg yolks and cook till mixture thickens. Beat well. Beat whites stiffly. Mix with chocolate and beat well. The more beating the softer the mousse will be.

10

MADEIRA

This cluster of lava cones rising sheer from the Atlantic has long been a popular winter resort for British people, and now Americans are discovering its year-round warmth. The climate, coupled with an extraordinarily industrious and patient population, have made it a lush floral and fruit paradise. Unpeopled till found by Henry the Navigator's sailors in the fifteenth century, the barren lava rock, which supported little apart from thick forests, has been made to produce bananas and grapes in particular. The rain which falls thickly in the high central plateau has been channelled by hand down *levadas*, or watercourses, whose thin silver threads can be seen cutting through the cultivated terraces niched into the rocks. Even the skirts of Cabo Girão's suicidal plunge to the sea have been cultivated.

With both water and sun, flowers and fruit abound. More northern apples – made into cider in Machico and Camacha – are coupled with bananas, the island's number one industry, grapes, chestnuts, custard apples, avocados, superb vegetables and thick, waxy flowers and orchids. The juice of the passion fruit is made into a pleasant cocktail drink with soda and *aguardente* (local brandy).

The visitor should go to the market at Funchal on Saturday morning to see the colourful array of local produce tenderly laid out in trumpet-shaped wickerwork baskets behind which sit women as colourful as their produce, in red- and yellow-striped pleated

Madeira

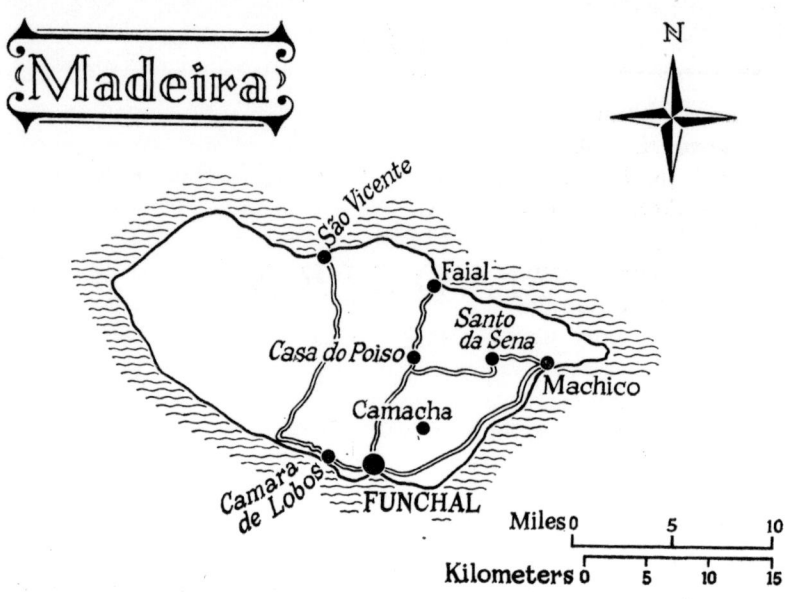

skirts and shawls and wearing untanned leather boots. Their men are dressed in white cotton tunics and loose trousers.

The fish section of the market displays the *espada*, a hideous-looking, yard-long fish with black and white smudges on its flattish body. This fish is found only in the deep water off Madeira and also off Japan, and in Madeira at least, I was told, one had never yet been caught alive. It turns up frequently in local cooking, often served with fried bananas. Other local fish include lobster, crab, shrimp and swordfish. Tuna is seen in the market, sold like great blood-streaked steaks.

The meat on the island is often tough, and the beef is made the most of by marinating it in wine and then cooking it skewered on green laurel sticks with garlic, wine and olive oil. The *espetada*, as this kebab is called, is found everywhere. The best *espetada* restaurant, the Seta, is half way up to Monte above Funchal where the meat is accompanied in the traditional manner with new wine.

Perhaps this passion for kebabing stems from a nearness to Africa, because there is a local *couscous*, and fried maize is a popular dish accompaniment, especially with tuna. But the main inspiration remains similar to the dishes of the mainland from the

Minho, Lisbon and Algarve – the pork roast with cinnamon, the *bacalhau*, the fish soups and the *pudim flan*. The taste for sweetmeats is not lost; there are *bolo de mel*, honey cake; *queijadas*, sweet cheesecakes; and madeira cake – derived from an old English recipe. Madeira wine is not greatly used for cooking locally, though a classic sauce is made with it.

There are a number of cattle and pigs on the island, but they are rarely seen, since they live in charming, if smelly, thatched huts next to the peasant's house. The cows are taken for walks like a dog and pampered for their milk and excellent butter rather than for their meat. The high, flat, central plateau provides grazing for sheep, prized for cheese and meat. The shepherds wear thick woolly caps with earflaps, sold in Funchal to tourists for a few shillings.

The grapes of course are made into madeira wine, the rich, golden, fortified wines praised by Shakespeare. The visitor is welcome to taste these at the Madeira Wine Association's old beamed premises at Avenida Arriaga, 28, in Funchal.

The destruction of vines some years ago led to the introduction of the famous embroidery industry, from which the island now earns more than from its wine. An Englishwoman, alarmed at the possibility of the women of Madeira having little to employ them, taught them embroidery, which developed into a great export trade. With the wickerwork baskets and furniture made at Camacha, embroidery and wine, the tourist is off to a good start at souvenir shopping. The bazaars in the narrow streets running down to the quayside from the main square exist principally for the cruise trade (alas declining), and most of their wares are priced in sterling, dollars, francs, etc., as well as escudos, and all kinds of money will be accepted.

For the tourist with time to linger, dresses in cut-out lace work, linen skirts, handbags, blouses and other clothing will be made to measure and delivered to the hotel. Leather and polished inlaid wood items are other good buys; the shopkeepers happily bring out a bottle of madeira to seal a sale. Particularly amusing are the huge, gaily coloured dolls set round a stick, which appear to dance and play music when the base is moved, and are carried for local dances.

The best display is that of the Casa do Turista, which shows native handicrafts from Madeira and the mainland set out in the rooms and courtyard of a charming old house near the quayside. Multilingual girls help customers choose from the massive array, which includes glorious china reproductions of old designs and complete table settings. The packages are then superbly gift-wrapped. Other shops to see include Arte Fina (opposite the cathedral), Imperial Linens, Q. Farra and Company and Madeira Superbia.

Apart from shopping, trying the osier, tray-like toboggans down the cobbled streets from Monte above Funchal, or the slow oxen carts on wooden skates, the tourist has little to do except to swim, since Madeira, although conscious of its tourist trade, remains much as it was before the war, with the accent on peace and rest.

The focus of tourism is in Funchal and here are all the hotels, with the exception of one pension, the Fernendes at Porto Moniz in the north-west. Most of the restaurants, all the night-clubs, casino and shops are clustered in the natural amphitheatre bay. Car hire is reasonably inexpensive and enables the visitor to see the island's 35- by 20-mile surface as he wishes. But the ceaseless twist and curve of every road may deter the queasy from long drives. There are, however, one or two pleasant places within easy reach of Funchal which look like being the next to be developed for tourism: Câmara de Lobos and Machico. Apart from these two places communities are tiny villages or a grouping of farm houses, but there are a few restaurants to refresh the traveller away from Funchal.

The Casa da Chá at Faial in the north-east, in spite of its name, serves good local food and is perched on the side of an inevitable hill among the *levadas* a little inland. Near the airport is the Jardim do Sol at Caniço, where *espada* steaks and excellent *hors d'œuvres* are served; at São Vicente in the north of the island, reached by a beautiful but steep hill journey, is a friendly café-restaurant built in an old but still operational wine-press cellar. In harvest season the tourist can tread the grapes and then enjoy a harvester style meal alongside the presses. At any time the fare is simple but tasty, served at refectory-style tables by candlelight. There is the favourite *espetada* steak cooked on a laurel rod and served with warm unleavened bread, preceded by a thick stew soup which the locals make to take with them on pilgrimages into the hills.

Machico boasts no restaurants for tourists at present, but Camara de Lobos, the picture-postcard village, has the charming Riba-Mar overlooking the stony beach alongside the tiny square with a wrought-iron bandstand in its centre. On the beach by day the visitor can see swordfish hanging to dry in the sun while the fishermen drink away the proceeds of their last catch and play card games on the decks of their ships drawn up conveniently near the back doors of small taverns. The Riba-Mar has a terrace bar and a restaurant with whitewashed walls, gingham checked tables set with candles and a centrepiece of a full-sized boat which acts as a bar. The food is well cooked and reasonably priced; the tomato soup studded with an egg and bread is good and so are the *caldeirada* and other fish dishes. The plates of *hors d'œuvres* served automatically are tasty. On certain evenings an accordionist plays during dinner. Other of the island's restaurants to note are the Pensão-Restaurante Windsor at Terreiro da Luta in the high centre of the island, and the Pensão-Restaurante at Ribeiro Frio.

Back in Funchal the tourist can choose between dining at the larger hotels or in the handful of restaurants. Of the hotels Reid's, the doyen of them all, riding out the sea from its cliff-top site, provides formality and an international menu spiced with local specialities, some of which are described on pages 177, 180, 181. The newly reconstructed Savoy has a rooftop dining-room and good cuisine. Local specialities include fillets of *espada* with banana and tuna fish steaks with fried maize, the fish being first marinated with garlic, red pepper, bay leaf and vinegar. Drinks can be taken at any time in the bars of Reid's and the Savoy, which have superb views over the harbour. The Savoy also has a night-club. At the New Avenue Hotel, Avenida do Infante, the unpretentious *décor* belies good food, the proprietor being an enthusiastic gourmet. As well as a mini English-pub-style bar, the hotel boasts a discothèque – the Gemini, the most swinging spot in Madeira. At the Casino, in the Quinta Vigia, there is a dinner-cabaret, with an excellent Brazilian pianist and trio for dancing, while upstairs there is gambling. For atmosphere this is one of the friendliest and pleasantest casinos I know. Other night spots where drinks are reasonable are the Flamingo and Folklore, the latter, in spite of its name, excellent value and charming.

Of the restaurants, the best is considered to be the Combatentes, Rua de Ivens, 1–8, just to the back of the main square. This is *bistro* in atmosphere and extremely unpretentious, but the food is good and not expensive; try grilled sardines and shrimps. The Seta (arrow), half way up to Monte, serves the *espetada* on iron kebab sticks, supposed to represent arrows. The meat with bread and wine costs about 7s to 8s 6d ($0.85 to $1.00).

For an intimate and elegant dinner or more casual poolside lunch the Club de Turismo, Estrada Monumental, 179, is a pleasant spot. Built out on a terrace overlooking the harbour beyond Reid's, it has a small pool bar and restaurant. Tourists become temporary members for a small fee. The restaurant is superbly panelled in polished wood with antique style *décor* and a beautiful coffee lounge upstairs. Another club to which tourists can belong during their stay is the British Country Club near the Club de Turismo, which has floodlit tennis courts. The Clube Naval accepts visitors as honorary members free of charge during their stay. The Savoy Hotel has plans shortly for building a beachside restaurant with a few hotel rooms, and Reid's has a new grillroom just opened.

MADEIRAN RECIPES

Although Madeirans do not use a great deal of their famed wine in their cooking – they leave that mainly to the French – there are one or two recipes which make use of madeira. In many cases the English influence and local traditions have become inextricably mixed, as in the case of madeira cake, which is made in Madeira but based on an old British recipe.

A simple recipe using madeira as a sauce flavouring is not from the island but is one invented by my friend Mr Castelo Branco at the Casa de Portugal in London.

GAMMON STEAK CASTELO BRANCO

Gently fry a gammon steak in its own fat (don't add any) till golden brown on both sides. Remove from the pan and keep hot.

Add a tablespoon or two of madeira to the frying-pan and heat, mixing with the meat juices in the pan, and use this sauce with the gammon.

SOPE DE TOMATE CEBOLA
(TOMATO AND ONION SOUP)
from Reid's Hotel

FOR FOUR TO FIVE

2 lb. tomatoes	salt, pepper
2 lb. onions	1 oz. butter
1 bay leaf	1 oz. lard
1 clove garlic	olive oil to taste
basil	3–4 eggs
2 slices bread and butter	3–4 oz. cheese

Cut the onions in rounds and fry in the olive oil, butter and lard, with the bay leaf and garlic. Meanwhile put the tomatoes in boiling water briefly to remove the skin. Cut into small pieces and add to the frying onions. Leave to cook for a while with water and seasoning, adding some basil. Butter bread, cut into small pieces and place some in each soup bowl with some grated cheese (fried or toasted bread and cheese can be used as an alternative). Blend the tomato and onion to a *purée*, reheat and serve. A poached egg can be added to each serving if wished.

SOPA DE TOMATE CEBOLA À PORTUGUESA
(PORTUGUESE ONION AND TOMATO SOUP)

A more rich and robust version of this soup, which makes use of bread to give added body, was described to me on Madeira. The consistency of this type of soup, which the Riba-Mar at Camara de Lobos makes most tastily, is such that one can almost literally stand a spoon up in it.

FOR FIVE TO SIX

½ pint olive oil
5 large onions
5 large tomatoes
4 oz. butter
4 oz. cheese (grated)
5 or 6 eggs
seasoning
½ loaf white bread
a little sugar

Slice the onions and fry slowly in the oil till a golden colour. Add sliced tomatoes with a little sugar. Simmer till thick. Add sufficient water for 5–6 people and bring to the boil again and simmer. Melt butter, cool a little and add to the beaten eggs, together with the grated cheese. Add everything to the soup and beat well until it curdles. Reheat gently just before serving. Scatter broken bread on top until part of the soup is absorbed. Serve with a poached egg for each person.

PESCADA MADEIRA
(HAKE IN MADEIRA WINE)

This recipe comes from the Escondidinho restaurant in Oporto, but shows how the Portuguese use madeira in cooking.

Season hake steaks with salt and lemon juice. Coat with flour and fry in butter. When cooked, place on warm dish with the butter in which they were fried. Heat a little madeira wine and pour over the steaks.

BIFES DE ATUM (TUNA STEAKS)

FOR FIVE TO SIX

In Madeira fresh tuna is used. At home tinned tuna can be substituted, but will not need soaking in water prior to marinating and will not need marinating so long. The vinegar sauce gives the fish a pleasant tang.

2 lb. tuna
1 lb. onions
seasoning, bay leaf, parsley
sufficient water and vinegar to cover fish when cut into steaks
olive oil or cooking fat for frying

Slice fish into steaks or form into portions and cover with the finely chopped onion, parsley, bay leaf and seasonings. Pour over the vinegar solution and leave to soak an hour or so. Drain, then fry in heated olive oil and place in ovenproof dish. Pour vinegar mixture into pan, thicken with a little cornflour and pour over steaks.

A variation on this theme, using garlic and marjoram and a stronger sauce, was given me by the chef at Reid's Hotel. Dry white wine can be used instead of vinegar in both these recipes.

    2 lb. tuna olive oil
   1 clove garlic parsley, marjoram and
    1 bay leaf   vinegar to taste
  salt, pepper to taste

Marinate the tuna for an hour or so in the olive oil, vinegar, chopped garlic, bay leaf, pepper, chopped parsley, marjoram and salt. Fry the drained steaks in olive oil, adding when steaks are nearly cooked the liquid in which they were marinated, which can be thickened with the addition of a flour and water paste.

Wine, bay leaf and garlic are used to marinate the Madeira pork, and similar marinades are used to soften the fairly tough beef for the *espetada*. These recipes are in the direct mainland Portuguese tradition. Some of the Madeiran recipes call for marinades of eight days!

CARNE DE VINHO E ALHOS
(PORK IN WINE AND GARLIC)
from the Clube de Turismo

FOR TWO TO THREE

  1 lb. fillet of pork a little vinegar
  a little white wine lard
  garlic and bay leaf parsley
 salt, pepper, sweet paprika

Cut the meat in small pieces and marinate for 24 hours in a mixture of the above seasonings. Remove the meat and drain well. Heat some lard in a frying-pan and when hot fry the meat until it is half done, then add a little of the marinade. Put a lid on the frying-pan and when the meat is well done serve with boiled potatoes and finely chopped parsley.

MILHO FRITO (FRIED MEAL 'STICKS')

This is a Madeiran version of chips, made from a basis of meal flour and water, and is served at Reid's Hotel.

>   2½ pints water   salt to taste
>   1 lb. meal flour   olive oil
>   1 oz. lard

Heat the water with the lard and salt. When tepid, add the meal flour and mix well, constantly, until it forms a thick porridge. Simmer it for about 1 hour. When cooked turn out into a china or earthenware tray or flat platter about ½ inch deep. Leave overnight or for several hours then cut into thin, chip-sized pieces and fry in hot olive oil, turning when golden. Serve with meat, fish or egg dishes.

PUDIM MADEIRA (MADEIRA PUDDING)

This is a basic *pudim flan* recipe flavoured with madeira wine.

>   ½ lb. sugar   6 yolks
>   a little vinegar   ¾ pint milk
>   2 whole eggs   small port glass madeira

Make some caramel (see page 180) and coat mould with it. Put sugar into bowl and add vinegar, eggs and yolks. Beat thoroughly together. Heat milk. When hot, but not boiling, add slowly to egg mixture with the madeira. Beat together thoroughly and put in the mould previously covered with caramel. Cook in a *bain-marie* or double boiler for about 1–1½ hours on top of the stove or in a moderately hot oven until set.

PUDIM MADEIRA À CLUBE DE TURISMO

(MADEIRA PUDDING FROM THE TOURIST CLUB)

>   ½ lb. flour   madeira wine (sweet)
>   ½ lb. sugar   ¼ lb. butter
>   4 eggs   1–2 oz. raisins

Mix together flour, sugar and eggs, add melted butter and mix in well. Cook in well-buttered mould in a *bain-marie* or double boiler. Serve with a hot sauce made by cooking together madeira wine, in which the raisins have been previously soaked, raisins, finely grated lemon rind, a stick of cinnamon, water and sugar to taste.

PUDIM DE LARANJA FRIO
(COLD ORANGE PUDDING)
from Reid's Hotel

FOR SIX

a good ¾ pint milk   1 oz. gelatine
3 oranges   4¼ oz. sugar
6 egg yolks   1 glass curaçao liqueur

Heat thin strips of orange rind in the milk till infused. Mix eggs, sugar and milk and strain back into the pan; cook (without boiling) until thick. Allow to cool. Soak gelatine in ⅛ pint water for 5 minutes, then heat to dissolve. Stir the orange juice and liqueur into the custard, add the dissolved gelatine, stirring as it cools. Whisk the egg whites stiffly and fold into the thickening mixture. Rinse some moulds in cold water, pour the pudding mixture into them and chill. To serve, place moulds in warm water briefly and turn out at once on to a serving dish.

11

TRANSLATING FOR THE TABLE

This is an ingredients guide to help make these recipes at home in the Portuguese manner, and to indicate, where the exact ingredients are unobtainable, the best substitute. There are no specialist Portuguese shops in London or New York, but, in general, Spanish grocers will have many products similar to the Portuguese. In London the best source of products is Gomez Ortega in Soho's Old Compton Street, although the delicatessen departments of large supermarkets or food halls of the better departmental stores will provide most things.

FISH

BACALHAU. Obtainable from grocers from Spain and from Italy. The Spanish term to note on packs is *bacalao*, the Italian *baccala*. It is imperative to get this dried cod for any of the *bacalhau* recipes mentioned in this book. The flakes of *bacalhau*, even when soaked, produce a lighter dish than do those of fresh or frozen codfish; and they taste completely different. *Bacalhau* when unpacked looks like grey, chewed cardboard which has rather a pungent smell. It should be kept in a cool, dry place, well

TRANSLATING FOR THE TABLE

wrapped and away from other foodstuffs which might absorb the smell.

SARDINES (*sardinhas*). Another vital fish. Fresh sardines flown in from France are available from better fishmongers and supermarkets. Frozen sardines are also imported and these come from Portugal. They are perfect for the plainly grilled sardine dishes in this book. It is possible to use tinned sardines for grilling if they are well drained of oil, and they can also be used in *hors d'œuvres* and pastry dishes. However, it seems to be the southern English who have a passion for the tiny, crammed-together scraps that have given rise to the 'packed like sardines' phrase. The Americans, northern English and Scottish like their sardines larger, packed four to a tin instead of six. Marie Elisabeth is a leading Portuguese brand of tinned sardines obtainable everywhere.

AMÊIJOAS, usually translated as 'clams', are necessary for the *cataplana* and pork and clam dishes (see pages 163, 164). These are certainly not 'clams' in the larger American sense, but the equivalent of English cockles: small, fan-shaped shells about half an inch across, white in colour. These are often available fresh (e.g. in Brewer Street Market, London, occasionally), and also in bottled form.

OYSTERS (*ostras*). If no fresh oysters are available tinned or bottled oysters could be used for the recipes on pages 125 and 162.

SQUIDS (*lulas*). Stuffed squids are delicious, but although they are available in some leading fish shops around London there may be a little difficulty in getting them. The squid sold in Britain are from local waters and are probably a little smaller than the Portuguese. Imported frozen squid are also available at some shops.

TUNA. Fresh tuna is unobtainable in Britain but plentiful in tinned form, which is perfectly acceptable for use in most of the recipes in this book, though strictly the Madeira recipes should be made with fresh tuna.

FRESH FISH

The seasons for fish in Britain which are mentioned in these recipes are as follows:

COD. Best from October to the beginning of February, particularly round Christmas.

EEL. All the year, fewer in winter, very scarce in May.

HAKE (*pescada*). Best from June to January.

HALIBUT (*cherne*). All the year, fewer in May and June.

MACKEREL (*carapau*). Winter and spring.

RED MULLET (*salmonetes*). Best in summer, most found in the south and on south-west coasts.

SOLE (*linguado*). All the year.

WHITING (*pescadinhas*). Best in December, January and February.

There are, of course, many fish used in Portuguese cooking which are not found elsewhere; but these are the most common home water fish readily available and suitable for the recipes.

QUANTITIES TO BUY

Fillets, 1 lb. for 3 people. Cutlets and steaks, 6 oz. per person (less needed of halibut as it is a much richer fish).

FROZEN FISH

Frozen fillets of cod and hake are available. Prawns, shrimps, crab meat can be bought frozen or tinned.

MEAT

American cuts are much nearer to Portuguese butchery than the English ones. However, the cuts mentioned in this book's recipes do not, I think, present any great problems. A leg of pork is used in some recipes. For the veal and pork meat in other dishes it is best to get a boned leg. The *lombo* of pork much used in Portuguese cooking is the fillet, though in Britain the grain is different. It is best to ask for a big fillet.

TRANSLATING FOR THE TABLE

SAUSAGES

None of the Portuguese sausages are available in Britain, but other continental sausages can be used as substitutes in the various recipes, and a Spanish *chouriço* type is widely available. The most common types used in recipes in this book and their substitutes are as follows:

CHOURIÇO. A crude sausage of pork pepped up with garlic and paprika. It is about seven inches long and an inch in diameter. Substitute a garlic sausage.

PRESUNTO. This is a fine quality cured ham; the Italian *prosciutto* can easily be used instead.

MURCELA. A blood sausage from the north. For *caldo verde* soup etc. Italian, French or German blood sausage can be used in small pieces.

PAIO. This is a smoked pork loin meat.

OLIVE OIL

This is the breath of Portuguese cooking and for the Anglicized palate an acquired taste. In much Portuguese regional cooking the harsh oils are used; but even the better, refined oil has a salty tang to it that is unique. Oil is used as much for flavouring as for cooking action, but margarine and lard are increasingly becoming becoming alternatives among young Portuguese housewives. The salty tang of margarine is probably nearer to the original taste than the substitution of Spanish or Italian olive oil easily obtainable at home. (Buy large cans for economy.)

TOUCINHO (*lard*). Many recipes call for a pure white pork fat. A good quality lard such as American lard is a suitable substitute.

SPICES AND FLAVOURINGS

For sardines the rough rock salt used for cooking is best, rubbed into the skin before cooking. The Portuguese rarely add olive oil; their big sardines contain enough of their own. Chopped fresh *mint* stuffed inside the sardine for filling is an easily obtainable alternative.

PARSLEY (*salsa*) is used in great quantities in Portugal, particularly in Algarve cooking. The Portuguese *salsa* is stronger than its English equivalent and should be added to taste. Add just before serving as the pungency is soon destroyed in cooking.

GARLIC (*alho*). Again liberally used; the Portuguese pile in whole cloves with abandon. It depends on personal taste and you may well want to cut down to a minimum. Lawry's Garlic Salt is an excellent seasoning for just a slight suspicion of a Portuguese garlic flavour.

PIRI-PIRI is a hot chilli sauce used to spice up certain dishes and sauces, particularly in the Algarve. Ready-made *piri-piri* sauces are available in Britain in the McCormick foods range and also from Spanish grocery shops and continental grocers. A home-made sauce is described on page 194.

TOMATO PURÉE can be used in many recipes instead of cooked fresh tomatoes; in some recipes tomato *purée* only is needed. Tomato *purée* and tinned tomatoes produced in Portugal are found in most grocers everywhere.

COENTROS. Fresh coriander may be difficult to get, but a pungent herb like basil which marries well with tomatoes can be substituted.

COLORAU. A ground spice of peppers which is another flavouring ingredient basic to many dishes. This has no real equivalent, the nearest being cayenne, or paprika for the 'sweet'.

SAFFRON is expensive, but used to colour and flavour many of the rice dishes of the north; it would not, however, be essential to the recipe.

CLOVES, common here, are used a great deal.

WHITE WINE VINEGAR appears frequently in marinating sauces and could be used occasionally as a substitute for the dry white wine recommended.

BAY LEAVES. Almost universally used in most Portuguese dishes. Fresh bay is easily grown in most gardens, or dried bay leaves are available at better grocers. The Portuguese refer to 'laurel leaves' in their recipes, and while laurel is the same family as the bay the leaf is poisonous and should never be used in cookery.

ORANGES AND LEMONS are frequently used as flavouring, and a Portuguese touch can always be achieved when serving meat by adding a wedge of orange or even lemon.

VEGETABLES

I have already described the kinds of dark cabbage which can be used for the *caldo verde* soup (see page 23). There should not otherwise be any difficulty in getting the right vegetable ingredients.

The *favas* used for bean soup are white beans and should be soaked overnight (see page 140); red beans can also be used soaked overnight for the soup on page 126. Another translation of *fava* is the runner or French bean, fresh and whole, which is used for the 'garden fish' recipe on page 88.

CHEESES

There are no Portuguese cheeses available in Britain, but in the recipes alternatives can easily be found. Parmesan can be used for most of the dishes calling for grated cheese finishes and in the cheese pudding on page 127.

WINES

Many recipes call for wine either in the sauce or as a marinade. Port and madeira can be used in flavouring. For any recipe calling for wine it is pointless to use an expensive grade. Portuguese wines are plentifully available in Britain and some are inexpensive. The red and white Dãos and the Vila Reals from the north are dry wines, excellent for cooking. Occasionally, where a slightly sharper flavour is required, the sparkling red or white *vinhos verdes* of the north should be used. These are more expensive, but go well with some of the richer pork dishes for flavourings and drinking alongside.

SETTING A PORTUGUESE TABLE

Presentation helps a lot to set the atmosphere of your Portuguese meal. The Portuguese swear the food tastes different cooked in their earthenware pots. Many of the recipes are started on top of the stove and finished in the oven, then brought to the table wrapped in a clean white linen napkin. This way of cooking may shorten the life of the pot and an asbestos mat should be used; if not available a Pyrosil ware dish will do. Buy little casserole dishes for the *frigideira* way of cooking beef. Inexpensive earthenware dishes are sold in many big stores, Selfridges and John Lewis shops being good sources. In London there is a Portuguese Shop at Kensington Market (49 Kensington High Street, London, W.8). Large stores also sell Portuguese embroidery napkins, tablecloths and aprons.

COOKING UTENSILS

The small cast-iron Portuguese barbecue *fogareiro* is not on sale, but any small portable charcoal barbecue will do equally well. The sardines for grilling are best held within a double thickness of wire with handles; a rough holder can be made from chicken wire, and it should be large enough to take several, but the smaller holders are available from barbecue suppliers.

Cataplanas are also not available, but the same effect can be obtained by using a frying-pan or top-of-stove casserole with a tightly fitting lid (for other ideas see page 150).

Many of the Portuguese dishes like *cozido* call for large saucepans and long, slow simmering; these can, of course, be speeded in a pressure-cooker but if this is the case the initial quantity of liquid should be halved. Frequently the Portuguese will talk about boiling when they really mean 'simmering'.

In cases of difficulty in obtaining ingredients and Portuguese articles write to the trade department of the Casa de Portugal (address on page 11).

12

CAPTURING THE FLAVOUR: BASIC PORTUGUESE RECIPES

This chapter is intended to outline some of the basic cooking procedures and customs in Portuguese cuisine. Without these the Portuguese flavour is lost, and some of the basics listed here are common to many of the recipes in the book.

BACALHAU

The national staple dish of dried cod needs careful preparation. Thin fish pieces should be soaked for 24 hours; thicker pieces for 48 hours. Cover the dried fish with plain cold water and change the water once or twice during this time so that more of the salt is removed. When cooking, boil slowly till quite soft; this will take about 2–3 hours. Don't boil too quickly, rather simmer gently. The potatoes for cod recipes can be added during this boiling, but they should not be overboiled.

There are literally hundreds of regional variations in the cooking of *bacalhau*. The most common way found all over Portugal is as follows:

BACALHAU GOMES DE SÁ

FOR FOUR

1 lb. salted cod
2 lb. potatoes
1 lb. onions
4 hard-boiled eggs
1 cup of pure olive oil

½ cup of black olives
2 small spoons chopped parsley
garlic (optional)
pepper

Soak the cod overnight in cold water. Then boil the fish and cubed or sliced potatoes in water until the potatoes are cooked. Flake the fish into small pieces, removing bones and skin. Shell and slice the hard-boiled eggs. Fry the sliced onions in hot olive oil with crushed garlic and pepper until tender but not brown. Then add the fish, potatoes and olives, stirring gently until well mixed. Serve hot with the sliced eggs on top and parsley.

Many of the *bacalhau* dishes are basically boiled cod and potatoes mixed with a cheese sauce and baked in the oven. Variations are sauces made with wine, eggs or with vegetables added to the mixture as shown in the recipes below. Of these the following is one of the most popular.

BACALHAU À BRÁS

Cut the well-soaked and desalted cod into very fine pieces, do the same with the potatoes (cutting them long and thin and frying like chips) and onions. Pour some olive oil into a frying pan, add one crushed clove of garlic (remove when browned). Fry the cod, add potatoes previously fried, mix well and when cooked add well-beaten eggs (allowing 3 eggs per portion). Take care not to overcook.

BACALHAU WITH VEGETABLES

FOR FOUR

After the cod has been well soaked and desalted, place in a saucepan and cover with boiling water, cover and leave for 15 minutes away from the stove. Take the fish out of the water and remove skin and bones, and flake.

Boil 4 eggs till hard, 4 large sliced carrots, 6 oz. spinach or spring greens. Place in layers half the codfish in a baking-dish, the boiled eggs cut in slices, half the cabbage greens or spinach and carrots, repeat the process with the remaining ingredients and then pour olive oil over it all. (The Portuguese would use about ½ pint for this amount of vegetables.)

Boil 1 lb. potatoes, add 2 whole eggs, 5½ tablespoons olive oil, 1½ oz. melted butter, flavoured with salt and pepper. Mix well and cover the fish, egg, carrot and cabbage layers with the potatoes, brush the top with a yolk of egg and bake in a fairly hot oven: 425° F., Gas 6, for 15–20 minutes.

BACALHAU FANTASY

FOR SIX TO EIGHT

Simmer two sliced onions, parsley, one bay leaf, one small teaspoon ground pepper and three crushed garlic cloves in olive oil. As soon as the onion begins to brown lightly, add the previously cooked, well-soaked cod (2 lb., skinned and boneless) cut into thick pieces. Cook over strong heat. Remove when done. Boil 1 lb. potatoes, slice and cook in the above sauce. Remove when cooked. Beat 2 egg yolks with the juice of half a lemon, 1 teaspoon vinegar and parsley and add to the sauce in which the potatoes and cod were cooked. Simmer until it thickens, pour over the potatoes and cod mixed together and serve immediately.

ROAST BACALHAU IN VINHO VERDE

Soak and remove skin and bones from cod, keeping it in one piece. Place raw flaked fish or shellfish on top and roll cod up round this. Tie with string.

Place in ovenproof dish with chopped tomatoes, olive oil, chopped onion and dry white *vinho verde*. Cover with greaseproof paper. Bake for ½ hour. Strain off the gravy, add a little butter, stirring well, and sprinkle over the fish.

BACALHAU WITH PODRE SAUCE

BATTER

2 egg yolks   flour
2 egg whites   milk

SAUCE

olive oil in which fish was fried   1 egg yolk
3 tablespoons water or milk   1 oz. butter
  1 tablespoon grated cheese (preferably ewes' milk cheese)

Soak 1 lb. cod overnight, scald with boiling water to soften, then remove skins and bones and break into small pieces. Make a batter with the egg yolks, flour, milk and stiffly beaten egg whites. Dip the pieces of cod in the batter, fry and drain. Boil ½ lb. potatoes, slice and fry in hot olive oil.

For the sauce add water or milk to the olive oil, egg yolk and butter and cook well for 4–5 minutes, stirring continuously to prevent curdling. Add grated cheese until well dissolved. Place at the bottom of a baking dish a layer of potatoes and then one of fried cod, cover with a layer of breadcrumbs and one of grated cheese. Lastly, pour the sauce over and bake in the oven until a light brown in colour.

PASTEIS (or BALINHOS) DE BACALHAU

A delightful way of serving the dried cod, and can be cooked in bulk and stored, wrapped in foil, in the freezer.

12 oz. dried cod   1 well chopped onion
1 lb. potatoes   1 spoonful chopped parsley
5 eggs   olive oil

Prepare cod as on page 189. Mash cod with boiled potatoes till smooth. Add egg yolks one by one with onion and parsley. Beat well. Then stir in stiffly beaten egg whites. Drop spoonfuls of the mixture into very hot olive oil to cover and, when puffy and golden, drain on kitchen paper. Serve hot or cold with salad.

BACALHAU FRICASSÉ

The potatoes are omitted for those with weight problems.

FOR FOUR

1 onion (finely chopped) chopped parsley
butter lemon juice
a little water 2 egg yolks
1 lb. cod fillets

Fry onion in butter, add water, and pass through fine wire mesh sieve. Season and add the cod fillets and cook gently for 10–15 minutes. Mix egg yolks and a lot of chopped parsley and lemon juice. Add to fish at last minute, stirring all the time over flame.

BACALHAU PUDDING

Can be made soufflé light with the addition of beaten egg whites.

FOR FOUR

¾ lb. dried cod 4 eggs
1 lb. potatoes

Cook the prepared cod first, cool and mix with cooked, boiled potatoes and a plain basic white sauce. Beat in the egg yolks and fold in the beaten whites. Chopped parsley, a little nutmeg or crushed garlic can be added. Bake in an ovenproof dish in a moderate oven.

CALDEIRADA

This fish soup starts with a basis of onion cooked to a pulp in olive oil. Use a huge saucepan and cover bottom with olive oil and onion. Top with selected fish (see page 88) in layers interspersed with sliced tomatoes. Add stock and potatoes. *Bacalhau* can be used for this if the thicker lumps are carefully soaked first. White wine, coriander, bay leaves and sliced green pepper can all be added to this fish stew. The Lisbon variety includes a small glass of dry port.

COZIDO

The Portuguese are very fond of boiling everything. The basic *cozido* of boiled meat recipe is given on page 27 and many recipes will refer to 'boiling'; in fact in most cases the ingredients should be simmered slowly and carefully and not over boiled. When boiling several items together it is a Portuguese habit to strain the meat and vegetables out of the liquid in which they have been cooked and arrange them separately on a serving platter, often with the addition of rice. The cooking liquid is then served alongside in soup bowls.

SAUCES

PIRI-PIRI

This hot chilli sauce is added to several dishes, e.g. chicken. It is also brushed on chicken, pork and shellfish before they are grilled. A home-made *piri-piri* sauce can be made by infusing small, very hot chillies in olive oil.

FOR ½ PINT OLIVE OIL

a small handful of chillies a piece of lemon rind
1 bay leaf (about ½ inch in diameter)

Take the top off each chilli with the thumb-nail before tipping them into the olive oil, add crushed bay leaf and grated lemon rind and leave the mixture to infuse for several hours at the bottom of a very slow oven or on the lowest possible heat on the top of the stove.

Seal and store for at least 24 hours before using.

(The Portuguese make *piri-piri* by standing the seasoned oil out in the noonday sun but, alas, we do not have sun of that strength.)

GREEN PEPPER PASTE

Used to coat meat in several of the Alentejo recipes. This paste is a method of preserving the peppers out of season and a thick pulp of fresh peppers spread over the meat can be used instead.

Pound together, or liquidize, de-seeded peppers with a little ginger, onion and salt. Put paste in a jar and cover with olive oil. Store before using to improve the flavour. This stores well if the paste remains covered with oil.

TOMATO SAUCE

Essential for garnishing many dishes, and widely used for cooking fish in an ovenproof dish. It can also be poured over the cheese pudding described on page 127.

2 tablespoons olive oil
1 finely chopped onion
½ clove garlic
1 tin peeled tomatoes
salt, pepper
bay leaf

Fry onion and crushed garlic in olive oil in a thick saucepan (do not allow to brown). Add chopped tomatoes, salt, pepper and bay leaf. Simmer for 1 hour without cover. Add water to taste, heat and use as a sauce.

MEAT

PORK. The favourite meat of the Portuguese. It should be marinated in white wine to which an onion or chopped garlic is added for at least 3 hours in advance of cooking. Paprika should be rubbed into the skin. The meat should be cooked slowly. More wine can be added when it is roasted.

Chunks of soaked pork can be fried with potatoes or the fillet cooked more plainly with lemon juice and served, as is customary, with finely chopped pickled cucumbers.

PORTUGUESE FILLETS OF PORK

pork chops can be cooked in the same way

At least 3 hours before cooking salt the pork. The best fillets are from the loin or leg and must be well pounded and flattened. Place on a warm serving dish and put on top of each piece of meat 1 oz. butter, a few drops lemon juice, pepper and chopped parsley. Orange slices go well with grilled or fried pork, or lemon and chopped parsley can also be used as a garnish for pork fillets.

PORTUGUESE STEAK AND ONIONS

BEEF. A soft tomato and onion sauce spiced with vinegar helps to make tough steaks more palatable. Without the typical *frigideira* (see page 36) a Portuguese style steak can be cooked as follows:

FOR FIVE TO SEVEN

> 2 lb. sirloin or rump steak
> 2 large onions (sliced)
> 2 oz. butter
> 2 tablespoons tomato *purée* or
> 4 tomatoes
> 1 tablespoon white vinegar
> 2 cloves garlic
> 1 sprig parsley
> salt, pepper

Fry butter, onions, tomato *purée* or chopped tomatoes, crushed garlic, salt and pepper to flavour. When onion is browned add the vinegar, simmer until the vinegar is well blended. Check salt and pepper flavourings. Grill the steaks. Pour sauce over steaks, garnish with chopped parsley and serve hot with boiled or fried potatoes.

VEGETABLES, RICE AND POTATOES

POTATOES. The most common way of cooking is the Irish way of boiling with the skins still on. The skin is then peeled off before serving. Fairly waxy potatoes should be selected.

REFOGADO. Most dishes start with this onion *purée*, whether it is a thick soup, a *bacalhau* dish or a garnishing sauce for meat or fish. The basic *refogado* is finely chopped onion cooked to a pulp in a frying-pan with 1 tablespoon olive oil. The pan is kept covered to keep the onion soft. Tinned or sieved tomatoes can be added. Salt and pepper are added to taste. Seasonings depend on the type of recipe for which the sauce is being prepared and can include garlic or bay leaf.

RICE. Brought to Portugal by the Indian voyages of discovery and colonization and now also grown in Portugal, rice is a common dish accompaniment. Uncle Ben rice is a good, plain, easy-to-cook rice to use. The Portuguese way is simple. Melt butter or use olive oil in a pan. Mix the dry rice in it till evenly coated over a low heat. Add twice the quantity of water to the rice. Cover the pan and boil for 20 minutes on a low heat: the rice will absorb all the moisture and be separated and fluffy.

TOMATO RICE

Flavoured with the favourite tomatoes and onions, this is a good dish accompaniment:

CAPTURING THE FLAVOUR: BASIC PORTUGUESE RECIPES

FOR SIX

4 tablespoons olive oil
2 onions (finely chopped)
1 clove garlic
1 tin whole tomatoes
1 small tin tomato *purée*
salt, pepper, bay leaf
2 teacups rice
3 teacups water

Gently fry the onions and garlic in olive oil. When golden, add tomatoes and tomato *purée*, salt, pepper and bay leaf. Simmer for ½ hour. Add rice and water and cook until liquid is absorbed.

For the Portuguese version of rice pudding see below.

SWEETS

SWEET RICE

Use lemon flavouring and a rich egg custard to make it much more appealing than our stodgier offering.

To 1 cup rice add 2 cups milk and boil slowly together with lemon peel or a stick of vanilla. When rice is thoroughly done stir in, little by little, 2 or 3 egg yolks, and continue stirring while it thickens. After the eggs have been added it must not boil. Pour the mixture on to a large flat dish and let it get cold, then sprinkle with cinnamon.

CARAMEL

Many of the egg pudding sweets in Portugal are lined with liquid caramel before being set in a metal mould. A *caramel sauce* can be made using the proportions of 3 oz. sugar to ⅛ pint water. Heat sugar and water together, stir until boiling. Remove the spoon and allow to boil without stirring until it is golden brown. Pour into a *warm* mould.

An alternative method was given to me by the cooks at the Pousada de São Brás in the Algarve. Scatter granulated sugar on the bottom of a frying-pan and cook till it burns. Then pour on a little boiling water, mix well, and remove from heat.

Some recipes call for a top decoration of *hard caramel*. This can be made by quickly boiling sugar and water mixed in the proportions of 8 oz. sugar to ½ pint water. When syrup is thick and golden pour onto a greased baking sheet as thinly as possible and chill till hard. Remove, break into pieces and scatter on the sweet.

Syrups are used a great deal in Portuguese pudding-making and a sugar thermometer would be a great asset to the cook.

PUDIM FLAN
a basic pudding flan egg custard
FOR EIGHT

4–6 eggs (depending on how firm you wish the pudding to be)
1 lb. sugar
1 pint milk
vanilla essence

Mix eggs well with the sugar, milk and a couple of drops of vanilla essence. Pour into a tin lined with caramel and put in a *bain-marie* or double boiler. Bake in the *bain-marie* in a medium oven for about 2 hours. Test with a knife to see when it is cooked; the knife should come away cleanly when it is just firm. The *pudim flan* improves in flavour if kept in a fridge – it will keep up to a week. Preferably use a ring mould and fill the centre with cream for serving.

Other basic pudding ingredients are almonds, oranges and a light sponge mixture. Two typical basic puddings are outlined below.

ALMOND PUDDING

Put 8 oz. ground almonds to soak in a mixture of ½ pint boiling milk, 8 oz. sugar and a small glass of port wine. Stir carefully and add 3 eggs and 3 whites beaten up. Put in a mould lined with caramel and steam in a *bain-marie* or double boiler. Leave to cool.

ORANGE PUDDING

10 oz. sugar   juice of 1½ oranges
6 eggs   rind of 2 oranges

Beat ingredients together in a bowl. Grease a mould with butter and cover with sugar. Pour in sugar and egg mixture. Cook in a moderate oven for 1 hour. Test with a toothpick or knife – it is ready if it comes out cleanly. Turn out of the mould on to a plate and garnish with whipped cream and fresh orange segments.

13

TABLE TALK: A MENU DICTIONARY

This section is a brief dictionary style coverage of the most common words you will come across in connection with Portuguese food. The translation is from Portuguese into English, listed alphabetically. This is of most help when faced with menu and busy waiter in a Portuguese restaurant. Descriptive translations of complete dishes are found in the following chapter.

HORS D'ŒUVRES (*acepipes*)
azeitonas, olives
pepinos pequenos, gherkins

SOUP (*sopa*)

FISH (*peixe*),
   SHELLFISH (*mariscos*)

amêijoas, cockles or clams
anchovas, anchovies
arenque, herring
atum, tuna
bacalhau, dried cod
caldeirada, fish chowder

camarões, shrimps (also used for scampi)
caranguejo, crab (small)
carapau, mackerel
cherne, grouper
   (English substitute, halibut)
chocos, cuttlefish

eirós, eels
enguia, eel
espadarte, swordfish

gambas, large prawns
gosta, lobster (big)
lagostins, Dublin Bay prawns

lampreia, lamprey
linguado, sole
lulas, squid

mexilhão, mussel

ostra, oyster

ovas, roes

pargo, seabream
peixe espada, scabbard fish
perceves, barnacles
pescada, hake
pescadinha, whiting
robalo, sea bass

salmão, salmon
salmonetes, red mullet
sarda, mackerel
sardinhas, sardines
savel, shad
solha, plaice

truta, trout

MEAT (*carne*), FOWL (*aves*), GAME (*caça*)

anho, lamb
bife, beefsteak (also any steak)
borrego, lamb
cabrito, kid
carneiro, mutton
codorniz, quail
coelho, rabbit
cordiero, lamb
costelata, chop
cozida à Portuguesa, stew (boiled)
dobrada, tripe
empadão de carne, minced meat pie
estufado, stew (braised)
faisão, pheasant
fiambre, ham
fígado, liver
filetes, fillets
frango, chicken
galinha, chicken
ganso, goose
iscas, liver (when cooked)
lebre, hare
leitão, sucking pig
língua, tongue
pato, duck
perdiz, partridge
perú, turkey
pombo, pigeon
porco, pork
presunto, smoked Parma ham
rins, kidneys
salsicha, sausage
toucinho, bacon (streaky)
tripas, tripe
veado, venison
vitela, veal

VEGETABLES (*legumes*)

agriões, watercress
aipo, celery
alcachofra, artichoke
alface, lettuce
alho(s), garlic
batata, potato
beterraba, beetroot
cebola, onion
cenoura, carrot
cogumelo, mushroom

couve, cabbage
couve-flor, cauliflower
ervilhas, green peas
esparagos, asparagus
espinafre, spinach
favas, broad beans
feijão, or *feijão verde*, french beans
grãos, chick-peas
nabo, turnip
pastinaça, parsnip
pepino, cucumber
salada, salad
tomate, tomato

DAIRY PRODUCTS
gelado, ice cream
manteiga, butter
nata, cream
ovo, egg
queijo, cheese

EGGS (*ovos*)
cozidos, hard-boiled
escalfados, poached
estrelados, fried
mexidos, scrambled
omeleta, omelette
quentes, boiled in the shell

DESSERTS (*sobremesa*),
 SWEETS (*doces*),
 FRUITS (*frutas*)
alperche, apricot
ameixa, plum

amora, blackberry
ananás, pineapple
arroz doce, Portuguese rice pudding
banana, banana
bolo, cake
cereja, cherry
compota, compôte, preserve *or* jam
damasco, apricot
figo, fig
framboesa, raspberry
laranja, orange
limão, lemon
maça, apple
melancia, water melon
melão, melon
morango, strawberry
pastelaria, pastries, *or* pâtisseries
pera, pear
pessego, peach
pudim flan, egg custard
ruibarbo, rhubarb
toranja, grapefruit
torta, tart
uva, grape

DRINKS (*bebidas*)
água, water
água potável, drinking water
aguardente, local brandy
águas minerais, mineral water
cacau, cocoa
café, coffee

café com leite, coffee with milk
cerveja, beer
chá, tea
cidra, cider

laranjada, orangeade
leite, milk
licor, liqueur
limonada, lemonade

rosé, rosé (wine)

vinho, wine
vinho branco, white wine
vinho da casa, wine of the house
vinho da região, wine of the district
vinho de mesa, table wine
vinho tinto, red wine
vinho verde, young wine, slightly sparkling

MISCELLANEOUS, SEASONINGS

açúcar, sugar
arroz, rice
azeite, olive oil

biscoito, biscuit

gelo, ice

molho, sauce
mostarda, mustard

oleo, oil

pão, bread
pimenta, pepper

sal, salt
salsa, parsley

torradas, toast

vinagre, vinegar

RESTAURANT WORDS

almoço, lunch
carta de vinhos, wine list
chávena, cup
chefe de mesa, head waiter
colher, spoon
com, with
conta, bill

ementa, menu
empregado de mesa, waiter

faca, knife

garfo, fork
gorjeta, tip
guardanapo, napkin

jantar, dinner

obrigada, thank you (when spoken by a woman)
obrigado, thank you (when spoken by a man)

pequeno, small
pequeno almoço, breakfast
pires, saucer
prato, plate

se faz favor, please
sem, without

toilette, w.c. (Ladies, *senhoras;* Gentlemen, *cavalheiros* or *homens;* Vacant, *livre;* Engaged, *ocupado*)

COOKING TERMS (*termos culinarios*)

assado, roasted
bem passada, well done

corado, browned
cozido, boiled

empada, pie
enrolado, rolled
estufado, braised

frito, fried
fumado, smoked

gratinado, au gratin
grelhado, grilled
guisado, a kind of stew

mal passado, underdone

na conta, just done (very colloquial)
nas brasas, cooked on a charcoal grill
no espeto, on the spit
no forno, in the oven

panada, fried with breadcrumbs
passado, minced *or* hashed
picado, sifted *or* finely minced
pure, mashed
salgada, salted
sateado, sauté

14

MENU PLANNER: INDEX TO RECIPES

This chapter lists all the recipes that are printed in full in this book, together with a brief description of their make-up. The page references are given alongside.

The recipes have been divided into the various meal courses for which they would normally be served. This may provide a rough guide to the most common national dishes for the diner in a Portuguese restaurant. It is also intended to help the housewife in a hurry to choose dishes which interest and appeal to her without scanning through every chapter in the book.

HORS D'ŒUVRES

Arroz de Tuna. Moulded rice blended with tuna and lettuce, served cold. (109)

Camarões com Creme e Vinho. Shrimps baked with cream, port and egg yolk. (44)

Cocktail de Peixe. Sea trout cocktail. (162)

Empadinha de Tuna. Smooth pâté made of tuna flavoured with spirits. (71)

Favas à Algarvia. Broad beans cooked with onion and sausage, ham and chicken stock. (167)

Favas à Saloia. Broad beans with chopped bacon and sausage. (89)

MENU PLANNER: INDEX TO RECIPES

Favas Quinta das Torres. Broad beans cooked with herbs and onion. (129)
Melão com Vinho do Porto. Melon served soaked in port. (44)
Milho Frito. Sticks made in Madeira from flour meal, flour and water. (180)
Ostras do Algarve. Shelled oysters baked in white wine and butter. (162)
Ostras Recheadas. Oysters with onions in cream sauce. (125)
Ovos à Minhota. Eggs baked in cocotte dishes served topped with onions and tomato. (24)
Ovos Verdes. 1. Hard-boiled eggs with yolks mixed with minced onion, curry powder and mayonnaise. 2. Hard-boiled eggs with stuffed yolks rolled in egg and breadcrumbs and deep fried. (127)
Peixinhos da Horta. Batter-fried runner beans. (88)
Rissóis. Deep-fried pastry cases filled with meat or fish. (109)
Sardinhas Portimão. Sardines, olives and tomato baked in puff pastry. (162)
Tomatada à Portuguesa. 3-4 vegetables mixed with tomato sauce and served with scrambled egg. (129)
Tomates Recheados. Tomatoes baked with bread and cheese filling. (109)
Tomato Rice. Tomato and onion cooked with rice, served cold. (196)

SOUPS

Açorda Alentejana. Garlic and coriander flavouring for a 'dry' bread soup. (138)
Amêijoas à Bulhão Pato. Broth of boiled cockles with garlic and herbs. (91)
Caldeirada à fragateira de Lisboa (88); *Caldeirada à Pescador* (111) Fish soups similar to bouillabaisse.
Caldo Verde. Potato soup with finely shredded green cabbage. (23)
Canja. Chicken broth including rice, ham or fresh mint flavourings. (110)
Gaspacho à Alentejana. Cold soup based on tomato, pepper, cucumber, gammon and breadcrumbs. (138)

Perdiz Açorda. Partridge meat and bread 'dry' soup. (46)
Red Bean Soup. Red beans cooked with rice and cabbage *purée*. (126)
Salmi de Perdiz. Boiled partridge and vegetables with bread slices. (112)
Simple Açorda. Garlic, bread and herb 'dry' soup. (137)
Sopa à Pescador. Almonds in fish soup. (161)
Sopa de Agriões. Watercress soup. (126)
Sopa de Alho. Fried bread, poached egg and garlic-flavoured broth. (140)
Sopa de Batata à Alentejana. Potato soup with garlic, parsley and onion flavouring. (139)
Sopa de Conquilhas. Mussels cooked with rice and potatoes. (161)
Sopa de Feijão Frade à Alentejana. Black eye beans simmered with vinegar, onions, herbs and minted bread slices. (139)
Sopa de Feijão Verde à Moda de Beira. Runner bean soup. (72)
Sopa de Legumes. Creamed vegetable soup. (45)
Sopa de Puré de Grão com Espinafres. Chick-pea and spinach soup with bacon. (91)
Sopa de Tomate à Alentejana. Sausage, green pepper and tomato soup. (139)
Sopa de Tomate Cebola. Onion, garlic and tomato with bread and cheese. (177)
Sopa de Tomate Cebola à Portuguesa. As above, thickened with beaten eggs and bread and poached egg. (177)
Sopa Transmontana. Pork and vegetables with bread slices. (48)

SAUCES

Amêijoas à Marinheira. Cockles cooked with tomatoes and onions, used with pork fillets and omelettes. (93)
Béchamel Sauce. (30)
Caramel. Hard and soft versions used for egg custard puddings. (197)
Green Pepper Paste. For preserving peppers. (194)
Molho à Portuguesa. Port, meat juice, lemon and a slice of bitter orange. (44)
Molho de Aves. Stock and port. (44)

Molho Escabeche. Onion, olive oil, garlic and white vinegar used cold on fish. (90)
Piri-piri Sauce. Hot chilli sauce for chicken. (194)
Refogado. Basic sauce of tomato and onion *purée.* (196)
Tomato Sauce. (195)

FISH DISHES

Amêijoas e Porco na Cataplana. Cockles cooked with pork and ham and onions in a *cataplana* dish. (164)
Amêijoas na Cataplana. As above with sausage instead of pork. (163)
Bacalhau à Brás. Fried dried cod strips with onion and potatoes cooked in beaten egg. (190)
Bacalhau à Chanceler. Dried cod with potatoes and cream mustard sauce. (93)
Bacalhau à Douro. Baked dried cod with cream sauce and cabbage. (48)
Bacalhau à Moda de Viana. Dried cod cooked in a cabbage leaf and served with onion sauce. (27)
Bacalhau à Moda do Porto. Dried cod fried in breadcrumbs and egg with onion and egg yolk sauce. (49)
Bacalhau Assado. Green pepper, onion and tomato sauce with cod fried, then simmered with dry white wine and olives. (116)
Bacalhau Assado à Vila Real. Charcoal-grilled dried cod. (49)
Bacalhau com Natas. Fried dried cod with onions and potatoes cooked in a cream sauce. (128)
Bacalhau Fantasy. Dried cod cooked with egg yolk sauce. (191)
Bacalhau Fricassé. Dried cod and onion cooked in lemon juice and egg yolk sauce. (193)
Bacalhau Gomes de Sà. Fried dried cod with onions, potatoes and sliced egg topping. (190)
Bacalhau Gratinado. Dried cod and potatoes baked in *béchamel* sauce topped with cheese. (128)
Bacalhau Hotel Grão Vasco. Fried dried cod, baked in *béchamel* sauce. (75)
Bacalhau Pudding. Soufflé of dried cod. (193)
Bacalhau with Podre Sauce. Batter-fried dried cod, baked with potato and cheese. (192)

Bacalhau with Vegetables. Dried cod baked in layers with cabbage or spinach, eggs and olive oil. (190)

Bife de Atum à Algarvia. Tuna cooked with bacon and onions in wine. (165)

Bifes de Atum. Tuna steaks with vinegar sauce. (178)

Camarão à Portuguesa. Scampi kebab with rice, brandy and Portuguese tomato and onion sauce. (115)

Delicias de Peixe Envoltas. Milk-poached fish fillets fried in breadcrumbs, and baked wrapped in ham slices with mayonnaise and grated cheese. (94)

Empada de Sardinhas. Sardines in bread dough case with onions. (50)

Filetes à Clube Naval. Whiting fillets cooked in garlic and egg yolk sauce. (130)

Filetes Pescador. Whiting or sole fillets fried in egg and flour with sauce flavoured with gherkins and cockles. (131)

Lagosta à Bar de Ofir. Lobster baked with *béchamel* sauce, onions and egg yolks. (30)

Lagosta à Muchaxo. Seasoned tomato and onion *purée* boiled with lobster and rice. (114)

Lagosta à Portuguesa. Lobster simmered with tomato and onion sauce and brandy. (115)

Lagosta Barraca. Fried lobster *flambéed* in cognac and served with rice. (114)

Lagosta Suada. Lobster simmered with madeira or port and served with tomatoes and onions. (113)

Linguado à Lisboa; Linguado Recheado. Sole stuffed with chicken, onions and ham. (92)

Lulas à Pousada. Casseroled squid rings with tomatoes and onions. (111)

Lulas Recheadas. Squids stuffed with minced ham, onion and egg yolks with tomato sauce. (130)

Mexilhões à Francillon. Mussels with port wine sauce. (44)

Pasteis (or *Balinhos*) *de Bacalhau.* Puffy spoonfuls of dried cod and potato mixture, deep fried. (192)

Peixe Assado. Fish baked with onions, tomatoes and port wine. (45)

MENU PLANNER: INDEX TO RECIPES

Peixe Assado à Ofir. Fish baked with potatoes in white wine. (29)
Peixe Creme. Fish baked in cream sauce with beans. (90)
Pentéolas à Portuguesa. Scallops with minced pork, tomatoes and onion. (96)
Pescada à Maiata. Hake and potatoes with mayonnaise. (28)
Pescada Hotel Faro. Hake baked with potatoes, mayonnaise and white wine. (163)
Pescada Madeira. Hake with madeira sauce. (178)
Pudim de Bacalhau. Baked dried cod with milk and breadcrumbs and egg yolk sauce. (49)
Roast Bacalhau in Vinho Verde. Dried cod rolled round raw fish or shellfish and baked with tomatoes and onion in *vinho verde*. (191)
Robalo no Forno à Portuguesa. Baked bass with onions, tomato and lemon juice. (94)
Salada de Tuna e Amêndoas. Tuna and almonds blended with mayonnaise and seasonings. (165)
Salmonete Vladimiro. Red mullet baked with tomato and onions and cockles. (164)
Salmonetes Setubalense. Red mullet in sauce made from fish livers, lemon and butter. (131)
Santola no Carro. Seasoned crab meat baked in its shell. (113)
Sardinhas de Cascais. Baked sardines with tomatoes and onions in white wine. (110)
Sardinhas Fritas. Sardines fried in batter. Tinned sardines may be used in this recipe. (126)
Trutas de Escabeche Manteigas. Cold trout in *escabeche* sauce. (72)

MEAT, GAME AND POULTRY DISHES

Arroz de Frango à Portuguesa. Fried chicken joints simmered with white wine and garlic sausage or ham and rice. Finished in casserole. (74)
Arroz de Frango de Cabidela. Jugged chicken, white rice and garlic sausage. (24)
Arroz Monção. Rice and chicken with chopped bacon and onion. (26)

PORTUGUESE FOOD

Bife à Estalagem. Steak and wine and cream sauce; can be topped with fried egg and a ham slice. (29)
Bife à Frigideira. Fried beef steak with white wine and garlic served with fried bread and ham. (95)
Bife Chave Douro. As above with egg instead of ham. (96)
Bife Nicola. Steak with tomato and onion sauce. (96)
Bifes de Cebolada. Steaks casseroled with onions. (95)
Bifinhos de Vitela. Braised veal strips in port. (98)
Bola de Carne. Dough case filled with chopped smoked ham and stewed chicken. (51)
Caçarola de Cabrito. Baby kid (or lamb) casseroled according to the region. (166)
Carne de Porco à Alentejana. Cockles with chopped pork fried to-together with onion and tomato. (141)
Carne de Vinho e Alhos. Marinated pork cubes simmered in madeira wine with spices. (179)
Carneiro à Transmontana. Cold mutton soaked in wine sauce and coated with beaten egg and breadcrumbs. (53)
Coelho à Minhota. Marinated rabbit, fried, served with tomato sauce and fried bread triangles. (26)
Coelho em Vinho Verde. Garlic and rabbit casseroled in *vinho verde*. (53)
Coelho na Cataplana. Rabbit with onion, cooked in a *cataplana* dish. (164)
Costelatas à Moda de Braga. Cutlets fried with chopped onion and ham. (25)
Costelatas de Carneiro à Barcelense. Chops fried in herbs and breadcrumbs. (24)
Costelatas de Porco à Alentejana. Pork cutlets marinated in green pepper paste and fried, served with orange slices. (142)
Cozido à Portuguesa. Meat stew with beef, gammon, smoked sausage, vegetables and rice. (27)
Dobrada com Grão. Chopped tripe, boiled with chick-peas and chopped bacon, onions and tomatoes. (97)
Empadinhas de Castelo Branco. Veal cooked in wine and garlic; used in soft crust pies. (74)
Ensopada de Borrego. Lamb stew with bread slices; the meat is usually served separately from the flavoured broth. (140)

MENU PLANNER: INDEX TO RECIPES

Ensopada de Lebre à Alentejana. Hare stew as above. (143)

Entrecosto de Viana. Cutlets fried with tomatoes and onion *purée.* (25)

Ervilhas com Paio. Peas and pork sausages topped with poached egg. (89)

Faisão Estufado. Pheasant soaked in cognac and port and fried with almonds cooked in wine sauce. (143)

Frangainho Hotel Eva. Chicken cooked with mushrooms and rice served with rosemary sauce. (165)

Frango à Castelo Vide. Boiled chicken and rice casseroled with tomatoes and mushrooms and topped with beaten egg crust. (129)

Frango à Moda da Beira. Chicken roast with cottage cheese and cream sauce. (73)

Frango na Pucara. Chicken casseroled with mustard, brandy, port and seasonings. (117)

Galinha com Vinho do Porto à Alentejana. Fried chicken simmered in port. (142)

Galinha de Fricassé à Moda da Beira. Chicken fricassée with egg yolk sauce. (72)

Gammon Steak Castelo Branco. Gammon steak fried in madeira wine. (176)

Íscas à Portuguesa. Thin slices of liver marinated in white wine and herbs and fried with ham. (95)

Língua à Beiroa. Beef tongue cooked in wine sauce with onions and carrots. (73)

Lombo Assado à Alentejana. Loin of pork flavoured with green pepper paste and roast in a wine sauce. (142)

Lombo de Porco de Monção. Loin of pork with wine, cloves and bay-leaf-flavoured sauce. (25)

Peitos de Frango à Varanda. Boned chicken breasts fried and served with white wine, brandy, port, tomato and mustard sauce. (94)

Perdiz Assado. Partridge and onions roasted in white wine and served with vegetables in a cream sauce. (112)

Perdizes Convento de Alcantara. A rich dish of partridge stuffed with pâté and marinated with, then simmered in, wine and served with a wine sauce. (97)

Portuguese Fillets of Pork. Fillets cooked in a lemon flavouring. (195)

Portuguese Steak and Onions. Grilled steaks with onions, and tomato simmered in vinegar. (195)

Rojoes à Moda do Minho. Chopped pork Minho style, marinated in white wine with onions. (28)

Tournedos Hotel Eva. Fillet steak with *béarnaise* sauce and poached eggs). (167)

Tripas à Moda do Porto. Tripe and sausage, ham, rice and beans. (51)

Vitela Assada. Veal, ham, tomatoes and onions in port wine. (45)

Vitela Assada no Espeto. Spit-roasted veal basted with olive oil, garlic and bay leaf. (52)

CHEESE DISHES

Pudim de Queijo. Cheese and egg soufflé cooked in *bain-marie* mould and covered with tomato sauce. (127)

Queijo Phillipa. Small cheese scooped out, filled with scrambled egg and briefly baked in the oven. (128)

DESSERTS

Almond Pudding. Almonds, sugar and wine baked with eggs. (198)

Cerica. Egg and lemon soufflé topped with cinnamon. (144)

Creme à Moda de Régua. Hot egg custard topped with burnt sugar coating. (55)

Crepes à Escondidinho. Pancakes filled with liqueur sauce. (55)

Delicia de Laranja. Baked orange sponge topped with orange sugar cream. (56)

Doce de Ovos São Brás. Yolk and sugar pudding beaten with egg white and topped with cinnamon. (168)

Doce Rapido. Sliced oranges soaked in juice and marmalade, chilled and sprinkled with coconut. (131)

Farofias. Beaten egg whites cooked in sweet milk and served covered with egg custard and cinnamon. (98)

Manjar de Principe. Minced almonds and bread baked in syrup with egg yolks. (132)

MENU PLANNER: INDEX TO RECIPES

Morangos com Vinho do Porto. Strawberries served with dry port and sliced orange. (45)
Mousse Chocolate à Togi. Soft chocolate mousse. (170)
Mousse de Ananas. Pineapple mousse. (170)
Orange Pudding. Orange-flavoured egg custard. (198)
Papos de Anjo. Syrup-covered baked egg custards. (57)
Pudim Creme. Creamy custard topped with burnt sugar coating. (53)
Pudim de Laranja Frio. Cold orange-flavoured milk pudding. (181)
Pudim de Laranjas São Filipe. Orange-flavoured egg custard. (132)
Pudim de Leite. Milk pudding with caramel sauce. (170)
Pudim de Nozes. Spice and walnuts baked in egg custard. (119)
Pudim de Ovos de Coimbra. Egg pudding. (77)
Pudim de Presunto de Monção. Caramel egg custard flavoured with cinnamon and ham. (32)
Pudim Flan. Egg custard lined with caramel sauce. (198)
Pudim Flan de Monção. Lemon-flavoured egg custard. (31)
Pudim Madeira. Egg custards flavoured with madeira wine. (180)
Pudim Rapido de Bananas. Baked bananas with port and egg whites. (45)
Rolo de Ovos. Light sponge, rolled like a swiss roll round beaten egg white. (56)
Salada de Laranjas. Liqueur-flavoured orange slices. (79)
Sopa Dourada. Bread in syrup with egg yolks and almonds, served with cinnamon. (54)
Sweet Rice. Rice pudding flavoured with lemon and cinnamon. (197)
Torta à Quinta do Passadouro. Almond tart. (56)
Toucinho de Céu. Baked almonds in syrup blended with egg yolks. (118)
Toucinhos. Shiny yellow egg custards. (169)

BISCUITS, CAKES, PRESERVES ETC.

Batatada. Potato flour and cinnamon cakes. (77)
Biscoitos de Coimbra. Cinnamon biscuits. (78)
Biscoitos de Lamego. Biscuits rich in egg and butter. (57)
Biscoitos de Sintra. Cinnamon biscuits. (118)

Bolas de Figo. Almonds, figs, orange peel and chocolate blended with syrup and rolled in small balls. (169)
Bolo de Mel de Castelo Branco. Honey-flavoured sponge cakes. (76)
Bolo de Ouro Alentejano. Rich, light, egg sponge cake. (145)
Broas de Mel de Castelo Branco. Lemon-flavoured honey cakes. (75)
Delicias. Small, lemon-flavoured sponge cakes. (77)
Emmanuels. Almond egg paste baked in small slices. (145)
Esquecidos. Tiny, puffy, lemon-flavoured pastries. (75)
Fidalguinhos. Plaited sweet dough biscuits. (30)
Figos Recheados à Algarvia. Almonds and chocolate stuffing in baked figs. (168)
Frutas Regionais de Amêndoa. Almond sugar and egg paste made into fruit shapes. (167)
Marmelada. Quince jelly preserve. (7)
Ouricos Alentejanos. Sugar and egg mixture baked on wafer biscuits and stuck with sliced almonds. (145)
Ovos Moles. Very sweet egg and white wine custards topped with cream and almonds cooked in caramel sauce. (78)
Pão Constipado. Fried bread coated with sugar and cinnamon. (146)
Pão de ló. Rich golden sponge cake, soft and runny. (76)
Queijadas de Évora. Pastry cases filled with sweetened cheese mixture. (144)
Queijadas de Sintra. Box-shaped pastry cases filled with cream cheese, almond and coconut mixture. (117)
Rabanadas. Fried slices of bread soaked in sugar, milk and beaten eggs. (54)
Sonhos. Puffy, cinnamon-flavoured, deep-fried dough. (31)
Tijelinhas de Nata. Puff pastry cases filled with custard. (55)
Trás-Os-Montes Cristas. Pastries filled with jam. (57)